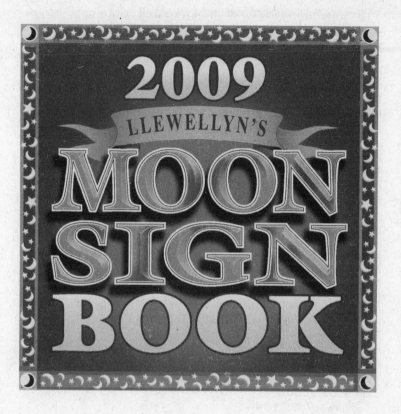

Llewellyn's 2009 Moon Sign Book

ISBN 978-0-7387-0720-4.

Cover Design & Art: Gavin Dayton Duffy
Editor/Designer: Sharon Leah
Interior Photographs © IndexOpen
Stock photography model(s) used for illustrative purposes only and may not endorse or represent the book's subject.
Copyright 2008 Llewellyn Worldwide. All rights reserved.
Typography owned by Llewellyn Worldwide.

Any Internet references contained in this work are current at publication time, but the publisher cannot guarantee that a specific location will continue to be maintained.

You can order Llewellyn annuals and books from *New Worlds*, Llewellyn's catalog. To request a free copy of the catalog, call toll-free 1-877-NEW-WRLD, or visit our Web site at www.llewellyn.com.

Llewellyn is a registered trademark of Llewellyn Worldwide, Ltd.
2134 Wooddale Drive, Woodbury, MN 55125-2989 USA
Printed in the USA

Llewellyn Worldwide
Dept. 978-0-7387-0720-4
2143 Wooddale Drive
Woodbury, MN 55125-3989
www.llewellyn.com

Table of Contents

What's Different About the Moon Sign Book?

Readers have asked why the *Moon Sign Book* says that the Moon is in Taurus when some almanacs indicate that the Moon is in the previous sign of Aries on the same date. It's because there are two different zodiac systems in use today: the tropical and the sidereal. The *Moon Sign Book* is based on the tropical zodiac.

The tropical zodiac takes 0 degrees of Aries to be the Spring Equinox in the Northern Hemisphere. This is the time and date when the Sun is directly overhead at noon along the equator, usually about March 20–21. The rest of the signs are positioned at 30 degree intervals from this point.

The sidereal zodiac, which is based on the location of fixed stars, uses the positions of the fixed stars to determine the starting point of

0 degrees of Aries. In the sidereal system, 0 degrees of Aries always begins at the same point. This does create a problem though, because the positions of the fixed stars, as seen from Earth, have changed since the constellations were named. The term "precession of the equinoxes" is used to describe the change.

Precession of the equinoxes describes an astronomical phenomenon brought about by the Earth's wobble as it rotates and orbits the Sun. The Earth's axis is inclined toward the Sun at an angle of about 23½ degrees, which creates our seasonal weather changes. Although the change is slight, because one complete circle of the Earth's axis takes 25,800 years to complete, we can actually see that the positions of the fixed stars seem to shift. The result is that each year, in the tropical system, the Spring Equinox occurs at a slightly different time.

Does Precession Matter?

There is an accumulative difference of about 23 degrees between the Spring Equinox (0 degrees Aries in the tropical zodiac and 0 degrees Aries in the sidereal zodiac) so that 0 degrees Aries at Spring Equinox in the tropical zodiac actually occurs at about 7 degrees Pisces in the sidereal zodiac system. You can readily see that those who use the other almanacs may be planting seeds (in the garden and in their individual lives) based on the belief that it is occurring in a fruitful sign, such as Taurus, when in fact it would be occurring in Gemini, one of the most barren signs of the zodiac. So, if you wish to plant and plan activities by the Moon, it is helpful to follow the *Moon Sign Book*. Before we go on, there are important things to understand about the Moon, her cycles, and their correlation with everyday living. For more information about gardening by the Moon, see page 61.

Weekly Almanac

Your Guide to Lunar Gardening & Good Timing for Activities

I think having land and not ruining it is the most beautiful art anyone could want to own.

~Andy Warhol

♉ January

January 1–3

If we had no winter, spring would not be so pleasant.

— ANNE BRADSTREET

Date	Qtr.	Sign	Activity
Dec 31, 7:27 pm– Jan 3, 4:50 pm	1st	Pisces	Plant grains, leafy annuals. Fertilize (chemical). Graft or bud plants. Irrigate. Trim to increase growth.

Did you know that it takes between 500 and 1000 years to make an inch of topsoil? For this reason topsoil is considered a nonrenewable resource. Snow and frost actually assist the production of topsoil in areas that have organic matter, such as leaves and grasses, that can be broken down and decomposed. But 500 years is a long time, so do what you can now to protect the topsoil that we do have.

———————————————————————

———————————————————————

———————————————————————

———————————————————————

JANUARY						
S	M	T	W	T	F	S
				1	2	3
4	5	6	7	8	9	10
11	12	13	14	15	16	17
18	19	20	21	22	23	24
25	26	27	28	29	30	31

January 4–10 ♉

To be a successful farmer one must first know the nature of the soil.

~XENOPHON, OECONOMICUS

Date	Qtr.	Sign	Activity
Jan 5, 10:46 am–Jan 7, 1:11 pm	2nd	Taurus	Plant annuals for hardiness. Trim to increase growth.
Jan 9, 1:14 pm–Jan 10:27 pm	2nd	Cancer	Plant grains, leafy annuals. Fertilize (chemical). Graft or bud plants. Irrigate. Trim to increase growth.
Jan 10, 10:27 pm–Jan 11, 12:41 pm	3rd	Cancer	Plant biennials, perennials, bulbs and roots. Prune. Irrigate. Fertilize (organic).

In the organic agriculture and the organic movement, *The Living Soil* (1943) by Lady Eve Balfour is considered a classic. The book is based on Balfour's agricultural and medical research, and the initial findings of the first three years of the Haughley Experiment, the first scientific, side-by-side farm trial to compare organic and chemical-based farming. The full text of this out-of-print book is available online in the Agriculture Library at *www.soilandhealth.org/*

Resource: *www.wikipedia.com*

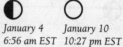

January 4
6:56 am EST

January 10
10:27 pm EST

JANUARY

S	M	T	W	T	F	S
				1	2	3
4	5	6	7	8	9	10
11	12	13	14	15	16	17
18	19	20	21	22	23	24
25	26	27	28	29	30	31

January 11–17

While the farmer holds the title to the land, actually it belongs to all the people because civilization itself rests upon the soil.

~THOMAS JEFFERSON

Date	Qtr.	Sign	Activity
Jan 10, 10:27 pm– Jan 11, 12:41 pm	3rd	Cancer	Plant biennials, perennials, bulbs and roots. Prune. Irrigate. Fertilize (organic).
Jan 11, 12:41 pm– Jan 13, 1:33 pm	3rd	Leo	Cultivate. Destroy weeds and pests. Harvest fruits and root crops for food. Trim to retard growth.
Jan 13, 1:33 pm– Jan 15, 5:30 pm	3rd	Virgo	Cultivate, especially medicinal plants. Destroy weeds and pests. Trim to retard growth.

Side effects of population growth—such as deforestation, soil erosion, and pollution—are placing great stress on the global environmental systems. If economic development and food and energy supplies cannot keep pace, widespread discontent and political instability could erupt into conflict. However, economic development does not always imply regional peace. Aggressive states can use such prosperity to impose their will on others.

Written by Mort Rolleston in 1997, the "Strategic Environment of 2010," is online at *www.ndu.edu/inss/Strforum/SF118/forum118. html/*

January 17
9:46 pm EST

JANUARY

S	M	T	W	T	F	S
				1	2	3
4	5	6	7	8	9	10
11	12	13	14	15	16	17
18	19	20	21	22	23	24
25	26	27	28	29	30	31

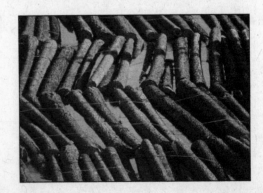

January 18–24

Red sky at night, shepherds delight,
Red sky in morning, shepherds take warning.

~AUTHOR UNKNOWN

Date	Qtr.	Sign	Activity
Jan 18, 1:20 am– Jan 20, 12:30 pm	4th	Scorpio	Plant biennials, perennials, bulbs and roots. Prune. Irrigate. Fertilize (organic).
Jan 20, 12:30 pm– Jan 23, 1:18 am	4th	Sagittarius	Cultivate. Destroy weeds and pests. Harvest fruits and root crops for food. Trim to retard growth.
Jan 23, 1:18 am– Jan 25, 1:56 pm	4th	Capricorn	Plant potatoes and tubers. Trim to retard growth.

When a cold front moves east, the setting sun reflects off the tops of clouds causing the sky to appear red at dusk. The cold front causes a rise in pressure and a couple of days of good weather will usually follow. The sky is red in the morning when the sun reflects off an ice cloud, which scatters light. A red sky in the morning can mean an approaching weather front and rain within twelve hours.

_____

_____

_____

JANUARY

S	M	T	W	T	F	S
				1	2	3
4	5	6	7	8	9	10
11	12	13	14	15	16	17
18	19	20	21	22	23	24
25	26	27	28	29	30	31

～～ January 25–31

The foolish man seeks happiness in the distance, the wise grows it under his feet.

~JAMES OPPENHEIM

Date	Qtr.	Sign	Activity
Jan 25, 1:56 pm– Jan 26, 2:55 am	4th	Aquarius	Cultivate. Destroy weeds and pests. Harvest fruits and root crops for food. Trim to retard growth.
Jan 28, 1:12 am– Jan 30, 10:25 am	1st	Pisces	Plant grains, leafy annuals. Fertilize (chemical). Graft or bud plants. Irrigate. Trim to increase growth.

The Chinese New Year begins on the first day of a New Moon in a new year, which is January 26 in 2009. New clothing is usually worn on the Chinese New Year, the color red is used in many decorations, and small gifts wrapped in red are often given. The color red is so widely used because it symbolizes good luck. The period around the Chinese New Year is also the time of Chunyun, when many Chinese travel home to have reunion dinners with their families.

_____

_____

_____

January 26
2:55 am EST

JANUARY

S	M	T	W	T	F	S
				1	2	3
4	5	6	7	8	9	10
11	12	13	14	15	16	17
18	19	20	21	22	23	24
25	26	27	28	29	30	31

February ~~~

February 1–7

Away in a meadow all covered with snow, the little old groundhog looks for his shadow. The clouds in the sky determine our fate, if winter will leave us all early or late.

~DON HALLEY

Date	Qtr.	Sign	Activity
Feb 1, 5:08 pm– Feb 2, 6:13 pm	1st	Taurus	Plant annuals for hardiness. Trim to increase growth.
Feb 2, 6:13 pm– Feb 3, 9:14 pm	2nd	Taurus	Plant annuals for hardiness. Trim to increase growth.
Feb 5, 11:05 pm– Feb 7, 11:43 pm	2nd	Cancer	Plant grains, leafy annuals. Fertilize (chemical). Graft or bud plants. Irrigate. Trim to increase growth.

Since 1900, the groundhog has seen his shadow 94 out of 107 years in Punxsutawney, New York. But the Punxsutawney groundhog is only right 39 percent of the time according to records kept by StormFax, Inc. On Groundhog Day in 1961, it was 25 degrees below zero. In 1999, the warmest Groundhog Day on record in Punxsutawney, it was 37 degrees above zero.

Resource: *www.stormfax.com*

○

February 2
6:13 pm EST

FEBRUARY

S	M	T	W	T	F	S
1	2	3	4	5	6	7
8	9	10	11	12	13	14
15	16	17	18	19	20	21
22	23	24	25	26	27	28

~~~ February 8–14

Without love, what are we worth? Eighty-nine cents! Eighty-nine cents worth of chemicals walking around lonely.

~HAWKEYE, FROM MASH

Date	Qtr.	Sign	Activity
Feb 9, 9:49 am–Feb 10, 12:38 am	3rd	Leo	Cultivate. Destroy weeds and pests. Harvest fruits and root crops for food. Trim to retard growth.
Feb 10, 12:38 am–Feb 12, 3:33 am	3rd	Virgo	Cultivate, especially medicinal plants. Destroy weeds and pests. Trim to retard growth.
Feb 14, 9:50 am–Feb 16, 4:37 pm	3rd	Scorpio	Plant biennials, perennials, bulbs and roots. Prune. Irrigate. Fertilize (organic).

Valentine's Day falls on Saturday this year, making it a prime date night. Start early and go all out with a special invitation that you write and deliver to your "date." Get out the cloth napkins and special dinnerware, and don't forget candles and flowers. Keep dinner simple. Dim the lights and have your favorite music playing in the background. Going with a Greek or Italian theme (music, wine, and food) would set the stage, and you could follow up dinner with a movie. *My Big Fat Greek Wedding* (2002) or *Roman Holiday* with Audrey Hepburn (1953) would be perfect.

February 9
9:49 am EST

FEBRUARY

S	M	T	W	T	F	S
1	2	3	4	5	6	7
8	9	10	11	12	13	14
15	16	17	18	19	20	21
22	23	24	25	26	27	28

February 15–21

A cloak of loose, soft material, held to the earth's hard surface by gravity, is all that lies between life and lifelessness.

~ WALLACE H. FULLER, SOILS OF THE DESERT SOUTHWEST, 1975

Date	Qtr.	Sign	Activity
Feb 16, 4:37 pm–Feb 16, 7:53 pm	4th	Scorpio	Plant biennials, perennials, bulbs and roots. Prune. Irrigate. Fertilize (organic).
Feb 16, 7:53 pm–Feb 19, 8:25 am	4th	Sagittarius	Cultivate. Destroy weeds and pests. Harvest fruits and root crops for food. Trim to retard growth.
Feb 19, 8:25 am–Feb 21, 9:06 pm	4th	Capricorn	Plant potatoes and tubers. Trim to retard growth.

Winter aconite, snowdrops, and grape hyacinths bloom in early spring as soon as the soil warms enough to let them pop through. These hardy spring-flowering bulbs will withstand sleet and snow, so don't worry if bad weather arrives after they've begun blooming. You'll want to plant the bulbs the previous fall in soil that gets good drainage to enjoy these early spring bloomers. If you have trouble with squirrels digging up the bulbs, cover the area with chicken wire and cover the wire with mulch.

February 16
4:37 pm EST

FEBRUARY

S	M	T	W	T	F	S
1	2	3	4	5	6	7
8	9	10	11	12	13	14
15	16	17	18	19	20	21
22	23	24	25	26	27	28

February 22–28

It is not what you do for your children, but what you have taught them to do for themselves that will make them successful human beings.

~ANN LANDERS

Date	Qtr.	Sign	Activity
Feb 21, 9:06 pm– Feb 24, 7:59 am	4th	Aquarius	Cultivate. Destroy weeds and pests. Harvest fruits and root crops for food. Trim to retard growth.
Feb 24, 7:59 am– Feb 24, 8:35 pm	4th	Pisces	Plant biennials, perennials, bulbs and roots. Prune. Irrigate. Fertilize (organic).
Feb 24, 8:35 pm– Feb 26, 4:24 pm	1st	Pisces	Plant grains, leafy annuals. Fertilize (chemical). Graft or bud plants. Irrigate. Trim to increase growth.

Some vines and deciduous trees can be pruned in the spring while they are still dormant. It's easier to see the framework of the tree before the leaf buds develop. Remove dead branches, those branches that cross one another, and branches that appear to be attacked by disease or insects. Shrubs that bloom in the spring should not be pruned now.

_____

_____

_____

February 24
8:35 pm EST

FEBRUARY

S	M	T	W	T	F	S
1	2	3	4	5	6	7
8	9	10	11	12	13	14
15	16	17	18	19	20	21
22	23	24	25	26	27	28

March

March 1–7

When March goes on forever, and April's twice as long, who gives a damn if spring has come, as long as winter's gone.

~R. L. Ruzicka

Date	Qtr.	Sign	Activity
Feb 28, 10:33 pm–Mar 3, 2:59 am	1st	Taurus	Plant annuals for hardiness. Trim to increase growth.
Mar 5, 6:07 am–Mar 7, 8:24 am	2nd	Cancer	Plant grains, leafy annuals. Fertilize (chemical). Graft or bud plants. Irrigate. Trim to increase growth.

It took a computer to figure out why we walk rather than run, and why we all have a unique walking speed. A couple of engineers from Cornell University used computer models that simulated measurements of leg and arm length, body velocity, and trajectory, and learned that walking is the most efficient use of our energy. Running, not walking fast, hopping, or skipping, is the most efficient way for humans to travel longer distances faster.

Resource: *www.livescience.com*

March 4
2:46 am EST

MARCH

S	M	T	W	T	F	S
1	2	3	4	5	6	7
8	9	10	11	12	13	14
15	16	17	18	19	20	21
22	23	24	25	26	27	28
29	30	31				

March 8–14

Up from the sea, the wild north wind is blowing, under the sky's gray arch; smiling I watch the shaken elm boughs, knowing it is the wind of March.

~WILLIAM WORDSWORTH

Date	Qtr.	Sign	Activity
Mar 10, 10:38 pm– Mar 11, 2:46 pm	3rd	Virgo	Cultivate, especially medicinal plants. Destroy weeds and pests. Trim to retard growth.
Mar 13, 8:22 pm– Mar 16, 5:21 am	3rd	Scorpio	Plant biennials, perennials, bulbs and roots. Prune. Irrigate. Fertilize (organic).

Global warming is impacting plant and animal life. According to a senior fellow with Stanford's Institute for International Studies, birds are laying their eggs earlier, animals are breaking out of their hibernation earlier, and plants are blooming earlier in the year than ever before. The rate of change appears to be about five days earlier per decade. Long-term, these changes will have a negative impact on habitat and animal life.

_____

_____

_____

_____

O
March 10
10:38 pm EDT
Daylight Saving Time begins
  March 8, 2:00 am

MARCH

S	M	T	W	T	F	S
						1	2	3	4	5	6	7
8	9	10	11	12	13	14
15	16	17	18	19	20	21
22	23	24	25	26	27	28
29	30	31

March 15–21

By working faithfully eight hours a day you may eventually get to be boss and work twelve hours a day.

~ROBERT FROST

Date	Qtr.	Sign	Activity
Mar 13, 8:22 pm– Mar 16, 5:21 am	3rd	Scorpio	Plant biennials, perennials, bulbs and roots. Prune. Irrigate. Fertilize (organic).
Mar 16, 5:21 am– Mar 18, 1:47 pm	3rd	Sagittarius	Cultivate. Destroy weeds and pests. Harvest fruits and root crops for food. Trim to retard growth.
Mar 18, 1:47 pm– Mar 18, 5:18 pm	4th	Sagittarius	Cultivate. Destroy weeds and pests. Harvest fruits and root crops for food. Trim to retard growth.
Mar 18, 5:18 pm– Mar 21, 6:06 am	4th	Capricorn	Plant potatoes and tubers. Trim to retard growth.

Botanists at the Smithsonian's National Museum of Natural History reviewed records on the spring bloom time of 100 common Washington D.C. area plants in 2003–04 to understand more about the effects of global warming. Eighty-nine of the 100 showed significantly earlier blooming—an average of thirty-nine days earlier than in 1970.

Resource: *www.smithsonianmag.com*

March 18
1:47 am EDT

MARCH

S	M	T	W	T	F	S
	1	2	3	4	5	6	7
8	9	10	11	12	13	14
15	16	17	18	19	20	21
22	23	24	25	26	27	28
29	30	31				

March 22–28

The world is mud-luscious and puddle-wonderful.

~E. E. CUMMINGS

Date	Qtr.	Sign	Activity
Mar 21, 6:06 am– Mar 23, 5:08 pm	4th	Aquarius	Cultivate. Destroy weeds and pests. Harvest fruits and root crops for food. Trim to retard growth.
Mar 23, 5:08 pm– Mar 26, 1:03 am	4th	Pisces	Plant biennials, perennials, bulbs and roots. Prune. Irrigate. Fertilize (organic).
Mar 26, 1:03 am– Mar 26, 12:06 pm	4th	Aries	Cultivate. Destroy weeds and pests. Harvest fruits and root crops for food. Trim to retard growth.
Mar 28, 6:09 am– Mar 30, 9:36 am	1st	Taurus	Plant annuals for hardiness. Trim to increase growth.

As the season changes from spring to summer in the Northern Hemisphere, the Moon appears further to the south and it is closer to the horizon as it travels through the night sky. This effect is due to the tilt of the Earth in its orbit around the Sun. Careful observers will notice that the crescent Moon looks like a bowl in the spring, and by summer, the "bowl" is tipped on its side. According to folklore, when the bowl tips, it loses its water and we get more rain.

March 26
12:06 pm EDT

MARCH

S	M	T	W	T	F	S
	1	2	3	4	5	6	7
8	9	10	11	12	13	14
15	16	17	18	19	20	21
22	23	24	25	26	27	28
29	30	31				

April

March 29–April 4

*In the spring, at the end of the day, you should smell
like dirt.*

~MARGARET ATWOOD

Date	Qtr.	Sign	Activity
Mar 28, 6:09 am– Mar 30, 9:36 am	1st	Taurus	Plant annuals for hardiness. Trim to increase growth.
Apr 1, 12:30 pm– Apr 2, 10:34 am	1st	Cancer	Plant grains, leafy annuals. Fertilize (chemical). Graft or bud plants. Irrigate. Trim to increase growth.

Every year new plant varieties are introduced to the market-place. Which ones will perform well in your area is always a concern to busy homeowners. Some people take up the challenge and give new varieties a trial. Others will wait until local garden centers have performed the trials and offer the varieties that require the least maintenance and the best uniformity and most continuous bloom. If it's been awhile since you tried a new variety, think about giving one a trial run this summer.

April 2
10:43 am EDT

APRIL

S	M	T	W	T	F	S
			1	2	3	4
5	6	7	8	9	10	11
12	13	14	15	16	17	18
19	20	21	22	23	24	25
26	27	28	29	30		

April 5–11

Many organic practices simply make sense, regardless of what overall agricultural system is used.

~DAVID SUZUKI, GENETICIST AND ENVIRONMENTAL ACTIVIST

Date	Qtr.	Sign	Activity
Apr 7, 11:22 pm– Apr 9, 10:56 am	2nd	Libra	Plant annuals for fragrance and beauty. Trim to increase growth.
Apr 10, 5:23 am– Apr 12, 2:00 pm	3rd	Scorpio	Plant biennials, perennials, bulbs and roots. Prune. Irrigate. Fertilize (organic).

There are some simple things you can do if you want to take a more organic approach to gardening.

- Deep watering will help plants develop deep root systems and protect the plants from drying out.

- Install a drip watering system that works on a timer.

- Add organic matter on a regular basis to increase soil nutrients.

- Add mulch to protect plants and preserve soil moisture.

○
April 8
10:56 am EDT

APRIL

S	M	T	W	T	F	S
			1	2	3	4
5	6	7	8	9	10	11
12	13	14	15	16	17	18
19	20	21	22	23	24	25
26	27	28	29	30		

April 12–18 ♈

Never yet was a springtime, when the buds forgot to bloom.
~MARGARET ELIZABETH SANGSTER

Date	Qtr.	Sign	Activity
Apr 10, 5:23 am– Apr 12, 2:00 pm	3rd	Scorpio	Plant biennials, perennials, bulbs and roots. Prune. Irrigate. Fertilize (organic).
Apr 12, 2:00 pm– Apr 15, 1:27 am	3rd	Sagittarius	Cultivate. Destroy weeds and pests. Harvest fruits and root crops for food. Trim to retard growth.
Apr 15, 1:27 am– Apr 17, 9:36 am	3rd	Capricorn	Plant potatoes and tubers. Trim to retard growth.
Apr 17, 9:36 am– Apr 17, 2:19 pm	4th	Capricorn	Plant potatoes and tubers. Trim to retard growth.
Apr 17, 2:19 pm– Apr 20, 1:55 am	4th	Aquarius	Cultivate. Destroy weeds and pests. Harvest fruits and root crops for food. Trim to retard growth.

Container gardening is often the best solution for renters. Pots and planters come in a wide array of sizes and colors, and you won't have to worry about how often the landlord waters the grass—even if they would allow you to plant something in the yard. Containers need frequent watering to keep your plants healthy, but you can grow some awesome tomatoes in a plastic pot!

April 17
9:36 am EDT

APRIL

S	M	T	W	T	F	S
				1	2	3	4
5	6	7	8	9	10	11
12	13	14	15	16	17	18
19	20	21	22	23	24	25
26	27	28	29	30		

April 19–25

If the rain spoils our picnic, but saves a farmer's crop, who are we to say it shouldn't rain?

~TOM BARRETT

Date	Qtr.	Sign	Activity
Apr 17, 2:19 pm– Apr 20, 1:55 am	4th	Aquarius	Cultivate. Destroy weeds and pests. Harvest fruits and root crops for food. Trim to retard growth.
Apr 20, 1:55 am– Apr 22, 10:09 am	4th	Pisces	Plant biennials, perennials, bulbs and roots. Prune. Irrigate. Fertilize (organic).
Apr 22, 10:09 am– Apr 24, 2:46 pm	4th	Aries	Cultivate. Destroy weeds and pests. Harvest fruits and root crops for food. Trim to retard growth.
Apr 24, 2:46 pm– Apr 24, 11:22 pm	4th	Taurus	Plant potatoes and tubers. Trim to retard growth.
Apr 24, 11:22 pm– Apr 26, 5:02 pm	1st	Taurus	Plant annuals for hardiness. Trim to increase growth.

April showers bring May flowers, but where do flowers bloom best? The annual precipitation in places around the U.S. varies a lot.

- Albany, NY: 35.74 inches of precipitation in 134 days

- Las Vegas, NV: 4.19 inches of precipitation in 26 days

- New Orleans, LA: 59.74 inches of precipitation in 114 days

April 24
11:22 pm EDT

APRIL

S	M	T	W	T	F	S
			1	2	3	4
5	6	7	8	9	10	11
12	13	14	15	16	17	18
19	20	21	22	23	24	25
26	27	28	29	30		

May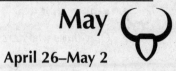

April 26–May 2

The true harvest of my life is intangible—a little star dust
caught, a portion of the rainbow I have clutched.

~HENRY DAVID THOREAU

Date	Qtr.	Sign	Activity
Apr 28, 6:38 pm– Apr 30, 8:56 pm	1st	Cancer	Plant grains, leafy annuals. Fertilize (chemical). Graft or bud plants. Irrigate. Trim to increase growth.

Green vegetables are packed with nutrients and cancer-fighting phytochemicals. Some phytochemicals aid digestion and keep bacteria out of your stomach. Broccoli is especially good for that. Eating green vegetables will help keep your eyes healthy, and those rich in potassium help your heart to beat correctly and your muscles to contract. Broccoli, kale, Brussel sprouts, spinach, okra, artichoke, romaine lettuce, bok choy, and green bell pepper are only a few of your choices. There are a lot more to choose from.

_____

_____

_____

_____

May 1
4:44 pm EDT

MAY

S	M	T	W	T	F	S
					1	2
3	4	5	6	7	8	9
10	11	12	13	14	15	16
17	18	19	20	21	22	23
24	25	26	27	28	29	30
31						

May 3–9

Only those who dare to fail greatly can ever achieve greatly.

~Robert F. Kennedy

Date	Qtr.	Sign	Activity
May 5, 5:51 am–May 7, 12:48 pm	2nd	Libra	Plant annuals for fragrance and beauty. Trim to increase growth.
May 7, 12:48 pm–May 9, 12:01 am	2nd	Scorpio	Plant grains, leafy annuals. Fertilize (chemical). Graft or bud plants. Irrigate. Trim to increase growth.
May 9, 12:01 am–May 9, 9:49 pm	3rd	Scorpio	Plant biennials, perennials, bulbs and roots. Prune. Irrigate. Fertilize (organic).

There is a Chinese proverb that says "The temptation to quit will always be greatest just before you are about to succeed." Union General George B. McClellan lost several engagements to his Confederate adversary, Robert E. Lee. McClellan's fear of loss was so great that it prevented him from winning even though he commanded the most powerful force ever assembled. Lee won because he was willing to risk failure.

May 9
12:01 am EDT

S	M	T	W	T	F	S
					1	2
3	4	5	6	7	8	9
10	11	12	13	14	15	16
17	18	19	20	21	22	23
24	25	26	27	28	29	30
31						

MAY

May 10–16

The thought you have now shapes your experience of the next
moment. Practice shaping the moment.

~TOM BARRETT

Date	Qtr.	Sign	Activity
May 9, 9:49 pm–May 12, 9:09 am	3rd	Sagittarius	Cultivate. Destroy weeds and pests. Harvest fruits and root crops for food. Trim to retard growth.
May 12, 9:09 am–May 14, 10:01 pm	3rd	Capricorn	Plant potatoes and tubers. Trim to retard growth.
May 14, 10:01 pm–May 17, 3:26 am	3rd	Aquarius	Cultivate. Destroy weeds and pests. Harvest fruits and root crops for food. Trim to retard growth.

There's more to planting onions than you might have thought. Some onion varieties—the Walla Walla and Ringmaster, for example—enjoy the 14- to 16-hour long summer days found in northern states. Candy and Superstar are intermediate-day varieties that require 12 to 14 hours of daylight. They do well in the middle tier of states. White Bermuda and Texas Super Sweet are short-day varieties. If you plant short-day onions in northern states, they mature faster and produce smaller bulbs than the same varieties will when planted in the south.

			MAY			
S	M	T	W	T	F	S
					1	2
3	4	5	6	7	8	9
10	11	12	13	14	15	16
17	18	19	20	21	22	23
24	25	26	27	28	29	30
31						

May 17–23

I can't stand to see red in my profit-or-loss column. I'm Taurus the bull, so I react to red. If I see it, I sell my stocks quickly.

~BARBRA STREISAND

Date	Qtr.	Sign	Activity
May 14, 10:01 pm– May 17, 3:26 am	3rd	Aquarius	Cultivate. Destroy weeds and pests. Harvest fruits and root crops for food. Trim to retard growth.
May 17, 3:26 am– May 17, 10:17 am	4th	Aquarius	Cultivate. Destroy weeds and pests. Harvest fruits and root crops for food. Trim to retard growth.
May 17, 10:17 am– May 19, 7:30 pm	4th	Pisces	Plant biennials, perennials, bulbs and roots. Prune. Irrigate. Fertilize (organic).
May 19, 7:30 pm– May 22, 12:40 am	4th	Aries	Cultivate. Destroy weeds and pests. Harvest fruits and root crops for food. Trim to retard growth.
May 22, 12:40 am– May 24, 2:34 am	4th	Taurus	Plant potatoes and tubers. Trim to retard growth.

According to a Gallup Poll, the number of Americans who thought the economy got better in 2007 were in the minority, at 27 percent. Sixty-seven percent believed the economy got worse. You can check out more poll results at *www.galluppoll.com/*

May 17
3:26 am EDT

	MAY					
S	M	T	W	T	F	S
					1	2
3	4	5	6	7	8	9
10	11	12	13	14	15	16
17	18	19	20	21	22	23
24	25	26	27	28	29	30
31						

May 24–30

Don't be afraid of opposition. Remember that a kite rises against, not with, the wind.

~ANONYMOUS

Date	Qtr.	Sign	Activity
May 22, 12:40 am–May 24, 2:34 am	4th	Taurus	Plant potatoes and tubers. Trim to retard growth.
May 24, 2:34 am–May 24, 8:11 am	4th	Gemini	Cultivate. Destroy weeds and pests. Harvest fruits and root crops for food. Trim to retard growth.
May 26, 2:58 am–May 28, 3:44 am	1st	Cancer	Plant grains, leafy annuals. Fertilize (chemical). Graft or bud plants. Irrigate. Trim to increase growth.

Organic fertilizers are not always the best choice for plants. Organic fertilizers contain compost, bone meal, blood meal, and manure, and these ingredients are slow to break down so their nutrients are released over a longer period of time. A good use of organic fertilizer would be when you want to add food to a planting hole. On the other hand, liquid inorganic plant foods are good for container plants. Use them when you want to give your flowering plants and vegetables a boost.

● ◑
May 24   *May 30*
8:11 am EDT 11:22 pm EDT

MAY

S	M	T	W	T	F	S
					1	2
3	4	5	6	7	8	9
10	11	12	13	14	15	16
17	18	19	20	21	22	23
24	25	26	27	28	29	30
31						

June

May 31–June 6

The difficult we do immediately; the impossible takes a little longer.

~AIR FORCE MOTTO

Date	Qtr.	Sign	Activity
Jun 1, 11:17 am– Jun 3, 6:43 pm	2nd	Libra	Plant annuals for fragrance and beauty. Trim to increase growth.
Jun 3, 6:43 pm– Jun 6, 4:23 am	2nd	Scorpio	Plant grains, leafy annuals. Fertilize (chemical). Graft or bud plants. Irrigate. Trim to increase growth.

Orchids take a little extra care if you want them to bloom. In addition to sunlight (plenty of it), humidity (plenty of it), and fertilizer, orchids also need cool night temperatures to help them bloom. Cool temperatures in the fall will stimulate the plant to bloom in winter. Set your orchids outside this summer in a sunny spot, but move them back inside in the fall.

JUNE

S	M	T	W	T	F	S
		1	2	3	4	5	6
7	8	9	10	11	12	13
14	15	16	17	18	19	20
21	22	23	24	25	26	27
28	29	30

June 7–13

My most brilliant achievement was my ability to be able to persuade my wife to marry me.

~WINSTON CHURCHILL

Date	Qtr.	Sign	Activity
Jun 7, 2:12 pm– Jun 8, 3:59 pm	3rd	Sagittarius	Cultivate. Destroy weeds and pests. Harvest fruits and root crops for food. Trim to retard growth.
Jun 8, 3:59 pm– Jun 11, 4:52 am	3rd	Capricorn	Plant potatoes and tubers. Trim to retard growth.
Jun 11, 4:52 am– Jun 13, 5:32 pm	3rd	Aquarius	Cultivate. Destroy weeds and pests. Harvest fruits and root crops for food. Trim to retard growth.

What does it mean when the tag that accompanies the plant you're looking at says that the plant needs "full sun?" It means you should have a spot in your yard that gets at least six hours of direct sun each day. While some plants will tolerate both sun and light shade, they may need more sunlight to produce optimal blooms.

○
June 7
2:12 pm EDT

		JUNE				
S	M	T	W	T	F	S
	1	2	3	4	5	6
7	8	9	10	11	12	13
14	15	16	17	18	19	20
21	22	23	24	25	26	27
28	29	30				

June 14–20

The planet will survive. Whether we get to be here and enjoy it, or enjoy life as we've known it, is what's questionable.

~TED DANSON

Date	Qtr.	Sign	Activity
Jun 13, 5:32 pm– Jun 15, 6:14 pm	3rd	Pisces	Plant biennials, perennials, bulbs and roots. Prune. Irrigate. Fertilize (organic).
Jun 15, 6:14 pm– Jun 16, 3:51 am	4th	Pisces	Plant biennials, perennials, bulbs and roots. Prune. Irrigate. Fertilize (organic).
Jun 16, 3:51 am– Jun 18, 10:20 am	4th	Aries	Cultivate. Destroy weeds and pests. Harvest fruits and root crops for food. Trim to retard growth.
Jun 18, 10:20 am– Jun 20, 1:00 pm	4th	Taurus	Plant potatoes and tubers. Trim to retard growth.
Jun 20, 1:00 pm– Jun 22, 1:12 pm	4th	Gemini	Cultivate. Destroy weeds and pests. Harvest fruits and root crops for food. Trim to retard growth.

Remember that water intake is reduced when the Moon is waning. Cutting or pruning done now in your yard or garden will cause less injury to the plants (trees, shrubs, etc.).

_____

_____

_____

_____

◐
June 15
6:14 pm EDT

JUNE

S	M	T	W	T	F	S
	1	2	3	4	5	6
7	8	9	10	11	12	13
14	15	16	17	18	19	20
21	22	23	24	25	26	27
28	29	30				

June 21–27

Three things cannot be long hidden: the sun, the moon, and the truth.

~BUDDHA

Date	Qtr.	Sign	Activity
Jun 20, 1:00 pm–Jun 22, 1:12 pm	4th	Gemini	Cultivate. Destroy weeds and pests. Harvest fruits and root crops for food. Trim to retard growth.
Jun 22, 1:12 pm–Jun 22, 3:35 pm	4th	Cancer	Plant biennials, perennials, bulbs and roots. Prune. Irrigate. Fertilize (organic).
June 22, 3:35 pm–Jun 24, 12:50 pm	1st	Cancer	Plant grains, leafy annuals. Fertilize (chemical). Graft or bud plants. Irrigate. Trim to increase growth.

Most flowers, especially annuals, will benefit from deadheading—snipping or cutting off faded blooms. Some flowers will stop blooming or die if spent blooms are not removed. A weekly trip through your gardens to deadhead plants will help extend the blooming period and give you more time to enjoy the colors and smells of summer flowers.

June 22
3:35 am EDT

JUNE

S	M	T	W	T	F	S
	1	2	3	4	5	6
7	8	9	10	11	12	13
14	15	16	17	18	19	20
21	22	23	24	25	26	27
28	29	30				

July

June 28–July 4

If the first of July be rainy weather, it will rain, more or less, for four weeks together.

~JOHN RAY

Date	Qtr.	Sign	Activity
Jun 28, 5:24 pm–Jun 29, 7:28 am	1st	Libra	Plant annuals for fragrance and beauty. Trim to increase growth.
Jul 29, 7:28 am–Jul 1, 12:18 am	2nd	Libra	Plant annuals for fragrance and beauty. Trim to increase growth.
Jul 1, 12:18 am–Jul 3, 10:10 am	2nd	Scorpio	Plant grains, leafy annuals. Fertilize (chemical). Graft or bud plants. Irrigate. Trim to increase growth.

Flavored iced tea drinks are replacing cold coffee drinks for some people. These iced teas, usually made from black tea that has fruit or herbal infusions, are refreshing on a hot summer day, but they also have health benefits. Tea is well-known to be an excellent source of immune system-building antioxidants.

_____

_____

_____

June 29
7:28 am EDT

JULY

S	M	T	W	T	F	S
			1	2	3	4
5	6	7	8	9	10	11
12	13	14	15	16	17	18
19	20	21	22	23	24	25
26	27	28	29	30	31	

July 5–11

Motivation is what gets you started. Habit is what keeps you going.

~JIM ROHN

Date	Qtr.	Sign	Activity
Jul 5, 10:07 pm– Jul 7, 5:21 am	2nd	Capricorn	Graft or bud plants. Trim to increase growth.
Jul 7, 5:21 am– Jul 8, 11:03 am	3rd	Capricorn	Plant potatoes and tubers. Trim to retard growth.
Jul 8, 11:03 am– Jul 10, 11:44 pm	3rd	Aquarius	Cultivate. Destroy weeds and pests. Harvest fruits and root crops for food. Trim to retard growth.
Jul 10, 11:44 pm– Jul 13, 10:40 am	3rd	Pisces	Plant biennials, perennials, bulbs and roots. Prune. Irrigate. Fertilize (organic).

Moon gardens are designed to be seen at dusk and beyond. Moon gardeners design with white flowers and silvery-leafed plants that will reflect light. Moon gardens are made more interesting by using plants with different sized flowers and leaves, and lighting the path with solar-powered lights can add a special touch, too.

○
July 7
5:21 am EDT

JULY

S	M	T	W	T	F	S
			1	2	3	4
5	6	7	8	9	10	11
12	13	14	15	16	17	18
19	20	21	22	23	24	25
26	27	28	29	30	31	

July 12–18

*I know I am but summer to your heart, and not the full four
seasons of the year.*

~EDNA ST. VINCENT MILLAY

Date	Qtr.	Sign	Activity
Jul 10, 11:44 pm– Jul 13, 10:40 am	3rd	Pisces	Plant biennials, perennials, bulbs and roots. Prune. Irrigate. Fertilize (organic).
Jul 13, 10:40 am– Jul 15, 5:53 am	3rd	Aries	Cultivate. Destroy weeds and pests. Harvest fruits and root crops for food. Trim to retard growth.
Jul 15, 5:53 am– Jul 15, 6:30 pm	4th	Aries	Cultivate. Destroy weeds and pests. Harvest fruits and root crops for food. Trim to retard growth.
Jul 15, 6:30 pm– Jul 17, 10:41 pm	4th	Taurus	Plant potatoes and tubers. Trim to retard growth.
Jul 17, 10:41 pm– Jul 19, 11:51 pm	4th	Gemini	Cultivate. Destroy weeds and pests. Harvest fruits and root crops for food. Trim to retard growth.

Lunar winds move across the surface of the Earth twice daily, just as do ocean tides. Moving at about ¹⁄₂₀ mph, they flow east the morning and west in the afternoon.

SOURCE: *THE LUNAR GARDEN* BY E. A. CRAWFORD

_____

_____

_____

_____

July 15
5:53 am EDT

JULY

S	M	T	W	T	F	S
			1	2	3	4
5	6	7	8	9	10	11
12	13	14	15	16	17	18
19	20	21	22	23	24	25
26	27	28	29	30	31	

July 19–25

If the New Moon is seen for the first time straight ahead, it predicts good fortune until the next New Moon.

~FOLK LORE

Date	Qtr.	Sign	Activity
Jul 19, 11:51 pm– Jul 21, 10:34 pm	4th	Cancer	Plant biennials, perennials, bulbs and roots. Prune. Irrigate. Fertilize (organic).
Jul 21, 10:34 pm– Jul 21, 11:27 pm	1st	Cancer	Plant grains, leafy annuals. Fertilize (chemical). Graft or bud plants. Irrigate. Trim to increase growth.

The relationship of Saturn to the Moon is taken into consideration by lunar gardeners when planting perennials that need to be hardy and long lasting. Good dates to plant perennials (according to this rule) are: July 29, August 3, and October 8. If you find success with this rule and you'd like to apply it to other times of the year, check either our astrology calendar or an astrology datebook for dates when the Moon and Saturn are sextile or trine each other (and don't forget to take the Moon's phase into consideration).

_____

_____

_____

_____

July 21
10:34 pm EDT

JULY

S	M	T	W	T	F	S
			1	2	3	4
5	6	7	8	9	10	11
12	13	14	15	16	17	18
19	20	21	22	23	24	25
26	27	28	29	30	31	

August

July 26–August 1

Angel of hope and calendars, do you know despair? That hole
I crawl into with a box of Kleenex . . .

~Anne Sexton

Date	Qtr.	Sign	Activity
Jul 26, 1:25 am–Jul 28, 6:56 am	1st	Libra	Plant annuals for fragrance and beauty. Trim to increase growth.
Jul 28, 6:56 am–Jul 28, 6:00 pm	1st	Scorpio	Plant grains, leafy annuals. Fertilize (chemical). Graft or bud plants. Irrigate. Trim to increase growth.
Jul 28, 6:00 pm–Jul 30, 4:10 pm	2nd	Scorpio	Plant grains, leafy annuals. Fertilize (chemical). Graft or bud plants. Irrigate. Trim to increase growth.

Plant fragrant flowers near the house, where you visit them often and get more enjoyment from them. Also, heat reflected from patios or driveways will intensify flower scents, as will planting fragrant flowers in places that are protected from the wind. An enclosed or sheltered space will allow the fragrance to collect and intensify.

July 28
6:00 pm EDT

		JULY				
S	M	T	W	T	F	S
				1	2	3	4
5	6	7	8	9	10	11
12	13	14	15	16	17	18
19	20	21	22	23	24	25
26	27	28	29	30	31	

August 2–8 ♌

Either you run the day or the day runs you.

—JIM ROHN

Date	Qtr.	Sign	Activity
Aug 2, 4:08 am–Aug 4, 5:08 pm	2nd	Capricorn	Graft or bud plants. Trim to increase growth.
Aug 5, 8:55 pm–Aug 7, 5:34 am	3rd	Aquarius	Cultivate. Destroy weeds and pests. Harvest fruits and root crops for food. Trim to retard growth.
Aug 7, 5:34 am–Aug 9, 4:23 pm	3rd	Pisces	Plant biennials, perennials, bulbs and roots. Prune. Irrigate. Fertilize (organic).

Lawns don't like drought conditions. They turn brown and crispy if dry conditions last too long, but when heavy watering isn't an option, you can minimize lawn damage by rethinking where you plant grass and what kind of plants you have in your yard. Removing four feet of grass next to the driveway and replacing it with mulch and a few drought-tolerant shrubs or trees not only adds interest to the landscape, it is an eco-friendly solution, too.

○

August 5
8:55 pm EDT

AUGUST

S	M	T	W	T	F	S
						1
2	3	4	5	6	7	8
9	10	11	12	13	14	15
16	17	18	19	20	21	22
23	24	25	26	27	28	29
30	31					

August 9–15

A perfect summer day is when the sun is shining, the breeze is blowing, the birds are singing, and the lawn mower is broken.

~James Dent

Date	Qtr.	Sign	Activity
Aug 9, 4:23 pm– Aug 12, 12:49 am	3rd	Aries	Cultivate. Destroy weeds and pests. Harvest fruits and root crops for food. Trim to retard growth.
Aug 12, 12:49 am– Aug 13, 2:55 pm	3rd	Taurus	Plant potatoes and tubers. Trim to retard growth.
Aug 13, 2:55 pm– Aug 14, 6:25 am	4th	Taurus	Plant potatoes and tubers. Trim to retard growth.
Aug 14, 6:25 am– Aug 16, 9:13 am	4th	Gemini	Cultivate. Destroy weeds and pests. Harvest fruits and root crops for food. Trim to retard growth.

If you want to apply an organic insect spray to your plants, try the following recipe. Combine 1 pint of water, 1 teaspoon of Tabasco, ½ teaspoon cayenne pepper, and 2 large crushed garlic cloves in a container with a spray nozzle. Spray your plants with this mixture during the waning Moon.

August 13
2:55 pm EDT

August

S	M	T	W	T	F	S
						1
2	3	4	5	6	7	8
9	10	11	12	13	14	15
16	17	18	19	20	21	22
23	24	25	26	27	28	29
30	31					

August 16–22 ♌

Don't knock the weather; nine-tenths of the people couldn't
start a conversation if it didn't change once in a while.

~KIN HUBBARD

Date	Qtr.	Sign	Activity
Aug 16, 9:13 am– Aug 18, 9:56 am	4th	Cancer	Plant biennials, perennials, bulbs and roots. Prune. Irrigate. Fertilize (organic).
Aug 18, 9:56 am– Aug 20, 6:01 am	4th	Leo	Cultivate. Destroy weeds and pests. Harvest fruits and root crops for food. Trim to retard growth.
Aug 22, 11:12 am– Aug 24, 3:16 pm	1st	Libra	Plant annuals for fragrance and beauty. Trim to increase growth.

Fruits and vegetables meant to be eaten immediately are best harvested during the waxing phase of the Moon. If you plan to store the fruits or vegetables for a time before you eat them, harvest during the waning Moon phase.

August 20
6:01 am EDT

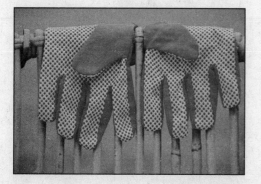

AUGUST

S	M	T	W	T	F	S
						1
2	3	4	5	6	7	8
9	10	11	12	13	14	15
16	17	18	19	20	21	22
23	24	25	26	27	28	29
30	31					

♍ August 23–29

The coldest winter I ever spent was a summer in San Francisco.

~MARK TWAIN, ATTRIBUTED

Date	Qtr.	Sign	Activity
Aug 22, 11:12 am–Aug 24, 3:16 pm	1st	Libra	Plant annuals for fragrance and beauty. Trim to increase growth.
Aug 24, 3:16 pm–Aug 26, 11:16 pm	1st	Scorpio	Plant grains, leafy annuals. Fertilize (chemical). Graft or bud plants. Irrigate. Trim to increase growth.
Aug 29, 10:44 am–Aug 31, 11:43 pm	2nd	Capricorn	Graft or bud plants. Trim to increase growth.

Plant those peach pits! The tree that grows from a peach pit will not be the same as the tree that bore the fruit (those trees are grafted), but the fruit from your own tree will be good nonetheless. Plant them about a foot apart in your garden in the fall and cover over with four inches of soil and some mulch—pine needles, straw, etc.—and water. Many of the pits will germinate in the spring. You can then transplant them to a new location or put them in pots.

_____

_____

_____

_____

August 27
7:42 am EDT

AUGUST

S	M	T	W	T	F	S
						1
2	3	4	5	6	7	8
9	10	11	12	13	14	15
16	17	18	19	20	21	22
23	24	25	26	27	28	29
30	31					

September ♍

August 30–September 5

*The conservative argument is that the economy is like the
weather, that it just operates automatically.*

~Sidney Blumenthal

Date	Qtr.	Sign	Activity
Aug 29, 10:44 am– Aug 31, 11:43 pm	2nd	Capricorn	Graft or bud plants. Trim to increase growth.
Sep 3, 11:58 am– Sep 4, 12:02 pm	2nd	Pisces	Plant grains, leafy annuals. Fertilize (chemical). Graft or bud plants. Irrigate. Trim to increase growth.
Sep 4, 12:02 pm– Sep 5, 10:14 pm	3rd	Pisces	Plant biennials, perennials, bulbs and roots. Prune. Irrigate. Fertilize (organic).
Sep 5, 10:14 pm– Sep 8, 6:17 am	3rd	Aries	Cultivate. Destroy weeds and pests. Harvest fruits and root crops for food. Trim to retard growth.

Tulip bulbs can be placed in the refrigerator (at about 40° F) for at least ten weeks if you want to force them to bloom this winter. Plan ahead now if you want to decorate your rooms with red and white blooms over the holidays. 'Apricot Beauty,' 'Diana,' 'Merry Christmas,' and 'Abba' are good choices for indoor forcing.

○
September 4
12:02 pm EDT

SEPTEMBER

S	M	T	W	T	F	S
		1	2	3	4	5
6	7	8	9	10	11	12
13	14	15	16	17	18	19
20	21	22	23	24	25	26
27	28	29	30			

♍ September 6–12

September: it was the most beautiful of words, he'd always felt, evoking orange-flowers, swallows, and regret.

~ALEXANDER THEROUX

Date	Qtr.	Sign	Activity
Sep 5, 10:14 pm–Sep 8, 6:17 am	3rd	Aries	Cultivate. Destroy weeds and pests. Harvest fruits and root crops for food. Trim to retard growth.
Sep 8, 6:17 am–Sep 10, 12:17 pm	3rd	Taurus	Plant potatoes and tubers. Trim to retard growth.
Sep 10, 12:17 pm–Sep 11, 10:16 pm	3rd	Gemini	Cultivate. Destroy weeds and pests. Harvest fruits and root crops for food. Trim to retard growth.
Sep 11, 10:16 pm–Sep 12, 4:19 pm	4th	Gemini	Cultivate. Destroy weeds and pests. Harvest fruits and root crops for food. Trim to retard growth.

Citrus trees make wonderful indoor houseplants. They need a warm room that gets five to six hours of sun, and a high-nitrogen, acid fertilizer; and in return, they'll reward you with year-round fragrant blooms, and maybe even some fruit.

Resource: *www.colostate.edu/Depts/CoopExt/4DMG/Plants/ citrus.htm/*

September 11
10:16 pm EDT

SEPTEMBER

S	M	T	W	T	F	S
		1	2	3	4	5
6	7	8	9	10	11	12
13	14	15	16	17	18	19
20	21	22	23	24	25	26
27	28	29	30			

September 13–19 ♍

One sees great things from the valley, only small things from the peak.

~G. K. CHESTERTON

Date	Qtr.	Sign	Activity
Sep 12, 4:19 pm– Sep 14, 6:39 pm	4th	Cancer	Plant biennials, perennials, bulbs and roots. Prune. Irrigate. Fertilize (organic).
Sep 14, 6:39 pm– Sep 16, 7:56 pm	4th	Leo	Cultivate. Destroy weeds and pests. Harvest fruits and root crops for food. Trim to retard growth.
Sep 16, 7:56 pm– Sep 18, 2:44 pm	4th	Virgo	Cultivate, especially medicinal plants. Destroy weeds and pests. Trim to retard growth.
Sep 18, 9:26 pm– Sep 21, 12:52 am	1st	Libra	Plant annuals for fragrance and beauty. Trim to increase growth.

D id you know that human hair actually gets longer when humidity goes up? One weather watcher suggests that when hair becomes less manageable, it may be an indication that rain is on the way.

Resource: *http://wilstar.com/skywatch.htm#indicators/*

September 18
2:44 pm EDT

SEPTEMBER

S	M	T	W	T	F	S
		1	2	3	4	5
6	7	8	9	10	11	12
13	14	15	16	17	18	19
20	21	22	23	24	25	26
27	28	29	30			

♍ September 20–26

I'm not interested in age. People who tell me their age are silly. You're as old as you feel.

~ELIZABETH ARDEN

Date	Qtr.	Sign	Activity
Sep 18, 9:26 pm– Sep 21, 12:52 am	1st	Libra	Plant annuals for fragrance and beauty. Trim to increase growth.
Sep 21, 12:52 am– Sep 23, 7:43 am	1st	Scorpio	Plant grains, leafy annuals. Fertilize (chemical). Graft or bud plants. Irrigate. Trim to increase growth.
Sep 25, 6:19 pm– Sep 26, 12:50 am	1st	Capricorn	Graft or bud plants. Trim to increase growth.
Sep 26, 12:50 am– Sep 28, 7:06 am	2nd	Capricorn	Graft or bud plants. Trim to increase growth.

"When the dew is on the grass,
Rain will never come to pass.
When grass is dry at morning light,
Look for rain before the night."

September 26
12:50 am EDT

SEPTEMBER

S	M	T	W	T	F	S
		1	2	3	4	5
6	7	8	9	10	11	12
13	14	15	16	17	18	19
20	21	22	23	24	25	26
27	28	29	30			

October ⟋‿⟍

September 27–October 3

You'll never do a whole lot unless you're brave enough to try.

~Dolly Parton

Date	Qtr.	Sign	Activity
Sep 26, 12:50 am– Sep 28, 7:06 am	2nd	Capricorn	Graft or bud plants. Trim to increase growth.
Sep 30, 7:26 pm– Oct 3, 5:20 am	2nd	Pisces	Plant grains, leafy annuals. Fertilize (chemical). Graft or bud plants. Irrigate. Trim to increase growth.

Orchids like to be fed constantly. This is mostly due to the medium they're planted in—bark. Bark is very poor at holding nutrients, so plan on feeding your orchids with a weak fertilizer solution once a week. Keep your orchids in a room where the nighttime temperature is between 50 and 60 degrees Fahrenheit, and once they are blooming, the cool temperatures will help your plants produce more vivid blooms that last longer.

OCTOBER						
S	M	T	W	T	F	S
					1	2	3
4	5	6	7	8	9	10
11	12	13	14	15	16	17
18	19	20	21	22	23	24
25	26	27	28	29	30	31

♎ October 4–10

Fear of failure and making mistakes is the first real impediment to success.

~STEVEN STOWELL

Date	Qtr.	Sign	Activity
Oct 4, 2:10 am– Oct 5, 12:33 pm	3rd	Aries	Cultivate. Destroy weeds and pests. Harvest fruits and root crops for food. Trim to retard growth.
Oct 5, 12:33 pm– Oct 7, 5:46 pm	3rd	Taurus	Plant potatoes and tubers. Trim to retard growth.
Oct 7, 5:46 pm– Oct 9, 9:48 pm	3rd	Gemini	Cultivate. Destroy weeds and pests. Harvest fruits and root crops for food. Trim to retard growth.
Oct 9, 9:48 pm– Oct 11, 4:56 am	3rd	Cancer	Plant biennials, perennials, bulbs and roots. Prune. Irrigate. Fertilize (organic).

Weather systems usually move from west to east. A reddish evening sky can be caused by sunlight shining through dry dust particles in the western sky. This dry sky may move overhead by morning. If the morning is gray in the east, it means the clouds have already passed you. But if the evening is gray, it means the clouds have not yet reached you, and rain may be on its way.

○
October 4
2:10 am EDT

OCTOBER

S	M	T	W	T	F	S
				1	2	3
4	5	6	7	8	9	10
11	12	13	14	15	16	17
18	19	20	21	22	23	24
25	26	27	28	29	30	31

October 11–17 ♎

Farmers and gardeners, dependent on the whims of nature,
watch the Moon and study its effects.

~E. A. CRAWFORD

Date	Qtr.	Sign	Activity
Oct 11, 4:56 am– Oct 12, 1:02 am	4th	Cancer	Plant biennials, perennials, bulbs and roots. Prune. Irrigate. Fertilize (organic).
Oct 12, 1:02 am– Oct 14, 3:45 am	4th	Leo	Cultivate. Destroy weeds and pests. Harvest fruits and root crops for food. Trim to retard growth.
Oct 14, 3:45 am– Oct 16, 6:29 am	4th	Virgo	Cultivate, especially medicinal plants. Destroy weeds and pests. Trim to retard growth.

The potato, a member of the nightshade family, was originally cultivated in the Andes Mountains. It took about 250 years after the Spanish conquistadors brought potatoes back to Europe in 1570 before the general population accepted them. Until the early 1800s, potatoes were considered food for only the poor to eat.

_____

_____

_____

_____

October 11
4:56 am EDT

OCTOBER

S	M	T	W	T	F	S
				1	2	3
4	5	6	7	8	9	10
11	12	13	14	15	16	17
18	19	20	21	22	23	24
25	26	27	28	29	30	31

October 18–24

Even gardening is easier if we learn to work with nature
instead of trying to control our environment.

~JUDE C. TODD

Date	Qtr.	Sign	Activity
Oct 18, 1:33 am– Oct 18, 10:22 am	1st	Libra	Plant annuals for fragrance and beauty. Trim to increase growth.
Oct 18, 10:22 am– Oct 20, 4:49 pm	1st	Scorpio	Plant grains, leafy annuals. Fertilize (chemical). Graft or bud plants. Irrigate. Trim to increase growth.
Oct 23, 2:39 am– Oct 25, 3:08 pm	1st	Capricorn	Graft or bud plants. Trim to increase growth.

Snakes love gardens because there are so many places for them to hide. Did you know that you can make a fence to keep snakes out? A snake-proof fence can be made of heavy galvanized screen, about three-feet wide with a quarter-inch mesh. The fence should slant away from the garden at a thirty-degree angle and be buried six inches below the soil surface. Remove or closely mow any vegetation that may be near the fence.

Resource: *www.colostate.edu/Depts/CoopExt/4DMG/Pests/snakesin. htm/*

October 18
1:33 am EDT

OCTOBER

S	M	T	W	T	F	S
				1	2	3
4	5	6	7	8	9	10
11	12	13	14	15	16	17
18	19	20	21	22	23	24
25	26	27	28	29	30	31

October 25–31 ♏

Life is not measured by the number of breaths we take, but by the moments that take our breath away.

~UNKNOWN

Date	Qtr.	Sign	Activity
Oct 23, 2:39 am–Oct 25, 3:08 pm	1st	Capricorn	Graft or bud plants. Trim to increase growth.
Oct 28, 3:45 am–Oct 30, 1:56 pm	2nd	Pisces	Plant grains, leafy annuals. Fertilize (chemical). Graft or bud plants. Irrigate. Trim to increase growth.

Stress management is important if we want to enjoy life. We can think positive, which doesn't always work, or we can reframe how we think about some things—especially things that cause stress. If how you think about something has given you heartburn or high blood pressure, is it worth the risk you're taking? Perhaps the key is to focus on what is going on inside and spend much less energy worrying about what is happening around us. Breathe, and . . . release.

_____

_____

_____

_____

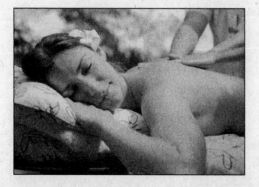

October 25
8:42 pm EDT

OCTOBER

S	M	T	W	T	F	S
				1	2	3
4	5	6	7	8	9	10
11	12	13	14	15	16	17
18	19	20	21	22	23	24
25	26	27	28	29	30	31

♏ November

November 1–7

When you lose touch with your inner stillness, you lose touch with yourself.

~ECKHART TOLLE

Date	Qtr.	Sign	Activity
Nov 1, 7:44 pm– Nov 2, 2:14 pm	2nd	Taurus	Plant annuals for hardiness. Trim to increase growth.
Nov 2, 2:14 pm– Nov 4, 11:53 am	3rd	Taurus	Plant potatoes and tubers. Trim to retard growth.
Nov 4, 11:53 am– Nov 6, 2:42 am	3rd	Gemini	Cultivate. Destroy weeds and pests. Harvest fruits and root crops for food. Trim to retard growth.
Nov 6, 2:42 am– Nov 8, 5:23 am	3rd	Cancer	Plant biennials, perennials, bulbs and roots. Prune. Irrigate. Fertilize (organic).

The herbs of Scorpio are antiseptic and cleansing in nature. The best known of these are horehound, horseradish, sarsaparilla, and leek. All of these stimulate the glandular system to eliminate waste that accumulates in the throat, bladder, and reproductive organs.

○
November 2
2:14 pm EST
Daylight Saving Time ends
    November 1, 2 am

NOVEMBER

S	M	T	W	T	F	S
1	2	3	4	5	6	7
8	9	10	11	12	13	14
15	16	17	18	19	20	21
22	23	24	25	26	27	28
29	30					

November 8–14 ♏

Part of critical thinking is the questioning of underlying assumptions, including our own.

~DAVID POLLARD

Date	Qtr.	Sign	Activity
Nov 6, 2:42 am– Nov 8, 5:23 am	3rd	Cancer	Plant biennials, perennials, bulbs and roots. Prune. Irrigate. Fertilize (organic).
Nov 8, 5:23 am– Nov 9, 10:56 am	3rd	Leo	Cultivate. Destroy weeds and pests. Harvest fruits and root crops for food. Trim to retard growth.
Nov 9, 10:56 am– Nov 10, 8:30 am	4th	Leo	Cultivate. Destroy weeds and pests. Harvest fruits and root crops for food. Trim to retard growth.
Nov 10, 8:30 am– Nov 12, 12:22 pm	4th	Virgo	Cultivate, especially medicinal plants. Destroy weeds and pests. Trim to retard growth.
Nov 14, 5:24 pm– Nov 16, 2:14 pm	4th	Scorpio	Plant biennials, perennials, bulbs and roots. Prune. Irrigate. Fertilize (organic).

Snowbird alert! If you're a gardener, and you're planning to relocate to the southwest, where it's warmer and dryer in the winter, learn about xeriscaping. Xeriscaping requires less water, fertilizer, and maintenance than many other types of landscaping, and it's beautiful. Xeriscaping can be used in any location, though, and you may want to consider incorporating the principles of xeriscaping in your lawn design.

November 9
10:56 am EST

NOVEMBER

S	M	T	W	T	F	S
1	2	3	4	5	6	7
8	9	10	11	12	13	14
15	16	17	18	19	20	21
22	23	24	25	26	27	28
29	30					

♏ November 15–21

Fame always brings loneliness. Success is as ice cold and lonely as the North Pole.

~VICKI BAUM

Date	Qtr.	Sign	Activity
Nov 14, 5:24 pm– Nov 16, 2:14 pm	4th	Scorpio	Plant biennials, perennials, bulbs and roots. Prune. Irrigate. Fertilize (organic).
Nov 16, 2:14 pm– Nov 17, 12:22 am	1st	Scorpio	Plant grains, leafy annuals. Fertilize (chemical). Graft or bud plants. Irrigate. Trim to increase growth.
Nov 19, 10:00 am– Nov 21, 10:11 pm	1st	Capricorn	Graft or bud plants. Trim to increase growth.

W inter is approaching in many areas of the United States and the world. With winter comes dry air and brittle fingernails. Some gardeners recommend eating plenty of cucumbers to help prevent brittle and splitting nails.

—————————————————————

—————————————————————

—————————————————————

—————————————————————

●
November 16
2:14 pm EST

NOVEMBER

S	M	T	W	T	F	S
1	2	3	4	5	6	7
8	9	10	11	12	13	14
15	16	17	18	19	20	21
22	23	24	25	26	27	28
29	30	31				

November 22–28

If you want to turn your life around, try thankfulness. It will change your life mightily.

~GERALD GOOD

Date	Qtr.	Sign	Activity
Nov 24, 11:07 am–Nov 24, 4:39 pm	1st	Pisces	Plant grains, leafy annuals. Fertilize (chemical). Graft or bud plants. Irrigate. Trim to increase growth.
Nov 24, 4:39 pm–Nov 26, 10:10 pm	2nd	Pisces	Plant grains, leafy annuals. Fertilize (chemical). Graft or bud plants. Irrigate. Trim to increase growth.

Adults who eat apples, applesauce, or drink apple juice lower their risk of metabolic syndrome, a cluster of health-related problems including diabetes and cardiovascular disease. The results of a study released in early 2008 indicate that eating that apple a day may still be one of the best things we can do for ourselves. For more information, check out *www.medicalnewstoday.com/articles/103341.php/*

November 24
4:39 pm EST

NOVEMBER

S	M	T	W	T	F	S
1	2	3	4	5	6	7
8	9	10	11	12	13	14
15	16	17	18	19	20	21
22	23	24	25	26	27	28
29	30	31				

December

November 29–December 5

Nothing purchased can come close to the renewed sense of gratitude for having family and friends.

~COURTLAND MALLOY

Date	Qtr.	Sign	Activity
Nov 29, 5:34 am–Dec 1, 9:23 am	2nd	Taurus	Plant annuals for hardiness. Trim to increase growth.
Dec 2, 2:30 am–Dec 3, 11:00 am	3rd	Gemini	Cultivate. Destroy weeds and pests. Harvest fruits and root crops for food. Trim to retard growth.
Dec 3, 11:00 am–Dec 5, 12:07 pm	3rd	Cancer	Plant biennials, perennials, bulbs and roots. Prune. Irrigate. Fertilize (organic).
Dec 5, 12:07 pm–Dec 7, 2:05 pm	3rd	Leo	Cultivate. Destroy weeds and pests. Harvest fruits and root crops for food. Trim to retard growth.

Firewood piled near a fireplace may be the source of unwelcome winter insect pests. They emerge after the wood is brought inside. Fortunately, they are harmless to humans, but you may want to leave wood outside until it's ready to use.

○
December 2
2:30 am EST

DECEMBER

S	M	T	W	T	F	S
		1	2	3	4	5
6	7	8	9	10	11	12
13	14	15	16	17	18	19
20	21	22	23	24	25	26
27	28	29	30	31		

December 6–12

*My soul can find no staircase to heaven unless it be through
Earth's loveliness.*

~MICHELANGELO

Date	Qtr.	Sign	Activity
Dec 5, 12:07 pm– Dec 7, 2:05 pm	3rd	Leo	Cultivate. Destroy weeds and pests. Harvest fruits and root crops for food. Trim to retard growth.
Dec 7, 2:05 pm– Dec 8, 7:13 pm	3rd	Virgo	Cultivate, especially medicinal plants. Destroy weeds and pests. Trim to retard growth.
Dec 8, 7:13 pm– Dec 9, 5:47 pm	4th	Virgo	Cultivate, especially medicinal plants. Destroy weeds and pests. Trim to retard growth.
Dec 11, 11:31 pm– Dec 14, 7:25 am	4th	Scorpio	Plant biennials, perennials, bulbs and roots. Prune. Irrigate. Fertilize (organic).

Simplify your holidays by following this sage advice: Every task must be handled so "do it, delegate it, or dump it." If the task isn't one of your top three priorities, give it to someone else or eliminate it altogether. This will allow you space to enjoy the days ahead.

◖
December 8
7:13 pm EST

DECEMBER

S	M	T	W	T	F	S
		1	2	3	4	5
6	7	8	9	10	11	12
13	14	15	16	17	18	19
20	21	22	23	24	25	26
27	28	29	30	31		

December 13–19

Most people are other people. Their thoughts are someone else's opinions, their lives a mimicry, their passions a quotation.

~Oscar Wilde

Date	Qtr.	Sign	Activity
Dec 11, 11:31 pm– Dec 14, 7:25 am	4th	Scorpio	Plant biennials, perennials, bulbs and roots. Prune. Irrigate. Fertilize (organic).
Dec 14, 7:25 am– Dec 16, 7:02 am	4th	Sagittarius	Cultivate. Destroy weeds and pests. Harvest fruits and root crops for food. Trim to retard growth.
Dec 16, 5:32 pm– Dec 19, 5:38 am	1st	Capricorn	Graft or bud plants. Trim to increase growth.

Vitamin D is known as the "sunshine" vitamin because the body makes vitamin D after being exposed to sunlight. It takes only fifteen minutes of exposure three times a week for the body to produce enough "sunshine" to keep away the winter blahs and promote absorption of calcium for our bones and teeth. Dairy products, fish, and fortified cereals are also good sources of vitamin D.

December 16
7:02 am EST

DECEMBER

S	M	T	W	T	F	S
		1	2	3	4	5
6	7	8	9	10	11	12
13	14	15	16	17	18	19
20	21	22	23	24	25	26
27	28	29	30	31		

December 20–26

True patriotism hates injustice in its own land more than anywhere else.

~CLARENCE S. DARROW

Date	Qtr.	Sign	Activity
Dec 21, 6:42 pm–Dec 24, 6:39 am	1st	Pisces	Plant grains, leafy annuals. Fertilize (chemical). Graft or bud plants. Irrigate. Trim to increase growth.
Dec 26, 3:26 pm–Dec 28, 8:13 pm	2nd	Taurus	Plant annuals for hardiness. Trim to increase growth.

A NASA study found that certain houseplants can remove up to 87 percent of indoor pollutants within twenty-four hours. English ivy, dracaena marginata, gerbena daisy, and peace lilies remove fumes from inks, oils, paints, plastic, tobacco smoke, and gasoline. Philodendron, spider plant, chrysanthemum, corn plant, golden pathos, mother-in-law's tongue, and bamboo palm will remove formaldehyde fumes emitted by foam insulation, grocery bags, waxed paper, fire retardants, floor coverings, and cigarette smoke.

December 24
12:36 pm EST

DECEMBER

S	M	T	W	T	F	S
		1	2	3	4	5
6	7	8	9	10	11	12
13	14	15	16	17	18	19
20	21	22	23	24	25	26
27	28	29	30	31		

December 27–January 2

Forgiveness is the fragrance the violet sheds on the heel that crushed it.

~MARK TWAIN

Date	Qtr.	Sign	Activity
Dec 26, 3:26 pm– Dec 28, 8:13 pm	2nd	Taurus	Plant annuals for hardiness. Trim to increase growth.
Dec 30, 9:45 pm– Dec 31, 2:13 pm	2nd	Cancer	Plant grains, leafy annuals. Fertilize (chemical). Graft or bud plants. Irrigate. Trim to increase growth.
Dec 31, 2:13 pm– Jan 1, 9:41 pm	3rd	Cancer	Plant biennials, perennials, bulbs and roots. Prune. Irrigate. Fertilize (organic).

Add cinnamon tea to your list of comfort aids. It smells, well—wonderful! It's refreshing, it eases cold symptoms and stomach upsets, and it improves circulation so you'll feel warmer. Some Chinese black teas have cinnamon in them, but you can find cinnamon as an ingredient in many herbal teas, too. Serve cinnamon tea with fruit or pastries, or after dinner on winter nights to drive away the cold.

_____

_____

_____

_____

○
December 31
2:13 pm EST

DECEMBER

S	M	T	W	T	F	S
		1	2	3	4	5
6	7	8	9	10	11	12
13	14	15	16	17	18	19
20	21	22	23	24	25	26
27	28	29	30	31		

Gardening by the Moon

Today, people often reject the notion of gardening according to the Moon's phase and sign. The usual nonbeliever is not a scientist but the city dweller who has never had any real contact with nature and little experience of natural rhythms.

Camille Flammarian, the French astronomer, testifies to the success of Moon planting, though:

"Cucumbers increase at Full Moon, as well as radishes, turnips, leeks, lilies, horseradish, and saffron; onions, on the contrary, are much larger and better nourished during the decline and old age of the Moon than at its increase, during its youth and fullness, which is the reason the Egyptians abstained from onions, on account of their antipathy to the Moon. Herbs gathered while the Moon increases are of great efficiency. If the vines are trimmed at night when the Moon is in the sign of the Lion, Sagittarius, the Scorpion, or the Bull, it will save them from field rats, moles, snails, flies, and other animals."

Dr. Clark Timmins is one of the few modern scientists to have conducted tests in Moon planting. Following is a summary of his experiments:

Beets: When sown with the Moon in Scorpio, the germination rate was 71 percent; when sown in Sagittarius, the germination rate was 58 percent.

Scotch marigold: When sown with the Moon in Cancer, the germination rate was 90 percent; when sown in Leo, the rate was 32 percent.

Carrots: When sown with the Moon in Scorpio, the germination rate was 64 percent; when sown in Sagittarius, the germination rate was 47 percent.

Tomatoes: When sown with the Moon in Cancer, the germination rate was 90 percent; but when sown with the Moon in Leo, the germination rate was 58 percent.

Two things should be emphasized. First, remember that this is only a summary of the results of the experiments; the experiments themselves were conducted in a scientific manner to eliminate any variation in soil, temperature, moisture, and so on, so that only the Moon sign is varied. Second, note that these astonishing results were obtained without regard to the phase of the Moon—the other factor we use in Moon planting, and which presumably would have increased the differential in germination rates.

Dr. Timmins also tried transplanting Cancer- and Leo-planted tomato seedlings while the Cancer Moon was waxing. The result was 100 percent survival. When transplanting was done with the waning Sagittarius Moon, there was 0 percent survival. Dr. Timmins' tests show that the Cancer-planted tomatoes had blossoms twelve days earlier than those planted under Leo; the Cancer-planted tomatoes had an average height of twenty inches at that time compared to fifteen inches for the Leo-planted; the first ripe tomatoes were gathered from the Cancer plantings eleven days ahead of the Leo plantings; and a count of the hanging fruit and its size and weight shows an advantage to the Cancer plants over the Leo plants of 45 percent.

Dr. Timmins also observed that there have been similar tests that did not indicate results favorable to the Moon planting theory. As a scientist, he asked why one set of experiments indicated a positive verification of Moon planting, and others did not. He checked these other tests and found that the experimenters had not followed the geocentric system for determining the Moon sign positions, but the heliocentric. When the times used in these other tests were converted to the geocentric system, the dates chosen often were found to be in barren, rather than fertile, signs. Without going into a technical explanation, it is sufficient to point out that geocentric and heliocentric positions often vary by as much as four days. This is a large enough differential to place the Moon in Cancer, for example, in the heliocentric system, and at the same time in Leo by the geocentric system.

Most almanacs and calendars show the Moon's signs heliocentrically—and thus incorrectly for Moon planting—while the *Moon Sign Book* is calculated correctly for planting purposes, using the geocentric system. Some readers are confused because the *Moon Sign Book* talks about first, second, third, and fourth quarters, while other almanacs refer to these same divisions as New Moon, first quarter, Full Moon, and fourth quarter. Thus the almanacs say first quarter when the *Moon Sign Book* says second quarter.

There is nothing complicated about using astrology in agriculture and horticulture in order to increase both pleasure and profit, but there is one very important rule that is often neglected—use common sense! Of course this is one rule that should be remembered in every activity we undertake, but in the case of gardening and farming by the Moon, if it is not possible to use the best dates for planting or harvesting, we must select the next best and just try to do the best we can.

This brings up the matter of the other factors to consider in your gardening work. The dates we give as best for a certain activity apply to the entire country (with slight time correction), but in your section of the country you may be buried under three feet of snow on a date we say is good to plant your flowers. So we have factors of weather, season, temperature and moisture variations, soil conditions, your own available time and opportunity, and so forth. Some astrologers like to think it is all a matter of science, but gardening is also an art. In art, you develop an instinctive identification with your work and influence it with your feelings and wishes.

The *Moon Sign Book* gives you the place of the Moon for every day of the year so that you can select the best times once you have become familiar with the rules and practices of lunar agriculture. We give you specific, easy-to-follow directions so that you can get right down to work.

We give you the best dates for planting, and also for various related activities, including cultivation, fertilizing, harvesting, irrigation, and getting rid of weeds and pests. But we cannot tell you exactly when it's good to plant. Many of these rules were learned by observation and experience; as the body of experience grew we could see various patterns emerging that allowed us to make judgments about new things. That's what you should do, too. After you have worked with lunar agriculture for a while and have gained a working knowledge, you will probably begin to try new things—and we hope you will share your experiments and findings with us. That's how the science grows.

Here's an example of what we mean. Years ago Llewellyn George suggested that we try to combine our bits of knowledge about what to expect in planting under each of the Moon signs in order to gain benefit from several lunar factors in one plant. From this came our rule for developing "thoroughbred seed." To develop thoroughbred seed, save the seed for three successive years from plants grown by the correct Moon sign and phase. You can plant in the first quarter phase and in the sign of Cancer for fruitfulness; the second year, plant seeds from the first year plants in Libra for beauty; and in the third year, plant the seeds from the second year plants in Taurus to produce hardiness. In a similar manner you can combine the fruitfulness of Cancer, the good root growth of Pisces, and the sturdiness and good vine growth of Scorpio. And don't forget the characteristics of Capricorn: hardy like Taurus, but drier and perhaps more resistant to drought and disease.

Unlike common almanacs, we consider both the Moon's phase and the Moon's sign in making our calculations for the proper timing of our work. It is perhaps a little easier to understand this if we remind you that we are all living in the center of a vast electromagnetic field that is the Earth and its environment in space. Everything that occurs within this electromagnetic field has an effect on everything else within the field. The Moon and the Sun are the most important of the factors affecting the life of the Earth, and it is their relative positions to the Earth that we project for each day of the year.

Many people claim that not only do they achieve larger crops gardening by the Moon, but that their fruits and vegetables are much tastier. A number of organic gardeners have also become lunar gardeners using the natural rhythm of life forces that we experience through the relative movements of the Sun and Moon. We provide a few basic rules and then give you day-by-day guidance for your gardening work. You will be able to choose the best dates to meet your own needs and opportunities.

Planting by the Moon's Phases

During the increasing or waxing light—from New Moon to Full Moon—plant annuals that produce their yield above the ground. An annual is a plant that completes its entire life cycle within one growing season and has to be seeded each year. During the decreasing or waning light—from Full Moon to New Moon—plant biennials, perennials, and bulb and root plants. Biennials include crops that are planted one season to winter over and produce crops the next, such as winter wheat. Perennials and bulb and root plants include all plants that grow from the same root each year.

A simpler, less-accurate rule is to plant crops that produce above the ground during the waxing Moon, and to plant crops that produce below the ground during the waning Moon. Thus the old adage, "Plant potatoes during the dark of the Moon." Llewellyn George's system divided the lunar month into quarters. The first two from New Moon to Full Moon are the first and second quarters, and the last two from Full Moon to New Moon the third and fourth quarters. Using these divisions, we can increase our accuracy in timing our efforts to coincide with natural forces.

First Quarter

Plant annuals producing their yield above the ground, which are generally of the leafy kind that produce their seed outside the fruit. Some examples are asparagus, broccoli, brussels sprouts, cabbage, cauliflower, celery, cress, endive, kohlrabi, lettuce, parsley, and spinach. Cucumbers are an exception, as they do best in the first quarter rather than the second, even though the seeds are inside the fruit. Also plant cereals and grains.

Second Quarter

Plant annuals producing their yield above the ground, which are generally of the viney kind that produce their seed inside the fruit. Some examples include beans, eggplant, melons, peas, peppers, pumpkins, squash, tomatoes, etc. These are not hard-and-fast divisions. If you can't plant during the first quarter, plant during the second, and vice versa. There are many plants that seem to do equally well planted in either quarter, such as watermelon, hay, and cereals and grains.

Third Quarter

Plant biennials, perennials, bulbs, root plants, trees, shrubs, berries, grapes, strawberries, beets, carrots, onions, parsnips, rutabagas, potatoes, radishes, peanuts, rhubarb, turnips, winter wheat, etc.

Fourth Quarter

This is the best time to cultivate, turn sod, pull weeds, and destroy pests of all kinds, especially when the Moon is in Aries, Leo, Virgo, Gemini, Aquarius, and Sagittarius.

The Moon in the Signs

Moon in Aries

Barren, dry, fiery, and masculine. Use for destroying noxious weeds.

Moon in Taurus

Productive, moist, earthy, and feminine. Use for planting many crops when hardiness is important, particularly root crops. Also used for lettuce, cabbage, and similar leafy vegetables.

Moon in Gemini

Barren and dry, airy and masculine. Use for destroying noxious growths, weeds, and pests, and for cultivation.

Moon in Cancer

Fruitful, moist, feminine. Use for planting and irrigation.

Moon in Leo
Barren, dry, fiery, masculine. Use for killing weeds or cultivation.

Moon in Virgo
Barren, moist, earthy, and feminine. Use for cultivation and destroying weeds and pests.

Moon in Libra
Semi-fruitful, moist, and airy. Use for planting crops that need good pulp growth. A very good sign for flowers and vines. Also used for seeding hay, corn fodder, and the like.

Moon in Scorpio
Very fruitful and moist, watery and feminine. Nearly as productive as Cancer; use for the same purposes. Especially good for vine growth and sturdiness.

Moon in Sagittarius
Barren and dry, fiery and masculine. Use for planting onions, seeding hay, and for cultivation.

Moon in Capricorn
Productive and dry, earthy and feminine. Use for planting potatoes and other tubers.

Moon in Aquarius
Barren, dry, airy, and masculine. Use for cultivation and destroying noxious growths and pests.

Moon in Pisces
Very fruitful, moist, watery, and feminine. Especially good for root growth.

A Guide to Planting

Plant	Quarter	Sign
Annuals	1st or 2nd	
Apple tree	2nd or 3rd	Cancer, Pisces, Virgo
Artichoke	1st	Cancer, Pisces
Asparagus	1st	Cancer, Scorpio, Pisces
Aster	1st or 2nd	Virgo, Libra
Barley	1st or 2nd	Cancer Pisces, Libra, Capricorn, Virgo
Beans (bush & pole)	2nd	Cancer, Taurus, Pisces, Libra
Beans (kidney, white, & navy)	1st or 2nd	Cancer, Pisces
Beech tree	2nd or 3rd	Virgo, Taurus
Beets	3rd	Cancer, Capricorn, Pisces, Libra
Biennials	3rd or 4th	
Broccoli	1st	Cancer, Scorpio, Pisces, Libra
Brussels sprouts	1st	Cancer, Scorpio, Pisces, Libra
Buckwheat	1st or 2nd	Capricorn
Bulbs	3rd	Cancer, Scorpio, Pisces
Bulbs for seed	2nd or 3rd	
Cabbage	1st	Cancer, Scorpio, Pisces, Taurus, Libra
Canes (raspberry, blackberry, & gooseberry)	2nd	Cancer, Scorpio, Pisces
Cantaloupe	1st or 2nd	Cancer, Scorpio, Pisces, Taurus, Libra
Carrots	3rd	Cancer, Scorpio, Pisces, Taurus, Libra
Cauliflower	1st	Cancer, Scorpio, Pisces, Libra
Celeriac	3rd	Cancer, Scorpio, Pisces
Celery	1st	Cancer, Scorpio, Pisces
Cereals	1st or 2nd	Cancer, Scorpio, Pisces, Libra
Chard	1st or 2nd	Cancer, Scorpio, Pisces
Chicory	2nd or 3rd	Cancer, Scorpio, Pisces
Chrysanthemum	1st or 2nd	Virgo
Clover	1st or 2nd	Cancer, Scorpio, Pisces

Plant	Quarter	Sign
Corn	1st	Cancer, Scorpio, Pisces
Corn for fodder	1st or 2nd	Libra
Coreopsis	2nd or 3rd	Libra
Cosmo	2nd or 3rd	Libra
Cress	1st	Cancer, Scorpio, Pisces
Crocus	1st or 2nd	Virgo
Cucumber	1st	Cancer, Scorpio, Pisces
Daffodil	1st or 2nd	Libra, Virgo
Dahlia	1st or 2nd	Libra, Virgo
Deciduous trees	2nd or 3rd	Cancer, Scorpio, Pisces, Virgo, Libra
Eggplant	2nd	Cancer, Scorpio, Pisces, Libra
Endive	1st	Cancer, Scorpio, Pisces, Libra
Flowers	1st	Cancer, Scorpio, Pisces, Libra, Taurus, Virgo
Garlic	3rd	Libra, Taurus, Pisces
Gladiola	1st or 2nd	Libra, Virgo
Gourds	1st or 2nd	Cancer, Scorpio, Pisces, Libra
Grapes	2nd or 3rd	Cancer, Scorpio, Pisces, Virgo
Hay	1st or 2nd	Cancer, Scorpio, Pisces, Libra, Taurus
Herbs	1st or 2nd	Cancer, Scorpio, Pisces
Honeysuckle	1st or 2nd	Scorpio, Virgo
Hops	1st or 2nd	Scorpio, Libra
Horseradish	1st or 2nd	Cancer, Scorpio, Pisces
Houseplants	1st	Cancer, Scorpio, Pisces, Libra
Hyacinth	3rd	Cancer, Scorpio, Pisces
Iris	1st or 2nd	Cancer, Virgo
Kohlrabi	1st or 2nd	Cancer, Scorpio, Pisces, Libra
Leek	1st or 2nd	Cancer, Pisces
Lettuce	1st	Cancer, Scorpio, Pisces, Libra, Taurus
Lily	1st or 2nd	Cancer, Scorpio, Pisces
Maple tree	2nd or 3rd	Taurus, Virgo, Cancer, Pisces
Melon	2nd	Cancer, Scorpio, Pisces
Moon vine	1st or 2nd	Virgo

Plant	Quarter	Sign
Morning glory	1st or 2nd	Cancer, Scorpio, Pisces, Virgo
Oak tree	2nd or 3rd	Taurus, Virgo, Cancer, Pisces
Okra	1st or 2nd	Cancer, Scorpio, Pisces, Libra
Oats	1st or 2nd	Cancer, Scorpio, Pisces, Libra
Onion seed	2nd	Cancer, Scorpio, Sagittarius
Onion set	3rd or 4th	Cancer, Pisces, Taurus, Libra
Pansies	1st or 2nd	Cancer, Scorpio, Pisces
Parsley	1st	Cancer, Scorpio, Pisces, Libra
Parsnip	3rd	Cancer, Scorpio, Taurus, Capricorn
Peach tree	2nd or 3rd	Cancer, Taurus, Virgo, Libra
Peanuts	3rd	Cancer, Scorpio, Pisces
Pear tree	2nd or 3rd	Cancer, Scorpio, Pisces, Libra
Peas	2nd	Cancer, Scorpio, Pisces, Libra
Peony	1st or 2nd	Virgo
Peppers	2nd	Cancer, Scorpio, Pisces
Perennials	3rd	
Petunia	1st or 2nd	Libra, Virgo
Plum tree	2nd or 3rd	Cancer, Pisces, Taurus, Virgo
Poppies	1st or 2nd	Virgo
Portulaca	1st or 2nd	Virgo
Potatoes	3rd	Cancer, Scorpio, Libra, Taurus, Capricorn
Privet	1st or 2nd	Taurus, Libra
Pumpkin	2nd	Cancer, Scorpio, Pisces, Libra
Quince	1st or 2nd	Capricorn
Radishes	3rd	Cancer, Scorpio, Pisces, Libra, Capricorn
Rhubarb	3rd	Cancer, Pisces
Rice	1st or 2nd	Scorpio
Roses	1st or 2nd	Cancer, Virgo
Rutabaga	3rd	Cancer, Scorpio, Pisces, Taurus
Saffron	1st or 2nd	Cancer, Scorpio, Pisces
Sage	3rd	Cancer, Scorpio, Pisces

Plant	Quarter	Sign
Salsify	1st	Cancer, Scorpio, Pisces
Shallot	2nd	Scorpio
Spinach	1st	Cancer, Scorpio, Pisces
Squash	2nd	Cancer, Scorpio, Pisces, Libra
Strawberries	3rd	Cancer, Scorpio, Pisces
String beans	1st or 2nd	Taurus
Sunflowers	1st or 2nd	Libra, Cancer
Sweet peas	1st or 2nd	
Tomatoes	2nd	Cancer, Scorpio, Pisces, Capricorn
Shade trees	3rd	Taurus, Capricorn
Ornamental trees	2nd	Libra, Taurus
Trumpet vine	1st or 2nd	Cancer, Scorpio, Pisces
Tubers for seed	3rd	Cancer, Scorpio, Pisces, Libra
Tulips	1st or 2nd	Libra, Virgo
Turnips	3rd	Cancer, Scorpio, Pisces, Taurus, Capricorn, Libra
Valerian	1st or 2nd	Virgo, Gemini
Watermelon	1st or 2nd	Cancer, Scorpio, Pisces, Libra
Wheat	1st or 2nd	Cancer, Scorpio, Pisces, Libra

Companion Planting Guide

Plant	Companions	Hindered by
Asparagus	Tomatoes, parsley, basil	None known
Beans	Tomatoes, carrots, cucumbers, garlic, cabbage, beets, corn	Onions, gladiolas
Beets	Onions, cabbage, lettuce, mint, catnip	Pole beans
Broccoli	Beans, celery, potatoes, onions	Tomatoes
Cabbage	Peppermint, sage, thyme, tomatoes	Strawberries, grapes
Carrots	Peas, lettuce, chives, radishes, leeks, onions, sage	Dill, anise
Citrus trees	Guava, live oak, rubber trees, peppers	None known
Corn	Potatoes, beans, peas, melon, squash, pumpkin, sunflowers, soybeans	Quack grass, wheat straw mulch
Cucumbers	Beans, cabbage, radishes, sunflowers, lettuce, broccoli, squash	Aromatic herbs
Eggplant	Green beans, lettuce, kale	None known
Grapes	Peas, beans, blackberries	Cabbage, radishes
Melons	Corn, peas	Potatoes, gourds
Onions, leeks	Beets, chamomile, carrots, lettuce	Peas, beans, sage
Parsnip	Peas	None known
Peas	Radishes, carrots, corn, cucumbers, beans, tomatoes, spinach, turnips	Onion, garlic
Potatoes	Beans, corn, peas, cabbage, hemp, cucumbers, eggplant, catnip	Raspberries, pumpkins, tomatoes, sunflowers
Radishes	Peas, lettuce, nasturtiums, cucumbers	Hyssop
Spinach	Strawberries	None known
Squash/Pumpkin	Nasturtiums, corn, mint, catnip	Potatoes
Tomatoes	Asparagus, parsley, chives, onions, carrots, marigolds, nasturtiums, dill	Black walnut roots, fennel, potatoes
Turnips	Peas, beans, brussels sprouts	Potatoes

Plant	Companions	Uses
Anise	Coriander	Flavor candy, pastry, cheeses, cookies
Basil	Tomatoes	Dislikes rue; repels flies and mosquitoes
Borage	Tomatoes, squash	Use in teas
Buttercup	Clover	Hinders delphinium, peonies, monkshood, columbine

Plant	Companions	Uses
Catnip		Repels flea beetles
Chamomile	Peppermint, wheat, onions, cabbage	Roman chamomile may control damping-off disease; use in herbal sprays
Chervil	Radishes	Good in soups and other dishes
Chives	Carrots	Use in spray to deter black spot on roses
Coriander	Plant anywhere	Hinders seed formation in fennel
Cosmos		Repels corn earworms
Dill	Cabbage	Hinders carrots and tomatoes
Fennel	Plant in borders away from garden	Disliked by all garden plants
Horseradish		Repels potato bugs
Horsetail		Makes fungicide spray
Hyssop		Attracts cabbage fly away from cabbage; harmful to radishes
Lavender	Plant anywhere	Use in spray to control insects on cotton, repels clothes moths
Lovage		Lures horn worms away from tomatoes
Marigolds		Pest repellent; use against Mexican bean beetles and nematodes
Mint	Cabbage, tomatoes	Repels ants, flea beetles, and cabbage worm butterflies
Morning glory	Corn	Helps melon germination
Nasturtiums	Cabbage, cucumbers	Deters aphids, squash bugs, and pumpkin beetles
Okra	Eggplant	Will attract leafhopper (use to trap insects away from other plants)
Parsley	Tomatoes, asparagus	Freeze chopped up leaves to flavor foods
Purslane		Good ground cover
Rosemary		Repels cabbage moths, bean beetles, and carrot flies
Savory		Plant with onions to give them added sweetness
Tansy		Deters Japanese beetles, striped cucumber beetles, and squash bugs
Thyme		Repels cabbage worms
Yarrow		Increases essential oils of neighbors

Moon Void-of Course

By Kim Rogers-Gallagher

The Moon circles the Earth in about twenty-eight days, moving through each zodiac sign in two-and-a-half days. As she passes through the thirty degrees of each sign, she "visits" with the planets in numerical order, forming aspects with them. Because she moves one degree in just two to two-and-a-half hours, her influence on each planet lasts only a few hours. She eventually reaches the planet that's in the highest degree of any sign, and forms what will be her final aspect before leaving the sign. From this point until she enters the next sign, she is referred to as void-of-course.

Think of it this way: the Moon is the emotional "tone" of the day, carrying feelings with her particular to the sign she's "wearing" at the moment. After she has contacted each of the planets, she symbolically "rests" before changing her costume, so her instinct is temporarily on hold. It's during this time that many people feel "fuzzy" or "vague." Plans or decisions made now often do not pan out. Without the instinctual "knowing" the Moon provides as she touches each planet, we tend to be unrealistic or exercise poor judgment. The traditional definition of the void Moon is that "nothing will come of this." Actions initiated under a void Moon are often wasted, irrelevant, or incorrect—usually because information is hidden, missing, or has been overlooked.

Although it's not a good time to initiate plans, routine tasks seem to go along just fine. This period is ideal for reflection. On the lighter side, remember there are good uses for the void Moon. It is the period when the universe seems to be most open to loopholes. It's a great time to make plans you don't want to fulfill or schedule things you don't want to do. See the table on pages 76–81 for a schedule of the Moon's void-of-course times.

Last Aspect **Moon Enters New Sign**

		January		
3	3:50 am	3	Aries	4:50 am
4	9:44 pm	5	Taurus	10:46 am
7	1:05 am	7	Gemini	1:11 pm
9	1:39 am	9	Cancer	1:14 pm
10	11:26 pm	11	Leo	12:41 pm
13	1:38 am	13	Virgo	1:33 pm
15	9:37 am	15	Libra	5:30 pm
17	9:46 pm	18	Scorpio	1:20 am
19	10:36 pm	20	Sagittarius	12:30 pm
22	11:23 am	23	Capricorn	1:18 am
25	4:08 am	25	Aquarius	1:56 pm
27	12:12 pm	28	Pisces	1:12 am
30	4:23 am	30	Aries	10:25 am
		February		
1	1:08 pm	1	Taurus	5:08 pm
3	8:27 pm	3	Gemini	9:14 pm
5	12:44 pm	5	Cancer	11:05 pm
7	2:07 pm	7	Leo	11:43 pm
9	2:28 pm	10	Virgo	12:38 am
11	11:17 pm	12	Libra	3:33 am
14	9:46 am	14	Scorpio	9:50 am
16	4:37 pm	16	Sagittarius	7:53 pm
18	8:36 pm	19	Capricorn	8:25 am
21	4:01 am	21	Aquarius	9:06 pm
23	9:08 pm	24	Pisces	7:59 am
26	1:09 pm	26	Aries	4:24 pm
28	12:51 pm	28	Taurus	10:33 pm

Last Aspect   ## Moon Enters New Sign

			March		
2	5:42 pm	3	Gemini	2:59 am
4	9:10 pm	5	Cancer	6:07 am
6	7:29 pm	7	Leo	8:24 am
9	3:56 am	9	Virgo	11:34 am
11	1:48 am	11	Libra	2:46 pm
13	6:39 pm	13	Scorpio	8:22 pm
15	8:43 pm	16	Sagittarius	5:21 am
18	1:47 pm	18	Capricorn	5:18 pm
20	4:06 pm	21	Aquarius	6:06 am
23	8:09 am	23	Pisces	5:08 pm
25	12:53 pm	26	Aries	1:03 am
27	10:17 pm	28	Taurus	6:09 am
30	2:00 am	30	Gemini	9:36 am
			April		
1	5:03 am	1	Cancer	12:30 pm
3	4:59 am	3	Leo	3:32 pm
5	11:38 am	5	Virgo	7:01 pm
7	12:52 pm	7	Libra	11:22 pm
9	9:45 pm	10	Scorpio	5:23 am
12	1:28 pm	12	Sagittarius	2:00 pm
15	12:07 am	15	Capricorn	1:27 am
17	12:42 pm	17	Aquarius	2:19 pm
19	6:15 pm	20	Pisces	1:55 am
22	9:29 am	22	Aries	10:09 am
24	8:11 am	24	Taurus	2:46 pm
26	11:42 am	26	Gemini	5:02 pm
28	12:22 pm	28	Cancer	6:38 pm
30	12:45 pm	30	Leo	8:56 pm

Last Aspect   **Moon Enters New Sign**

				May	
2	6:08 pm	3		Virgo	12:37 am
4	9:31 pm	5		Libra	5:51 am
7	6:00 am	7		Scorpio	12:48 pm
9	2:48 pm	9		Sagittarius	9:49 pm
12	1:55 am	12		Capricorn	9:09 am
14	8:58 am	14		Aquarius	10:01 pm
17	6:40 am	17		Pisces	10:17 am
19	5:43 pm	19		Aries	7:30 pm
21	6:36 pm	22		Taurus	12:40 am
23	8:48 pm	24		Gemini	2:34 am
25	9:17 pm	26		Cancer	2:58 am
27	11:06 pm	28		Leo	3:44 am
30	4:18 am	30		Virgo	6:17 am
				June	
1	4:32 am	1		Libra	11:17 am
3	2:00 pm	3		Scorpio	6:43 pm
5	10:18 pm	6		Sagittarius	4:23 am
8	9:51 am	8		Capricorn	3:59 pm
10	11:31 pm	11		Aquarius	4:52 am
13	5:04 pm	13		Pisces	5:32 pm
15	9:17 pm	16		Aries	3:51 am
18	5:35 am	18		Taurus	10:20 am
20	8:02 am	20		Gemini	1:00 pm
22	8:20 am	22		Cancer	1:12 pm
24	7:24 am	24		Leo	12:50 pm
26	8:28 am	26		Virgo	1:46 pm
28	11:26 am	28		Libra	5:24 pm
30	5:59 pm	1		Scorpio	12:18 am

Last Aspect   **Moon Enters New Sign**

		July		
3	6:03 am	3	Sagittarius	10:10 am
5	3:17 pm	5	Capricorn	10:07 pm
8	5:43 am	8	Aquarius	11:03 am
10	10:17 pm	10	Pisces	11:44 pm
13	4:03 am	13	Aries	10:40 am
15	11:07 am	15	Taurus	6:30 pm
17	4:48 pm	17	Gemini	10:41 pm
19	6:12 pm	19	Cancer	11:51 pm
21	10:34 pm	21	Leo	11:27 pm
23	4:28 pm	23	Virgo	11:22 pm
25	7:14 pm	26	Libra	1:25 am
27	10:53 pm	28	Scorpio	6:56 am
30	8:54 am	30	Sagittarius	4:10 pm
		August		
2	1:42 am	2	Capricorn	4:08 am
4	9:21 am	4	Aquarius	5:08 pm
6	8:19 pm	7	Pisces	5:34 am
9	8:44 am	9	Aries	4:23 pm
11	4:03 pm	12	Taurus	12:49 am
13	11:17 pm	14	Gemini	6:25 am
16	2:19 am	16	Cancer	9:13 am
18	3:09 am	18	Leo	9:56 am
20	6:01 am	20	Virgo	10:00 am
22	7:44 am	22	Libra	11:12 am
24	2:10 pm	24	Scorpio	3:16 pm
26	2:34 pm	26	Sagittarius	11:16 pm
29	1:26 am	29	Capricorn	10:44 am
31	2:09 pm	31	Aquarius	11:43 pm

Last Aspect   Moon Enters New Sign

		September		
3	1:19 am	3	Pisces	11:58 am
5	12:53 pm	5	Aries	10:14 pm
7	8:12 pm	8	Taurus	6:17 am
10	3:17 am	10	Gemini	12:17 pm
12	7:30 am	12	Cancer	4:19 pm
14	9:57 am	14	Leo	6:39 pm
16	12:10 pm	16	Virgo	7:56 pm
18	7:56 pm	18	Libra	9:26 pm
20	2:43 pm	21	Scorpio	12:52 am
22	11:32 pm	23	Sagittarius	7:43 am
25	10:15 am	25	Capricorn	6:19 pm
27	11:33 pm	28	Aquarius	7:06 am
30	7:34 am	30	Pisces	7:26 pm
		October		
2	11:29 pm	3	Aries	5:20 am
5	1:46 am	5	Taurus	12:33 pm
7	1:19 pm	7	Gemini	5:46 pm
9	9:35 pm	9	Cancer	9:48 pm
11	9:37 pm	12	Leo	1:02 am
13	5:20 pm	14	Virgo	3:45 am
16	6:18 am	16	Libra	6:29 am
18	1:33 am	18	Scorpio	10:22 am
20	2:57 pm	20	Sagittarius	4:49 pm
23	2:39 am	23	Capricorn	2:40 am
25	2:14 pm	25	Aquarius	3:08 pm
28	3:22 am	28	Pisces	3:45 am
30	12:56 am	30	Aries	1:56 pm

Last Aspect   Moon Enters New Sign

		November		
1	8:29 am	1	Taurus	7:44 pm
3	1:04 pm	4	Gemini	11:53 pm
5	10:47 pm	6	Cancer	2:42 am
7	5:26 pm	8	Leo	5:23 am
9	9:43 pm	10	Virgo	8:30 am
12	2:13 am	12	Libra	12:22 pm
14	6:10 am	14	Scorpio	5:24 pm
16	2:14 pm	17	Sagittarius	12:22 am
18	9:46 pm	19	Capricorn	10:00 am
21	10:04 pm	21	Aquarius	10:11 pm
23	10:35 pm	24	Pisces	11:07 am
26	9:17 am	26	Aries	10:10 pm
28	6:32 pm	29	Taurus	5:34 am
		December		
1	8:39 am	1	Gemini	9:23 am
3	5:27 am	3	Cancer	11:00 am
5	12:08 am	5	Leo	12:07 pm
7	3:57 am	7	Virgo	2:05 pm
9	5:04 am	9	Libra	5:47 pm
11	12:44 pm	11	Scorpio	11:31 pm
13	8:17 pm	14	Sagittarius	7:25 am
16	7:02 am	16	Capricorn	5:32 am
18	3:07 pm	19	Aquarius	5:38 am
21	7:53 am	21	Pisces	6:42 pm
24	3:09 am	24	Aries	6:39 am
26	6:44 am	26	Taurus	3:26 pm
28	12:54 pm	28	Gemini	8:13 pm
30	3:29 pm	30	Cancer	9:45 pm

The Moon's Rhythm

The Moon journeys around Earth in an elliptical orbit that takes about 27.33 days, which is known as a sidereal month (period of revolution of one body about another). She can move up to 15 degrees or as few as 11 degrees in a day, with the fastest motion occurring when the Moon is at perigee (closest approach to Earth). The Moon is never retrograde, but when her motion is slow, the effect is similar to a retrograde period.

Astrologers have observed that people born on a day when the Moon is fast will process information differently from those who are born when the Moon is slow in motion. People born when the Moon is fast process information quickly and tend to react quickly, while those born during a slow Moon will be more deliberate.

The time from New Moon to New Moon is called the synodic month (involving a conjunction), and the average time span between this Sun-Moon alignment is 29.53 days. Since 29.53 won't divide into 365 evenly, we can have a month with two Full Moons (December 2009) or two New Moons (August 2008).

Moon Aspects

The aspects the Moon will make during the times you are considering are also important. A trine or sextile, and sometimes a conjunction, are considered favorable aspects. A trine or sextile between the Sun and Moon is an excellent foundation for success. Whether or not a conjunction is considered favorable depends upon the planet the Moon is making a conjunction to. If it's joining the Sun, Venus, Mercury, Jupiter, or even Saturn, the aspect is favorable. If the Moon joins Pluto or Mars, however, that would not be considered favorable. There may be exceptions, but it would depend on what you are electing to do. For example, a trine to Pluto might hasten the end of a relationship you want to be free of.

It is important to avoid times when the Moon makes an aspect to or is conjoining any retrograde planet, unless, of course, you want the thing started to end in failure.

After the Moon has completed an aspect to a planet, that planetary energy has passed. For example, if the Moon squares Saturn at 10:00 am, you can disregard Saturn's influence on your activity if it will occur after that time. You should always look ahead at aspects the Moon will make on the day in question, though, because if the Moon opposes Mars at 11:30 pm on that day, you can expect events that stretch into the evening to be affected by the Moon-Mars aspect. A testy conversation might lead to an argument, or more.

Moon Signs

Much agricultural work is ruled by earth signs—Virgo, Capricorn, and Taurus; and the air signs—Gemini, Aquarius, and Libra—rule flying and intellectual pursuits.

Each planet has one or two signs in which its characteristics are enhanced or "dignified," and the planet is said to "rule" that sign. The Sun rules Leo and the Moon rules Cancer, for example. The ruling planet for each sign is listed below. These should not be considered complete lists. We recommend that you purchase a book of planetary rulerships for more complete information.

Aries Moon

The energy of an Aries Moon is masculine, dry, barren, and fiery. Aries provides great start-up energy, but things started at this time may be the result of impulsive action that lacks research or necessary support. Aries lacks staying power.

Use this assertive, outgoing Moon sign to initiate change, but have a plan in place for someone to pick up the reins when you're impatient to move on to the next thing. Work that requires skillful, but not necessarily patient, use of tools—hammering, cutting down trees, etc.—is appropriate in Aries. Expect things to occur rapidly but to also quickly pass. If you are prone to injury or accidents, exercise caution and good judgment in Aries-related activities.

RULER: Mars
IMPULSE: Action
RULES: Head and face

Taurus Moon

A Taurus Moon's energy is feminine, semi-fruitful, and earthy. The Moon is exalted—very strong—in Taurus. Taurus is known as the farmer's sign because of its associations with farmland and precipitation that is the typical day-long "soaker" variety. Taurus energy is good to incorporate into your plans when patience, practicality, and perseverance are needed. Be aware, though, that you may also experience stubbornness in this sign.

Things started in Taurus tend to be long lasting and to increase in value. This can be very supportive energy in a marriage election. On the downside, the fixed energy of this sign resists change or the letting go of even the most difficult situations. A divorce following a marriage that occurred during a Taurus Moon may be difficult and costly to end. Things begun now tend to become habitual and hard to alter. If you want to make changes in something you start, it would be better to wait for Gemini. This is a good time to get a loan, but expect the people in charge of money to be cautious and slow to make decisions.

RULER: Venus

IMPULSE Stability

RULES: Neck, throat, and voice

Gemini Moon

A Gemini Moon's energy is masculine, dry, barren, and airy. People are more changeable than usual and may prefer to follow intellectual pursuits and play mental games rather than apply themselves to practical concerns.

This sign is not favored for agricultural matters, but it is an excellent time to prepare for activities, to run errands, and write letters. Plan to use a Gemini Moon to exchange ideas, meet people, go on vacations that include walking or biking, or be in situations that require versatility and quick thinking on your feet.

RULER: Mercury

IMPULSE: Versatility

RULES: Shoulders, hands, arms, lungs, and nervous system

Cancer Moon

A Cancer Moon's energy is feminine, fruitful, moist, and very strong. Use this sign when you want to grow things—flowers, fruits, vegetables, commodities, stocks, or collections—for example. This sensitive sign stimulates rapport between people. Considered the most fertile of the signs, it is often associated with mothering. You can use this moontime to build personal friendships that support mutual growth.

Cancer is associated with emotions and feelings. Prominent Cancer energy promotes growth, but it can also turn people pouty and prone to withdrawing into their shells.

RULER: The Moon

IMPULSE Tenacity

RULES: Chest area, breasts, and stomach

Leo Moon

A Leo Moon's energy is masculine, hot, dry, fiery, and barren. Use it whenever you need to put on a show, make a presentation, or entertain colleagues or guests. This is a proud yet playful energy that exudes self-confidence and is often associated with romance.

This is an excellent time for fund-raisers and ceremonies, or to be straight forward, frank, and honest about something. It is advisable not to put yourself in a position of needing public approval or where you might have to cope with underhandedness, as trouble in these areas can bring out the worst Leo traits. There is a tendency in this sign to become arrogant or self-centered.

RULER: The Sun

IMPULSE: I am

RULES: Heart and upper back

Virgo Moon

A Virgo Moon is feminine, dry, barren, earthy energy. It is favorable for anything that needs painstaking attention—especially those things where exactness rather than innovation is preferred.

Use this sign for activities when you must analyze information, or when you must determine the value of something. Virgo is the sign of bargain hunting. It's friendly toward agricultural matters with an emphasis on animals and harvesting vegetables. It is an excellent time to care for animals, especially training them and veterinary work.

This sign is most beneficial when decisions have already been made and now need to be carried out. The inclination here is to see details rather than the bigger picture.

There is a tendency in this sign to overdo. Precautions should be taken to avoid becoming too dull from all work and no play. Build a little relaxation and pleasure into your routine from the beginning.

RULER: Mercury
IMPULSE: Discriminating
RULES: Abdomen and intestines

Libra Moon

A Libra Moon's energy is masculine, semi-fruitful, and airy. This energy will benefit any attempt to bring beauty to a place or thing. Libra is considered good energy for starting things of an intellectual nature. Libra is the sign of partnership and unions, which make it an excellent time to form partnerships of any kind, to make agreements, and to negotiate. Even though this sign is good for initiating things, it is crucial to work with a partner who will provide incentive and encouragement, however. A Libra Moon accentuates teamwork (particularly teams of two) and artistic work (especially work that involves color). Make use of this sign when you are decorating your home or shopping for better quality clothing.

RULER: Venus
IMPULSE: Balance
RULES: Lower back, kidneys, and buttocks

Scorpio Moon

The Scorpio Moon is feminine, fruitful, cold, and moist. It is useful when intensity (that sometimes borders on obsession) is needed. Scorpio is considered a very psychic sign. Use this Moon sign when you must back up something you strongly believe in, such as union or employer relations. There is strong group loyalty here, but a Scorpio Moon is also a good time to end connections thoroughly. This is also a good time to conduct research.

The desire nature is so strong here that there is a tendency to manipulate situations to get what one wants, or to not see one's responsibility in an act.

RULER: Pluto, Mars (traditional)

IMPULSE: Transformation

RULES: Reproductive organs, genitals, groin, and pelvis

Sagittarius Moon

The Moon's energy is masculine, dry, barren, and fiery in Sagittarius, encouraging flights of imagination and confidence in the flow of life. Sagittarius is the most philosophical sign. Candor and honesty are enhanced when the Moon is here. This is an excellent time to "get things off your chest," and to deal with institutions of higher learning, publishing companies, and the law. It's also a good time for sport and adventure.

Sagittarians are the crusaders of this world. This is a good time to tackle things that need improvement, but don't try to be the diplomat while influenced by this energy. Opinions can run strong and the tendency to proselytize is increased.

RULER: Jupiter

IMPULSE: Expansion

RULES: Thighs and hips

Capricorn Moon

In Capricorn the Moon's energy is feminine, semi-fruitful, and earthy. Because Cancer and Capricorn are polar opposites, the Moon's energy is thought to be weakened here. This energy encourages the need for structure, discipline, and organization. This is a good time to set goals and plan for the future, tend to family business, and to take care of details requiring patience or a businesslike manner. Institutional activities are favored. This sign should be avoided if you're seeking favors, as those in authority can be insensitive under this influence.

RULER: Saturn

IMPULSE: Ambitious

RULES: Bones, skin, and knees

Aquarius Moon

An Aquarius Moon's energy is masculine, barren, dry, and airy. Activities that are unique, individualistic, concerned with humanitarian issues, society as a whole, and making improvements are favored under this Moon. It is this quality of making improvements that has caused this sign to be associated with inventors and new inventions.

An Aquarius Moon promotes the gathering of social groups for friendly exchanges. People tend to react and speak from an intellectual rather than emotional viewpoint when the Moon is in this sign.

RULER: Uranus and Saturn

IMPULSE: Reformer

RULES: Calves and ankles

Pisces Moon

A Pisces Moon is feminine, fruitful, cool, and moist. This is an excellent time to retreat, meditate, sleep, pray, or make that dreamed-of escape into a fantasy vacation. However, things are not always what they seem to be with the Moon in Pisces. Personal boundaries tend to be fuzzy, and you may not be seeing things clearly. People tend to be idealistic under this sign, which can prevent them from seeing reality.

There is a live and let live philosophy attached to this sign, which in the idealistic world may work well enough, but chaos is frequently the result. That's why this sign is also associated with alcohol and drug abuse, drug trafficking, and counterfeiting. On the lighter side, many musicians and artists are ruled by Pisces. It's only when they move too far away from reality that the dark side of substance abuse, suicide, or crime takes away life.

RULER: Jupiter and Neptune

IMPULSE: Empathetic

RULES: Feet

More About Zodiac Signs

Element (Triplicity)

Each of the zodiac signs is classified as belonging to an element, and these are the four basic elements:

Fire Signs

Aries, Sagittarius, and Leo are action-oriented, outgoing, energetic, and spontaneous.

Earth Signs

Taurus, Capricorn, and Virgo are stable, conservative, practical, and oriented to the physical and material realm.

Air Signs

Gemini, Aquarius, and Libra are sociable and critical, and they tend to represent intellectual responses rather than feelings.

Water Signs

Cancer, Scorpio, and Pisces are emotional, receptive, intuitive, and can be very sensitive.

Quality (Quadruplicity)

Each zodiac sign is further classified as being cardinal, mutable, or fixed. There are four signs in each quadruplicity, one sign from each element.

Cardinal Signs

Aries, Cancer, Libra, and Capricorn represent beginnings and initiate new action. They initiate each new season in the cycle of the year.

Fixed Signs

Taurus, Leo, Scorpio, and Aquarius want to maintain the status quo through stubbornness and persistence; they represent that "between" time. For example, Leo is the month when summer really feels like summer.

Mutable Signs

Pisces, Gemini, Virgo, and Sagittarius adapt to change and tolerate situations. They represent the last month of each season, when things are changing in preparation for the coming season.

Nature and Fertility

In addition to a sign's element and quality, each sign is further classified as either fruitful, semi-fruitful, or barren. This classification is the most important for readers who use the gardening information in the *Moon Sign Book* because the timing of most events depends on the fertility of the sign occupied by the Moon. The water signs of Cancer, Scorpio, and Pisces are the most fruitful. The semi-fruitful signs are the earth signs Taurus and Capricorn, and the air sign Libra. The barren signs correspond to fire-signs Aries, Leo, and Sagittarius; air-signs Gemini and Aquarius; and earth-sign Virgo.

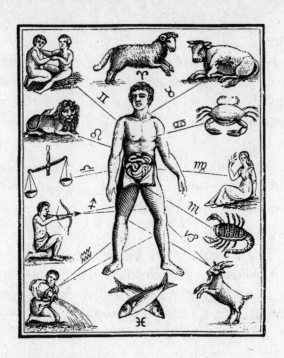

Good Timing

By Sharon Leah

Electional astrology is the art of electing times to begin any undertaking. Say, for example, you want to start a business. That business will experience ups and downs, as well as reach its potential, according to the promise held in the universe at the time the business was started—its birth time. The horoscope (birth chart) set for the date, time, and place that a business starts would indicate the outcome—its potential to succeed.

So, you might ask yourself the question: If the horoscope for a business start can show success or failure, why not begin at a time that is more favorable to the venture? Well, you can.

While no time is perfect, there are better times and better days to undertake specific activities. There are thousands of examples that prove electional astrology is not only practical, but that it can make a difference in our lives. There are rules for electing times to begin various activities—even shopping. You'll find detailed instructions about how to make elections beginning on page 108.

Personalizing Elections

The election rules in this almanac are based upon the planetary positions at the time for which the election is made. They do not depend on any type of birth chart. However, a birth chart based upon the time, date, and birthplace of an event has advantages. No election is effective for every person. For example, you may leave home to begin a trip at the same time as a friend, but each of you will have a different experience according to whether or not your birth chart favors the trip.

Not all elections require a birth chart, but the timing of very important events—business starts, marriages, etc.—would benefit from the additional accuracy a birth chart provides. To order a birth chart for yourself or a planned event, visit our Web site at www.llewellyn.com.

Some Things to Consider

You've probably experienced good timing in your life. Maybe you were at the right place at the right time to meet a friend whom you hadn't seen in years. Frequently, when something like that happens, it is the result of following an intuitive impulse—that "gut instinct." Consider for a moment that you were actually responding to planetary energies. Electional astrology is a tool that can help you to align with energies, present and future, that are available to us through planetary placements.

Significators

Decide upon the important significators (planet, sign, and house ruling the matter) for which the election is being made. The Moon is the most important significator in any election, so the

Moon should always be fortified (strong by sign, and making favorable aspects to other planets). The Moon's aspects to other planets are more important than the sign the Moon is in.

Other important considerations are the significators of the Ascendant and Midheaven—the house ruling the election matter, and the ruler of the sign on that house cusp. Finally, any planet or sign that has a general rulership over the matter in question should be taken into consideration.

Nature and Fertility

Determine the general nature of the sign that is appropriate for your election. For example, much agricultural work is ruled by the earth signs of Virgo, Capricorn, and Taurus; while the air signs—Gemini, Aquarius, and Libra—rule intellectual pursuits.

One Final Comment

Use common sense. If you must do something, like plant your garden or take an airplane trip on a day that doesn't have the best aspects, proceed anyway, but try to minimize problems. For example, leave early for the airport to avoid being left behind due to delays in the security lanes. When you have no other choice, do the best that you can under the circumstances at the time.

If you want to personalize your elections, please turn to page 106 for more information. If you want a quick and easy answer, you can refer to Llewellyn's Astro Almanac.

Llewellyn's Astro Almanac

The Astro Almanac tables, beginning on the next page, can help you find the dates best suited to particular activities. The dates provided are determined from the Moon's sign, phase, and aspects to other planets. Please note that the Astro Almanac does not take personal factors, such as your Sun and Moon sign, into account. The dates are general, and they will apply for everyone. Some activities will not have suitable dates during a particular month, so no dates will be shown.

Activity	January
Advertise in Print	5, 7, 18, 19, 20, 24
Automobile (Buy)	24, 25
Animals (Neuter or spay)	
Animals (Sell or buy)	3, 29
Build (Start excavation)	6, 24
Business (Start new)	6, 15, 24
Can Fruits and Vegetables	
Concrete (Pour)	25
Consultants (Begin work with)	5, 7
Contracts (Bid on)	25
Copyrights/Patents (Apply for)	3, 7, 15, 20
Cultivate	21, 22, 25
Cut Wood	
Entertain Guests	
Employee (Hire)	7
Fertilize and Compost (Chemical)	1, 2, 9, 10, 11
Fertilize and Compost (Organic)	18, 19, 20
Grafting or Budding (See p. 116)	1, 2, 10
Habits (Break)	23, 24
Hair (Cut)	5, 6
Harvest (Crops to dry)	12, 13
Harvest (Grain or root crops)	12, 13, 21
Job (Start new)	3, 29
Legal (To gain damages, start)	
Loan (Ask for)	
Massage (Relaxing)	5, 10
Mushrooms (Pick)	10
Promotion (Ask for)	1, 6, 15, 20, 31
Prune to Promote Healing	23, 24
Prune to Retard Growth	18, 19
Sauerkraut (Make)	
Spray Pests and Weeds	25, 26, 27
Wean Children	21, 22, 23, 24, 25
Weight (Reduce)	12, 21, 22

Activity	February
Advertise in Print	3, 14, 17, 27
Automobile (Buy)	3, 7, 16, 17, 21, 27
Animals (Neuter or spay)	
Animals (Sell or buy)	3, 17, 22, 27
Build (Start excavation)	2, 3
Business (Start new)	3
Can Fruits and Vegetables	
Concrete (Pour)	22, 23
Consultants (Begin work with)	3, 27
Contracts (Bid on)	12
Copyrights/Patents (Apply for)	3, 17, 22, 27
Cultivate	22, 23
Cut Wood	3
Entertain Guests	
Employee (Hire)	4
Fertilize and Compost (Chemical)	6, 7
Fertilize and Compost (Organic)	14, 15, 16
Grafting or Budding (See p. 116)	6, 7
Habits (Break)	19, 20, 21, 22
Hair (Cut)	3
Harvest (Crops to dry)	
Harvest (Grain or root crops)	22, 23
Job (Start new)	3, 17
Legal (To gain damages, start)	
Loan (Ask for)	16, 17
Massage (Relaxing)	3, 17
Mushrooms (Pick)	9
Promotion (Ask for)	19
Prune to Promote Healing	19, 20
Prune to Retard Growth	15, 16
Sauerkraut (Make)	
Spray Pests and Weeds	22, 23
Wean Children	17, 18
Weight (Reduce)	10, 11

Activity	March
Advertise in Print	4, 20, 22
Automobile (Buy)	4, 20
Animals (Neuter or spay)	16, 17, 18, 20, 21
Animals (Sell or buy)	
Build (Start excavation)	28, 29
Business (Start new)	28, 29
Can Fruits and Vegetables	24, 25
Concrete (Pour)	21, 22
Consultants (Begin work with)	29, 31
Contracts (Bid on)	3, 30
Copyrights/Patents (Apply for)	4, 20, 31
Cultivate	21, 22
Cut Wood	
Entertain Guests	
Employee (Hire)	4, 30, 31
Fertilize and Compost (Chemical)	5, 6
Fertilize and Compost (Organic)	14, 15
Grafting or Budding (See p. 116)	5, 6
Habits (Break)	19, 20, 21
Hair (Cut)	30
Harvest (Crops to dry)	17, 18
Harvest (Grain or root crops)	17, 18, 21, 22
Job (Start new)	12, 31
Legal (To gain damages, start)	3, 4, 18
Loan (Ask for)	24
Massage (Relaxing)	8, 22, 30
Mushrooms (Pick)	9, 10
Promotion (Ask for)	4, 6, 20 21
Prune to Promote Healing	19, 20
Prune to Retard Growth	14, 15
Sauerkraut (Make)	
Spray Pests and Weeds	21, 22, 23
Wean Children	17, 20, 21, 23
Weight (Reduce)	16, 17, 21, 22

Activity	April
Advertise in Print	16, 17, 30
Automobile (Buy)	16, 17
Animals (Neuter or spay)	13, 14
Animals (Sell or buy)	6, 20, 21
Build (Start excavation)	
Business (Start new)	6, 7, 25
Can Fruits and Vegetables	20, 21
Concrete (Pour)	18, 19
Consultants (Begin work with)	29, 30
Contracts (Bid on)	16
Copyrights/Patents (Apply for)	9, 24
Cultivate	18, 19, 22, 23
Cut Wood	
Entertain Guests	9
Employee (Hire)	6
Fertilize and Compost (Chemical)	1, 2, 3, 29, 30
Fertilize and Compost (Organic)	11, 12
Grafting or Budding (See p. 116)	1, 2, 29, 30
Habits (Break)	18, 19
Hair (Cut)	12, 17
Harvest (Crops to dry)	13, 14
Harvest (Grain or root crops)	18, 19, 22, 23
Job (Start new)	3, 9, 15
Legal (To gain damages, start)	
Loan (Ask for)	
Massage (Relaxing)	3, 26
Mushrooms (Pick)	8, 9
Promotion (Ask for)	16, 29
Prune to Promote Healing	15, 16, 17
Prune to Retard Growth	10, 11, 12
Sauerkraut (Make)	10
Spray Pests and Weeds	
Wean Children	13, 14, 15, 16, 17, 18, 19
Weight (Reduce)	

Activity	May
Advertise in Print	5, 14, 15, 19
Automobile (Buy)	21, 31
Animals (Neuter or spay)	10, 11, 12, 13, 14, 15, 16
Animals (Sell or buy)	19
Build (Start excavation)	28, 29
Business (Start new)	31
Can Fruits and Vegetables	17, 18, 19
Concrete (Pour)	22, 23
Consultants (Begin work with)	11, 14, 19, 25
Contracts (Bid on)	13, 14, 25
Copyrights/Patents (Apply for)	11, 14, 19, 21, 25, 27
Cultivate	10, 11, 15, 16
Cut Wood	
Entertain Guests	29, 30
Employee (Hire)	5, 25
Fertilize and Compost (Chemical)	7, 8, 9
Fertilize and Compost (Organic)	18, 19
Grafting or Budding (See p. 116)	7, 8, 26, 27
Habits (Break)	20, 21
Hair (Cut)	10, 29
Harvest (Crops to dry)	10, 11, 15, 16, 20, 21
Harvest (Grain or root crops)	20, 21
Job (Start new)	11, 15, 21, 25
Legal (To gain damages, start)	5, 6
Loan (Ask for)	11, 12
Massage (Relaxing)	10, 15, 29
Mushrooms (Pick)	8, 9
Promotion (Ask for)	14, 19, 27
Prune to Promote Healing	12, 13, 14
Prune to Retard Growth	
Sauerkraut (Make)	8, 9
Spray Pests and Weeds	
Wean Children	10, 11, 12, 13, 14, 15, 16
Weight (Reduce)	10, 11, 14, 15, 16, 19

Activity	June
Advertise in Print	8, 10, 16, 19, 23
Automobile (Buy)	8, 9, 10, 15, 19, 22
Animals (Neuter or spay)	6, 9, 10, 13, 14
Animals (Sell or buy)	
Build (Start excavation)	24, 25
Business (Start new)	27
Can Fruits and Vegetables	14, 15
Concrete (Pour)	11, 12, 13
Consultants (Begin work with)	3, 30
Contracts (Bid on)	9, 10
Copyrights/Patents (Apply for)	8, 13, 16, 17, 22, 30
Cultivate	16, 17
Cut Wood	
Entertain Guests	8
Employee (Hire)	27, 28
Fertilize and Compost (Chemical)	4, 5, 23, 24
Fertilize and Compost (Organic)	14, 15
Grafting or Budding (See p. 116)	
Habits (Break)	16, 17
Hair (Cut)	8, 19, 23
Harvest (Crops to dry)	11, 12
Harvest (Grain or root crops)	16, 17
Job (Start new)	2, 8, 19, 23, 30
Legal (To gain damages, start)	
Loan (Ask for)	15, 16
Massage (Relaxing)	8, 14, 19, 23
Mushrooms (Pick)	6, 7
Promotion (Ask for)	8, 18, 22
Prune to Promote Healing	9, 10
Prune to Retard Growth	
Sauerkraut (Make)	
Spray Pests and Weeds	
Wean Children	8, 9, 10, 11, 12, 13
Weight (Reduce)	

Activity	July
Advertise in Print	8, 12, 14, 17, 22, 27
Automobile (Buy)	3, 7, 11, 17, 27
Animals (Neuter or spay)	5, 7, 8, 9
Animals (Sell or buy)	12
Build (Start excavation)	22, 23
Business (Start new)	7
Can Fruits and Vegetables	11, 12, 20
Concrete (Pour)	8, 9, 10
Consultants (Begin work with)	5, 22, 26, 27
Contracts (Bid on)	18, 19
Copyrights/Patents (Apply for)	1, 3, 14, 15, 22
Cultivate	
Cut Wood	8, 25
Entertain Guests	26, 27
Employee (Hire)	24
Fertilize and Compost (Chemical)	1, 2, 29, 30
Fertilize and Compost (Organic)	11, 12, 20, 21
Grafting or Budding (See p. 116)	
Habits (Break)	18, 19
Hair (Cut)	27
Harvest (Crops to dry)	8, 9, 10
Harvest (Grain or root crops)	17, 18, 19
Job (Start new)	1, 8, 27
Legal (To gain damages, start)	3, 5, 27
Loan (Ask for)	13
Massage (Relaxing)	27
Mushrooms (Pick)	6, 7
Promotion (Ask for)	17, 27
Prune to Promote Healing	
Prune to Retard Growth	
Sauerkraut (Make)	
Spray Pests and Weeds	
Wean Children	8, 9, 10, 11, 12
Weight (Reduce)	8, 9, 10, 18, 19

Activity	August
Advertise in Print	7, 17
Automobile (Buy)	2, 3, 17, 26
Animals (Neuter or spay)	1, 3, 4
Animals (Sell or buy)	7
Build (Start excavation)	25, 26
Business (Start new)	3, 4
Can Fruits and Vegetables	8, 9
Concrete (Pour)	6, 12, 13
Consultants (Begin work with)	23, 24, 28
Contracts (Bid on)	3, 6, 15, 17, 23
Copyrights/Patents (Apply for)	6, 15, 17
Cultivate	6, 10, 11, 14, 15
Cut Wood	2, 3, 22, 30, 31
Entertain Guests	
Employee (Hire)	20, 21
Fertilize and Compost (Chemical)	25, 26
Fertilize and Compost (Organic)	7, 8, 16, 17
Grafting or Budding (See p. 116)	
Habits (Break)	14, 15, 18, 19
Hair (Cut)	
Harvest (Crops to dry)	6, 10, 11
Harvest (Grain or root crops)	14
Job (Start new)	6, 11, 17, 31
Legal (To gain damages, start)	1, 2, 8
Loan (Ask for)	18, 19
Massage (Relaxing)	17
Mushrooms (Pick)	5
Promotion (Ask for)	3, 6, 7, 17
Prune to Promote Healing	
Prune to Retard Growth	
Sauerkraut (Make)	
Spray Pests and Weeds	19
Wean Children	
Weight (Reduce)	14, 15, 18, 19

Activity	September
Advertise in Print	1, 10, 11, 14, 16, 18, 21
Automobile (Buy)	10, 11, 26, 27
Animals (Neuter or spay)	5
Animals (Sell or buy)	17, 18
Build (Start excavation)	21, 22
Business (Start new)	27, 28
Can Fruits and Vegetables	5, 13, 14
Concrete (Pour)	15, 16
Consultants (Begin work with)	21, 22, 24, 25, 26, 27, 28, 29
Contracts (Bid on)	10, 11, 26, 27
Copyrights/Patents (Apply for)	1, 2, 10, 11, 14, 16, 22, 27
Cultivate	15, 16, 17
Cut Wood	8, 9, 17, 18, 26, 27
Entertain Guests	11, 26
Employee (Hire)	
Fertilize and Compost (Chemical)	3, 21, 22
Fertilize and Compost (Organic)	13, 14
Grafting or Budding (See p. 116)	3, 4
Habits (Break)	15, 16
Hair (Cut)	21, 26
Harvest (Crops to dry)	6, 7, 10, 11
Harvest (Grain or root crops)	15, 16
Job (Start new)	2, 7, 11, 16, 21, 25, 29
Legal (To gain damages, start)	24
Loan (Ask for)	15, 16
Massage (Relaxing)	11, 16
Mushrooms (Pick)	3, 4
Promotion (Ask for)	22, 24, 28, 29
Prune to Promote Healing	
Prune to Retard Growth	
Sauerkraut (Make)	3, 4
Spray Pests and Weeds	15, 16
Wean Children	
Weight (Reduce)	15, 16

Activity	October
Advertise in Print	7, 12, 22
Automobile (Buy)	12
Animals (Neuter or spay)	
Animals (Sell or buy)	14, 15
Build (Start excavation)	19, 20
Business (Start new)	23, 24
Can Fruits and Vegetables	10
Concrete (Pour)	12, 13
Consultants (Begin work with)	21, 22, 23
Contracts (Bid on)	8, 26, 27
Copyrights/Patents (Apply for)	7, 8, 17, 22, 28
Cultivate	12, 13, 14, 15
Cut Wood	5, 6, 7, 14, 15, 16
Entertain Guests	
Employee (Hire)	
Fertilize and Compost (Chemical)	1, 2
Fertilize and Compost (Organic)	10, 11
Grafting or Budding (See p. 116)	1, 2, 29, 30
Habits (Break)	12, 13, 14, 15
Hair (Cut)	16, 21, 22
Harvest (Crops to dry)	8, 9
Harvest (Grain or root crops)	12, 13
Job (Start new)	8, 12, 16, 21, 22, 26
Legal (To gain damages, start)	21, 22
Loan (Ask for)	12, 13
Massage (Relaxing)	6, 13, 16
Mushrooms (Pick)	3, 4
Promotion (Ask for)	8, 22, 23
Prune to Promote Healing	
Prune to Retard Growth	
Sauerkraut (Make)	
Spray Pests and Weeds	11, 12
Wean Children	
Weight (Reduce)	11, 12, 13, 14, 15

Activity	November
Advertise in Print	5, 17, 22, 28
Automobile (Buy)	4, 5, 20, 21, 22
Animals (Neuter or spay)	
Animals (Sell or buy)	
Build (Start excavation)	22, 23
Business (Start new)	20, 21
Can Fruits and Vegetables	6, 7
Concrete (Pour)	8, 9
Consultants (Begin work with)	17, 22, 28
Contracts (Bid on)	5, 20, 21, 22
Copyrights/Patents (Apply for)	17, 22, 28
Cultivate	9, 10, 11
Cut Wood	
Entertain Guests	13
Employee (Hire)	
Fertilize and Compost (Chemical)	24, 25
Fertilize and Compost (Organic)	6, 7
Grafting or Budding (See p. 116)	24, 25
Habits (Break)	10, 11
Hair (Cut)	5, 10, 20, 26
Harvest (Crops to dry)	4, 5
Harvest (Grain or root crops)	8, 9, 10
Job (Start new)	5, 10, 17, 20
Legal (To gain damages, start)	4, 5, 17, 18
Loan (Ask for)	
Massage (Relaxing)	5, 10, 26
Mushrooms (Pick)	1, 2
Promotion (Ask for)	5
Prune to Promote Healing	
Prune to Retard Growth	
Sauerkraut (Make)	
Spray Pests and Weeds	
Wean Children	
Weight (Reduce)	4, 5, 8, 9, 10, 11

Activity	December
Advertise in Print	5, 12, 21, 23, 26
Automobile (Buy)	17, 18, 19, 29, 30
Animals (Neuter or spay)	
Animals (Sell or buy)	22
Build (Start excavation)	
Business (Start new)	27, 28, 29
Can Fruits and Vegetables	3, 4, 12, 13
Concrete (Pour)	
Consultants (Begin work with)	20, 21, 23, 26, 29
Contracts (Bid on)	2, 19, 20
Copyrights/Patents (Apply for)	5, 7, 11, 12, 21, 26
Cultivate	14, 15, 16
Cut Wood	2, 10, 15, 25
Entertain Guests	
Employee (Hire)	29, 30
Fertilize and Compost (Chemical)	22, 23, 31
Fertilize and Compost (Organic)	3, 4, 5, 12, 13
Grafting or Budding (See p. 116)	
Habits (Break)	
Hair (Cut)	5, 10, 21, 26
Harvest (Crops to dry)	5, 6
Harvest (Grain or root crops)	14, 15
Job (Start new)	5, 10, 11, 21, 26
Legal (To gain damages, start)	29, 30
Loan (Ask for)	5, 6, 11, 12
Massage (Relaxing)	5, 10, 21
Mushrooms (Pick)	1, 2
Promotion (Ask for)	6, 11, 14, 21, 26
Prune to Promote Healing	
Prune to Retard Growth	12, 13
Sauerkraut (Make)	
Spray Pests and Weeds	
Wean Children	14, 15, 16
Weight (Reduce)	14, 15

Choose the Best Time
for Your Activities

When rules for elections refer to "favorable" and "unfavorable" aspects to your Sun or other planets, please refer to the Favorable and Unfavorable Days Tables and Lunar Aspectarian for more information. You'll find instructions beginning on page 129 and the tables beginning on page 136.

The material in this section came from several sources including: *The New A to Z Horoscope Maker and Delineator* by Llewellyn George (Llewellyn, 1999), *Moon Sign Book* (Llewellyn, 1945), and *Electional Astrology* by Vivian Robson (Slingshot Publishing, 2000). Robson's book was originally published in 1937.

Advertise (Internet)

The Moon should be conjunct, sextile, or trine Mercury or Uranus; and in the sign of Gemini, Capricorn, or Aquarius.

Advertise (Print)

Write ads on a day favorable to your Sun. The Moon should be conjunct, sextile, or trine Mercury or Venus. Avoid hard aspects to Mars and Saturn. Ad campaigns produce the best results when the Moon is well aspected in Gemini (to enhance communication) or Capricorn (to build business).

Animals

Take home new pets when the day is favorable to your Sun, or when the Moon is trine, sextile, or conjunct Mercury, Venus, or Jupiter, or in the sign of Virgo or Pisces. However, avoid days when the Moon is either square or opposing the Sun, Mars, Saturn, Uranus, Neptune, or Pluto. When selecting a pet, have the Moon well aspected by the planet that rules the animal. Cats are ruled by the Sun, dogs by Mercury, birds by Venus, horses by Jupiter, and fish by Neptune. Buy large animals when the Moon is in Sagittarius or Pisces, and making favorable aspects to Jupiter or Mercury. Buy animals smaller than sheep when the Moon is in Virgo with favorable aspects to Mercury or Venus.

Animals (Breed)

Animals are easiest to handle when the Moon is in Taurus, Cancer, Libra, or Pisces, but try to avoid the Full Moon. To encourage healthy births, animals should be mated so births occur when the Moon is increasing in Taurus, Cancer, Pisces, or Libra. Those born during a semi-fruitful sign (Taurus and Capricorn) will produce leaner meat. Libra yields beautiful animals for showing and racing.

Animals (Declaw)

Declaw cats in the dark of the Moon. Avoid the week before and after the Full Moon and the sign of Pisces.

Animals (Neuter or spay)

Have livestock and pets neutered or spayed when the Moon is in Sagittarius, Capricorn, or Pisces; after it has passed through Scorpio, the sign that rules reproductive organs. Avoid the week before and after the Full Moon.

Animals (Sell or buy)

In either buying or selling, it is important to keep the Moon and Mercury free from any aspect to Mars. Aspects to Mars will create discord and increase the likelihood of wrangling over price and quality. The Moon should be passing from the first quarter to full and sextile or trine Venus or Jupiter. When buying race-horses, let the Moon be in an air sign. The Moon should be in air signs when you buy birds. If the birds are to be pets, let the Moon be in good aspect to Venus.

Animals (Train)

Train pets when the Moon is in Virgo or when the Moon trines Mercury.

Animals (Train dogs to hunt)

Let the Moon be in Aries in conjunction with Mars, which makes them courageous and quick to learn. But let Jupiter also be in aspect to preserve them from danger in hunting.

Automobiles

When buying an automobile, select a time when the Moon is conjunct, sextile, or trine to Mercury, Saturn, or Uranus; and in the sign Gemini or Capricorn.

Baking Cakes

Your cakes will have a lighter texture if you see that the Moon is in Gemini, Libra, or Aquarius, and in good aspect to Venus or Mercury. If you are decorating a cake or confections are being made, have the Moon placed in Libra.

Beauty Treatments (Massage, etc.)

See that the Moon is in Taurus, Cancer, Leo, Libra, or Aquarius, and in favorable aspect to Venus. In the case of plastic surgery, aspects to Mars should be avoided, and the Moon should not be in the sign ruling the part to be operated on.

Borrow (Money or goods)

See that the Moon is not placed between 15 degrees Libra and 15 degrees Scorpio. Let the Moon be waning and in Leo, Scorpio (16 to 30 degrees), Sagittarius, or Pisces. Venus should be in good aspect to the Moon, and the Moon should not be square, opposing, or conjunct either Saturn or Mars.

Brewing

Start brewing during the third or fourth quarter, when the Moon is in Cancer, Scorpio, or Pisces.

Build (Start foundation)

Turning the first sod for the foundation marks the beginning of the building. For best results, excavate the site when the Moon is in the first quarter of a fixed sign and making favorable aspects to Saturn.

Business (Start new)

When starting a business, have the Moon be in Taurus, Virgo, or Capricorn, and increasing. The Moon should be sextile or trine Jupiter or Saturn, but avoid oppositions or squares. The planet ruling the business should be well aspected, too.

Buy Goods

Buy during the third quarter, when the Moon is in Taurus for quality, or in a mutable sign (Gemini, Sagittarius, Virgo, or Pisces) for savings. Good aspects to Venus or the Sun are desirable. If you are buying for yourself, it is good if the day is favorable for your Sun sign. You may also apply rules for buying specific items.

Canning

Can fruits and vegetables when the Moon is in either the third or fourth quarter, and in the water sign Cancer or Pisces. Preserves and jellies use the same quarters and the signs Cancer, Pisces, or Taurus.

Clothing

Buy clothing on a day that is favorable for your Sun sign, and when Venus or Mercury is well aspected. Avoid aspects to Mars and Saturn. Buy your clothing when the Moon is in Taurus if you want to remain satisfied. Do not buy clothing or jewelry when the Moon is in Scorpio or Aries. See that the Moon is sextile or trine the Sun during the first or second quarters.

Collections

Try to make collections on days when your Sun is well aspected. Avoid days when the Moon is opposing or square Mars or Saturn. If possible, the Moon should be in a cardinal sign (Aries, Cancer, Libra, or Capricorn). It is more difficult to collect when the Moon is in Taurus or Scorpio.

Concrete

Pour concrete when the Moon is in the third quarter of the fixed sign Taurus, Leo, or Aquarius.

Construction (Begin new)

The Moon should be sextile or trine Jupiter. According to Hermes, no building should be begun when the Moon is in Scorpio or Pisces. The best time to begin building is when the Moon is in Aquarius.

Consultants (Work with)

The Moon should be conjunct, sextile, or trine Mercury or Jupiter.

Contracts (Bid on)

The Moon should be in Gemini or Capricorn, and either the Moon or Mercury should be conjunct, sextile, or trine Jupiter.

Copyrights/Patents

The Moon should be conjunct, trine, or sextile either Mercury or Jupiter.

Coronations and Installations

Let the Moon be in Leo and in favorable aspect to Venus, Jupiter, or Mercury. The Moon should be applying to these planets.

Cultivate

Cultivate when the Moon is in a barren sign and waning, ideally the fourth quarter in Aries, Gemini, Leo, Virgo, or Aquarius. The third quarter in the sign of Sagittarius will also work.

Cut Timber

Timber cut during the waning Moon does not become worm-eaten; it will season well, and not warp, decay, or snap during burning. Cut when the Moon is in Taurus, Gemini, Virgo, or Capricorn—especially in August. Avoid the water signs. Look for favorable aspects to Mars.

Decorating or Home Repairs

Have the Moon waxing, and in the sign of Libra, Gemini, or Aquarius. Avoid squares or oppositions to either Mars or Saturn. Venus in good aspect to Mars or Saturn is beneficial.

Demolition

Let the waning Moon be in Leo, Sagittarius, or Aries.

Dental and Dentists

Visit the dentist when the Moon is in Virgo, or pick a day marked favorable for your Sun sign. Mars should be marked sextile, conjunct, or trine; and avoid squares or oppositions to Saturn, Uranus, or Jupiter.

Teeth are best removed when the Moon is in Gemini, Virgo, Sagittarius, or Pisces, and during the first or second quarter. Avoid the Full Moon! The day should be favorable for your lunar cycle, and Mars and Saturn should be marked conjunct, trine, or sextile. Fillings should be done in the third or fourth quarters in the sign of Taurus, Leo, Scorpio, or Pisces. The same applies for dentures.

Dressmaking

William Lilly wrote in 1676: "Make no new clothes, or first put them on when the Moon is in Scorpio or afflicted by Mars, for they will be apt to be torn and quickly worn out." Design, repair, and sew clothes in the first and second quarters of Taurus, Leo, or Libra on a day marked favorable for your Sun sign. Venus, Jupiter, and Mercury should be favorably aspected, but avoid hard aspects to Mars or Saturn.

Egg-setting

Eggs should be set so chicks will hatch during fruitful signs. To set eggs, subtract the number of days given for incubation or gestation from the fruitful dates. Chickens incubate in twenty-one days, turkeys and geese in twenty-eight days.

A freshly laid egg loses quality rapidly if it is not handled properly. Use plenty of clean litter in the nests to reduce the number of dirty or cracked eggs. Gather eggs daily in mild weather and at least two times daily in hot or cold weather. The eggs should be placed in a cooler immediately after gathering and stored at 50 to 55 degrees Fahrenheit. Do not store eggs with foods or products that give off pungent odors since eggs may absorb the odors.

Eggs saved for hatching purposes should not be washed. Only clean and slightly soiled eggs should be saved for hatching. Dirty eggs should not be incubated. Eggs should be stored in a cool

place with the large ends up. It is not advisable to store the eggs longer than one week before setting them in an incubator.

Electricity and Gas (Install)

The Moon should be in a fire sign, and there should be no squares, oppositions, or conjunctions with Uranus (ruler of electricity), Neptune (ruler of gas), Saturn, or Mars. Hard aspects to Mars can cause fires.

Electronics (Buying)

Choose a day when the Moon is in an air sign (Gemini, Libra, Aquarius) and well aspected by Mercury and/or Uranus when buying electronics.

Electronics (Repair)

The Moon should be sextile or trine Mars or Uranus, and in a fixed sign (Taurus, Leo, Scorpio, Aquarius).

Entertain Friends

Let the Moon be in Leo or Libra and making good aspects to Venus. Avoid squares or oppositions to either Mars or Saturn by the Moon or Venus.

Eyes and Eyeglasses

Have your eyes tested and glasses fitted on a day marked favorable for your Sun sign, and on a day that falls during your favorable lunar cycle. Mars should not be in aspect with the Moon. The same applies for any treatment of the eyes, which should also be started during the Moon's first or second quarter.

Fence Posts

Set posts when the Moon is in the third or fourth quarter of the fixed sign Taurus or Leo.

Fertilize and Compost

Fertilize when the Moon is in a fruitful sign (Cancer, Scorpio, Pisces). Organic fertilizers are best when the Moon is waning. Use chemical fertilizers when the Moon is waxing. Start compost when the Moon is in the fourth quarter in a water sign.

Find Hidden Treasure

Let the Moon be in good aspect to Jupiter or Venus. If you erect a horoscope for this election, place the Moon in the Fourth House.

Find Lost Articles

Search for lost articles during the first quarter and when your Sun sign is marked favorable. Also check to see that the planet ruling the lost item is trine, sextile, or conjunct the Moon. The Moon rules household utensils; Mercury rules letters and books; and Venus rules clothing, jewelry, and money.

Fishing

During the summer months, the best time of the day to fish is from sunrise to three hours after, and from two hours before sunset until one hour after. Fish do not bite in cooler months until the air is warm, from noon to 3 pm. Warm, cloudy days are good. The most favorable winds are from the south and southwest. Easterly winds are unfavorable. The best days of the month for fishing are when the Moon changes quarters, especially if the change occurs on a day when the Moon is in a water sign (Cancer, Scorpio, Pisces). The best period in any month is the day after the Full Moon.

Friendship

The need for friendship is greater when the Moon is in Aquarius, or when Uranus aspects the Moon. Friendship prospers when Venus or Uranus is trine, sextile, or conjunct the Moon. The Moon in Gemini facilitates the chance meeting of acquaintances and friends.

Grafting or Budding

Grafting is the process of introducing new varieties of fruit on less desirable trees. For this process you should use the increasing phase of the Moon in fruitful signs such as Cancer, Scorpio, or Pisces. Capricorn may be used, too. Cut your grafts while trees are dormant, from December to March. Keep them in a cool, dark, not too dry or too damp place. Do the grafting before the sap starts to flow and while the Moon is waxing, and preferably while it is in Cancer, Scorpio, or Pisces. The type of plant should determine both cutting and planting times.

Habit (Breaking)

To end an undesirable habit, and this applies to ending everything from a bad relationship to smoking, start on a day when the Moon is in the fourth quarter and in the barren sign of Gemini, Leo, or

Aquarius. Aries, Virgo, and Capricorn may be suitable as well, depending on the habit you want to be rid of. Make sure that your lunar cycle is favorable. Avoid lunar aspects to Mars or Jupiter. However, favorable aspects to Pluto are helpful.

Haircuts

Cut hair when the Moon is in Gemini, Sagittarius, Pisces, Taurus, or Capricorn, but not in Virgo. Look for favorable aspects to Venus. For faster growth, cut hair when the Moon is increasing in Cancer or Pisces. To make hair grow thicker, cut when the Moon is full in the signs of Taurus, Cancer, or Leo. If you want your hair to grow more slowly, have the Moon be decreasing in Aries, Gemini, or Virgo, and have the Moon square or opposing Saturn.

Permanents, straightening, and hair coloring will take well if the Moon is in Taurus or Leo and trine or sextile Venus. Avoid hair treatments if Mars is marked as square or in opposition, especially if heat is to be used. For permanents, a trine to Jupiter is helpful. The Moon also should be in the first quarter. Check the lunar cycle for a favorable day in relation to your Sun sign.

Harvest Crops

Harvest root crops when the Moon is in a dry sign (Aries, Leo, Sagittarius, Gemini, Aquarius) and waning. Harvest grain for storage just after the Full Moon, avoiding Cancer, Scorpio, or Pisces. Harvest in the third and fourth quarters in dry signs. Dry crops in the third quarter in fire signs.

Health

A diagnosis is more likely to be successful when the Moon is in Aries, Cancer, Libra, or Capricorn; and less so when in Gemini, Sagittarius, Pisces, or Virgo. Begin a recuperation program when the Moon is in a cardinal or fixed sign and the day is favorable to your Sun sign. Enter hospitals at these times, too. For surgery, see "Surgical Procedures." Buy medicines when the Moon is in Virgo or Scorpio.

Home (Buy new)

If you desire a permanent home, buy when the New Moon is in a fixed sign—Taurus or Leo—for example. Each sign will affect your decision in a different way. A house bought when the Moon is in Taurus is likely to be more practical and have a country look—right down to the split-rail fence. A house purchased when the Moon is in Leo will more likely be a real showplace.

If you're buying for speculation and a quick turnover, be certain that the Moon is in a cardinal sign (Aries, Cancer, Libra, Capricorn). Avoid buying when the Moon is in a fixed sign (Leo, Scorpio, Aquarius, Taurus).

Home (Make repairs)

In all repairs, avoid squares, oppositions, or conjunctions to the planet ruling the place or thing to be repaired. For example, bathrooms are ruled by Scorpio and Cancer. You would not want to start a project in those rooms when the Moon or Pluto is receiving hard aspects. The front entrance, hall, dining room, and porch are ruled by the Sun. So you would want to avoid times when Saturn or Mars are square, opposing, or conjunct the Sun. Also, let the Moon be waxing.

Home (Sell)

Make a strong effort to list your property for sale when the Sun is marked favorable in your sign and in good aspect to Jupiter. Avoid adverse aspects to as many planets as possible.

Home Furnishings (Buy new)

Saturn days (Saturday) are good for buying, and Jupiter days (Thursday) are good for selling. Items bought on days when

Saturn is well aspected tend to wear longer and purchases tend to be more conservative.

Job (Start new)

Jupiter and Venus should be sextile, trine, or conjunct the Moon. A day when your Sun is receiving favorable aspects is preferred.

Legal Matters

Good Moon-Jupiter aspects improve the outcome in legal decisions. To gain damages through a lawsuit, begin the process during the increasing Moon. To avoid paying damages, a court date during the decreasing Moon is desirable. Good Moon-Sun aspects strengthen your chance of success. A well-aspected Moon in Cancer or Leo, making good aspects to the Sun, brings the best results in custody cases. In divorce cases, a favorable Moon-Venus aspect is best.

Loan (Ask for)

A first and second quarter phase favors the lender, the third and fourth quarters favor the borrower. Good aspects of Jupiter and Venus to the Moon are favorable to both, as is having the Moon in Leo or Taurus.

Machinery, Appliances, or Tools (Buy)

Tools, machinery, and other implements should be bought on days when your lunar cycle is favorable and when Mars and Uranus are trine, sextile, or conjunct the Moon. Any quarter of the Moon is suitable. When buying gas or electrical appliances, the Moon should be in Aquarius.

Make a Will

Let the Moon be in a fixed sign (Taurus, Leo, Scorpio, or Aquarius) to ensure permanence. If the Moon is in a cardinal sign (Aries, Cancer, Libra, or Capricorn), the will could be altered. Let the Moon be waxing—increasing in light—and in good aspect to

Saturn, Venus, or Mercury. In the case the will is made in an emergency during illness, and the Moon is slow in motion, void-of-course, combust, or under the Sun's beams, the testator will die and the will remain unaltered. There is some danger that it will be lost or stolen, however.

Marriage

The best time for marriage to take place is when the Moon is increasing, but not yet full. Good signs for the Moon to be in are Taurus, Cancer, Leo, or Libra.

The Moon in Taurus produces the most steadfast marriages, but if the partners later want to separate, they may have a difficult time. Make sure that the Moon is well aspected, especially to Venus or Jupiter. Avoid aspects to Mars, Uranus, or Pluto, and the signs Aries, Gemini, Virgo, Scorpio, or Aquarius.

The values of the signs are as follows:

- Aries is not favored for marriage
- Taurus from 0 to 19 degrees is good, the remaining degrees are less favorable
- Cancer is unfavorable unless you are marrying a widow
- Leo is favored, but it may cause one party to deceive the other as to his or her money or possessions
- Virgo is not favored except when marrying a widow
- Libra is good for engagements but not for marriage
- Scorpio from 0 to 15 degrees is good, but the last fifteen degrees are entirely unfortunate. The woman may be fickle, envious, and quarrelsome
- Sagittarius is neutral
- Capricorn, from 0 to 10 degrees, is difficult for marriage; however, the remaining degrees are favorable, especially when marrying a widow
- Aquarius is not favored

- Pisces is favored, although marriage under this sign can incline a woman to chatter a lot

These effects are strongest when the Moon is in the sign. If the Moon and Venus are in a cardinal sign, happiness between the couple may not continue long.

On no account should the Moon apply to Saturn or Mars, even by good aspect.

Medical Treatment for the Eyes

Let the Moon be increasing in light and motion and making favorable aspects to Venus or Jupiter, and be unaspected by Mars. Keep the Moon out of Taurus, Capricorn, or Virgo. If an aspect between the Moon and Mars is unavoidable, let it be separating.

Medical Treatment for the Head

If possible, have Mars and Saturn free of hard aspects. Let the Moon be in Aries or Taurus, decreasing in light, in conjunction or aspect with Venus or Jupiter, and free of hard aspects. The Sun should not be in any aspect to the Moon.

Medical Treatment for the Nose

Let the Moon be in Cancer, Leo, or Virgo, and not aspecting Mars or Saturn, and not in conjunction with a weak or retrograde planet.

Mining

Saturn rules mining. Begin work when Saturn is marked conjunct, trine, or sextile. Mine for gold when the Sun is marked conjunct, trine, or sextile. Mercury rules quicksilver, Venus rules copper, Jupiter rules tin, Saturn rules lead and coal, Uranus rules radioactive elements, Neptune rules oil, the Moon rules water. Mine for these items when the ruling planet is marked conjunct, trine, or sextile.

Move to New Home

If you have a choice, and sometimes we don't, make sure that Mars is not aspecting the Moon. Move on a day favorable to your Sun sign, or when the Moon is conjunct, sextile, or trine the Sun.

Mow Lawn

Mow in the first and second quarters (waxing phase) to increase growth and lushness, and in the third and fourth quarters (waning phase) to decrease growth.

Negotiate

When you are choosing a time to negotiate, consider what the meeting is about and what you want to have happen. If it is agreement or compromise between two parties that you desire, have the Moon be in the sign of Libra. When you are making contracts, it is best to have the Moon in the same element. For example, if your concern is communication, then elect a time when the Moon is in an air sign. If, on the other hand, your concern is about possessions, an earth sign would be more appropriate. Fixed signs are unfavorable, with the exception of Leo; so are cardinal signs, except for Capricorn. If you are negotiating the end of something, use the rules that apply to ending habits.

Occupational Training

When you begin training, see that your lunar cycle is favorable that day, and that the planet ruling your occupation is marked conjunct or trine.

Paint

Paint buildings during the waning Libra or Aquarius Moon. If the weather is hot, paint when the Moon is in Taurus. If the weather is cold, paint when the Moon is in Leo. Schedule the painting to start in the fourth quarter as the wood is drier and paint will penetrate wood better. Avoid painting around the New Moon, though, as the wood is likely to be damp, making the paint subject to scalding when hot weather hits it. If the temperature is below 70 degrees Fahrenheit, it is not advisable to paint while the Moon is in Cancer, Scorpio, or Pisces as the paint is apt to creep, check, or run.

Party (Host or attend)

A party timed so the Moon is in Gemini, Leo, Libra, or Sagittarius, with good aspects to Venus and Jupiter, will be fun and well attended. There should be no aspects between the Moon and Mars or Saturn.

Pawn

Do not pawn any article when Jupiter is receiving a square or opposition from Saturn or Mars, or when Jupiter is within 17 degrees of the Sun, for you will have little chance to redeem the items.

Pick Mushrooms

Mushrooms, one of the most promising traditional medicines in the world, should be gathered at the Full Moon.

Plant

Root crops, like carrots and potatoes, are best if planted in the sign Taurus or Capricorn. Beans, peas, tomatoes, peppers, and other fruit-bearing plants are best if planted in a sign that supports seed growth. Leaf plants, like lettuce, broccoli, or cauliflower, are best planted when the Moon is in a water sign.

It is recommended that you transplant during a decreasing Moon, when forces are streaming into the lower part of the plant. This helps root growth.

Promotion (Ask for)

Choose a day favorable to your Sun sign. Mercury should be marked conjunct, trine, or sextile. Avoid days when Mars or Saturn is aspected.

Prune

Prune during the third and fourth quarter of a Scorpio Moon to retard growth and to promote better fruit. Prune when the Moon is in cardinal Capricorn to promote healing.

Reconcile with People

If the reconciliation be with a woman, let Venus be strong and well aspected. If elders or superiors are involved, see that Saturn is receiving good aspects; if the reconciliation is between young people or between an older and younger person, see that Mercury is well aspected.

Romance

There is less control of when a romance starts, but romances begun under an increasing Moon are more likely to be permanent or satisfying, while those begun during the decreasing Moon tend to transform the participants. The tone of the relationship can be guessed from the sign the Moon is in. Romances begun with the Moon in Aries may be impulsive. Those begun in Capricorn will take greater effort to bring to a desirable conclusion, but they may be very rewarding. Good aspects between the Moon and Venus will have a positive influence on the relationship. Avoid unfavorable aspects to Mars, Uranus, and Pluto. A decreasing Moon, particularly the fourth quarter, facilitates ending a relationship, and causes the least pain.

Roof a Building

Begin roofing a building during the third or fourth quarter, when the Moon is in Aries or Aquarius. Shingles laid during the New Moon have a tendency to curl at the edges.

Sauerkraut

The best-tasting sauerkraut is made just after the Full Moon in the fruitful signs of Cancer, Scorpio, or Pisces.

Select a Child's Sex

Count from the last day of menstruation to the first day of the next cycle and divide the interval between the two dates in half. Pregnancy in the first half produces females, but copulation should take place with the Moon in a feminine sign. Pregnancy in the latter half, up to three days before the beginning of menstruation, produces males, but copulation should take place with the Moon in a masculine sign. The three-day period before the next period again produces females.

Sell or Canvass

Begin these activities during a day favorable to your Sun sign. Otherwise, sell on days when Jupiter, Mercury, or Mars is trine, sextile, or conjunct the Moon. Avoid days when Saturn is square or opposing the Moon, for that always hinders business and causes discord. If the Moon is passing from the first quarter to full, it is best to have the Moon swift in motion and in good aspect with Venus and/or Jupiter.

Sign Papers

Sign contracts or agreements when the Moon is increasing in a fruitful sign and on a day when the Moon is making favorable aspects to Mercury. Avoid days when Mars, Saturn, or Neptune are square or opposite the Moon.

Spray and Weed

Spray pests and weeds during the fourth quarter when the Moon is in the barren sign Leo or Aquarius, and making favorable aspects to Pluto. Weed during a waning Moon in a barren sign.

Staff (Fire)

Have the Moon in the third or fourth quarter, but not full. The Moon should not be square any planets.

Staff (Hire)

The Moon should be in the first or second quarter, and preferably in the sign of Gemini or Virgo. The Moon should be conjunct, trine, or sextile Mercury or Jupiter.

Stocks (Buy)

The Moon should be in Taurus or Capricorn, and there should be a sextile or trine to Jupiter or Saturn.

Surgical Procedures

Blood flow, like ocean tides, appears to be related to Moon phases. To reduce hemorrhage after a surgery, schedule it within one week before or after a New Moon. Schedule surgery to occur during the increase of the Moon if possible, as wounds heal better and vitality is greater than during the decrease of the Moon. Avoid surgery within one week before or after the Full Moon. Select a date when the Moon is past the sign governing the part of the body involved in the operation. For example, abdominal operations should be done when the Moon is in Sagittarius, Capricorn, or Aquarius. The further removed the Moon sign is from the sign ruling the afflicted part of the body, the better.

For successful operations, avoid times when the Moon is applying to any aspect of Mars. (This tends to promote inflammation and complications.) See the Lunar Aspectarian on odd pages 137–159 to find days with negative Mars aspects and positive Venus and Jupiter aspects. Never operate with the Moon in the same sign as a person's Sun sign or Ascendant. Let the Moon be in a fixed sign and avoid square or opposing aspects. The Moon should not be void-of-course. Cosmetic surgery should be done in the increase of the Moon, when the Moon is not square or in opposition to Mars. Avoid days when the Moon is square or opposing Saturn or the Sun.

Travel (Air)

Start long trips when the Moon is making favorable aspects to the Sun. For enjoyment, aspects to Jupiter are preferable; for visiting, look for favorable aspects to Mercury. To prevent accidents, avoid squares or oppositions to Mars, Saturn, Uranus, or Pluto. Choose a day when the Moon is in Sagittarius or Gemini and well aspected to Mercury, Jupiter, or Uranus. Avoid adverse aspects of Mars, Saturn, or Uranus.

Visit

On setting out to visit a person, let the Moon be in aspect with any retrograde planet, for this ensures that the person you're visiting will be at home. If you desire to stay a long time in a place, let the Moon be in good aspect to Saturn. If you desire to leave the place quickly, let the Moon be in a cardinal sign.

Wean Children

To wean a child successfully, do so when the Moon is in Sagittarius, Capricorn, Aquarius, or Pisces—signs that do not rule vital human organs. By observing this astrological rule, much trouble for parents and child may be avoided.

Weight (Reduce)

If you want to lose weight, the best time to get started is when the Moon is in the third or fourth quarter, and in the barren sign of Virgo. Review the section on How to Use the Moon Tables and Lunar Aspectarian beginning on page 129 to help you select a date that is favorable to begin your weight-loss program.

Wine and Drink Other Than Beer

Start brewing when the Moon is in Pisces or Taurus. Sextiles or trines to Venus are favorable, but avoid aspects to Mars or Saturn.

Write

Write for pleasure or publication when the Moon is in Gemini. Mercury should be making favorable aspects to Uranus and Neptune.

How to Use the Moon Tables and Lunar Aspectarian

Timing activities is one of the most important things you can do to ensure success. In many eastern countries, timing by the planets is so important that practically no event takes place without first setting up a chart for it. Weddings have occurred in the middle of the night because the influences were best then. You may not want to take it that far, but you can still make use of the influences of the Moon whenever possible. It's easy and it works!

In the *Moon Sign Book* is information to help you plan just about any activity: weddings, fishing, making purchases, cutting your hair, traveling, and more. We provide the guidelines you need to pick the best day out of the several from which you have to choose. The Moon Tables are the *Moon Sign Book's* primary method for choosing dates. Following are instructions, examples, and directions on how to read the Moon Tables.

More advanced information on using the tables containing the Lunar Aspectarian and favorable and unfavorable days (found on odd-numbered pages opposite the Moon Tables), Moon void-of-course and retrograde information to choose the dates best for you is also included.

The Five Basic Steps

Step 1: Directions for Choosing Dates

Look up the directions for choosing dates for the activity that you wish to begin, then go to step 2.

Step 2: Check the Moon Tables

You'll find two tables for each month of the year beginning on page 136. The Moon Tables (on the left-hand pages) include the day, date, and sign the Moon is in; the element and nature of the sign; the Moon's phase; and when it changes sign or phase. If there is a time listed after a date, that time is the time when the Moon moves into that zodiac sign. Until then, the Moon is considered to be in the sign for the previous day.

The abbreviation Full signifies Full Moon and New signifies New Moon. The times listed with dates indicate when the Moon changes sign. The times listed after the phase indicate when the Moon changes phase.

Turn to the month you would like to begin your activity. You will be using the Moon's sign and phase information most often when you begin choosing your own dates. Use the Time Zone Map on page 164 and the Time Zone Conversions table on page 165 to convert time to your own time zone.

When you find dates that meet the criteria for the correct Moon phase and sign for your activity, you may have completed the process. For certain simple activities, such as getting a haircut, the phase and sign information is all that is needed. If the directions for your activity include information on certain lunar aspects, however, you should consult the Lunar Aspectarian. An example of this would be if the directions told you not to perform a certain activity when the Moon is square (Q) Jupiter.

Step 3: Check the Lunar Aspectarian

On the pages opposite the Moon Tables you will find tables containing the Lunar Aspectarian and Favorable and Unfavorable Days. The Lunar Aspectarian gives the aspects (or angles) of the Moon to other planets. Some aspects are favorable, while others are not. To use the Lunar Aspectarian, find the planet that the directions list as favorable for your activity, and run down the column to the date desired. For example, you should avoid aspects to Mars if you are planning surgery. So you would look for Mars across the top and then run down that column looking for days where there are no aspects to Mars (as signified by empty boxes). If you want to find a favorable aspect (sextile (X) or trine (T)) to Mercury, run your finger down the column under Mercury until you find an X or T. Adverse aspects to planets are squares (Q) or oppositions (O). A conjunction (C) is sometimes beneficial, sometimes not, depending on the activity or planets involved.

Step 4: Favorable and Unfavorable Days

The tables listing favorable and unfavorable days are helpful when you want to choose your personal best dates because your Sun sign is taken into consideration. The twelve Sun signs are listed on the right side of the tables. Once you have determined which days meet your criteria for phase, sign, and aspects, you can determine whether or not those days are positive for you by checking the favorable and unfavorable days for your Sun sign.

To find out if a day is positive for you, find your Sun sign and then look down the column. If it is marked F, it is very favorable. The Moon is in the same sign as your Sun on a favorable day. If it is marked f, it is slightly favorable; U is very unfavorable; and u means slightly unfavorable. A day marked very unfavorable (U) indicates that the Moon is in the sign opposing your Sun.

Once you have selected good dates for the activity you are about to begin, you can go straight to "Using What You've Learned," beginning on the next page. To learn how to fine-tune your selections even further, read on.

Step 5: Void-of-Course Moon and Retrogrades

This last step is perhaps the most advanced portion of the procedure. It is generally considered poor timing to make decisions, sign important papers, or start special activities during a Moon void-of-course period or during a Mercury retrograde. Once you have chosen the best date for your activity based on steps one through four, you can check the Void-of-Course tables, beginning on page 76, to find out if any of the dates you have chosen have void periods.

The Moon is said to be void-of-course after it has made its last aspect to a planet within a particular sign, but before it has moved into the next sign. Put simply, the Moon is "resting" during the void-of-course period, so activities initiated at this time generally don't come to fruition. You will notice that there are many void periods during the year, and it is nearly impossible to avoid all of them. Some people choose to ignore these altogether and do not take them into consideration when planning activities.

Next, you can check the Retrograde Planets tables on page 160 to see what planets are retrograde during your chosen date(s).

A planet is said to be retrograde when it appears to move backward in the sky as viewed from the Earth. Generally, the farther a planet is away from the Sun, the longer it can stay retrograde. Some planets will retrograde for several months at a time. Avoiding retrogrades is not as important in lunar planning as avoiding the Moon void-of-course, with the exception of the planet Mercury.

Mercury rules thought and communication, so it is advisable not to sign important papers, initiate important business or legal work, or make crucial decisions during these times. As with the Moon void-of-course, it is difficult to avoid all planetary retrogrades when beginning events, and you may choose to ignore this step of the process. Following are some examples using some or all of the steps outlined above.

Using What You've Learned

Let's say it's a new year and you want to have your hair cut. It's thin and you would like it to look fuller, so you find the directions for hair care and you see that for thicker hair you should cut hair while the Moon is Full and in the sign of Taurus, Cancer, or Leo. You should avoid the Moon in Aries, Gemini, or Virgo. Look at the January Moon Table on page 136. You see that the Full Moon is on January 10 at 10:27 pm. The Moon moves into the sign of Leo the next day, and remains in Leo until January 13 at 1:33 pm, so January 1–11 meets both the phase and sign criteria.

Let's move on to a more difficult example using the sign and phase of the Moon. You want to buy a permanent home. After checking the instructions for purchasing a house: "Home (Buy new)" on page 118, you see that you should buy a home when the Moon is in Taurus, Cancer, or Leo. You need to get a loan, so you should also look under "Loan (Ask for)" on page 119. Here it says that the third and fourth quarters favor the borrower (you). You are going to buy the house in October so go to page 154. The Moon is in the third quarter October 27–31. The Moon is in Cancer from 9:48 pm on October 9 until October 11 at 4:56 am. The best days for obtaining a loan would be October 9–10, while the Moon is in Cancer.

Just match up the best sign and phase (quarter) to come up with the best date. With all activities, be sure to check the favorable and unfavorable days for your Sun sign in the table adjoining the Lunar Aspectarian. If there is a choice between several dates, pick the one most favorable for you. Because buying a home is an important business decision, you may also wish to see if the Moon is void or if Mercury is retrograde during these dates.

Now let's look at an example that uses signs, phases, and aspects. Our example is starting new home construction. We will use the month of April. Look under "Build (Start foundation)" on page 111 and you'll see that the Moon should be in the first quarter of Taurus or Leo. You should select a time when the Moon is not making unfavorable aspects to Saturn. (Conjunctions are usually considered good if they are not to Mars, Saturn, or Neptune.) Look in the April Moon Table. You will see that the Moon is in the first quarter April 24–30. The Moon is in Taurus from 2:46 pm on April 24 until April 26 at 5:02 pm. Now, look to the April Lunar Aspectarian. We see that there are no squares or oppositions to Saturn between April 24–26. These are good dates to start a foundation.

A Note About Time and Time Zones

All tables in the *Moon Sign Book* use Eastern Time. You must calculate the difference between your time zone and the Eastern Time Zone. Please refer to the Time Zone Conversions chart on 165 for help with time conversions. The sign the Moon is in at midnight is the sign shown in the Aspectarian and Favorable and Unfavorable Days tables.

How Does the Time Matter?

Due to the three-hour time difference between the east and west coasts of the United States, those of you living on the East Coast may be, for example, under the influence of a Virgo Moon, while those of you living on the West Coast will still have a Leo Moon influence.

We follow a commonly held belief among astrologers: whatever sign the Moon is in at the start of a day—12:00 am Eastern

Time—is considered the dominant influence of the day. That sign is indicated in the Moon Tables. If the date you select for an activity shows the Moon changing signs, you can decide how important the sign change may be for your specific election and adjust your election date and time accordingly.

Use Common Sense

Some activities depend on outside factors. Obviously, you can't go out and plant when there is a foot of snow on the ground. You should adjust to the conditions at hand. If the weather was bad during the first quarter, when it was best to plant crops, do it during the second quarter while the Moon is in a fruitful sign. If the Moon is not in a fruitful sign during the first or second quarter, choose a day when it is in a semi-fruitful sign. The best advice is to choose either the sign or phase that is most favorable, when the two don't coincide.

To Summarize

First, look up the activity under the proper heading, then look for the information given in the tables. Choose the best date considering the number of positive factors in effect. If most of the dates are favorable, there is no problem choosing the one that will fit your schedule. However, if there aren't any really good dates, pick the ones with the least number of negative influences. Please keep in mind that the information found here applies in the broadest sense to the events you want to plan or are considering. To be the most effective, when you use electional astrology, you should also consider your own birth chart in relation to a chart drawn for the time or times you have under consideration. The best advice we can offer you is: read the entire introduction to each section.

January Moon Table

Date	Sign	Element	Nature	Phase
1 Thu	Pisces	Water	Fruitful	1st
2 Fri	Pisces	Water	Fruitful	1st
3 Sat 4:50 am	Aries	Fire	Barren	1st
4 Sun	Aries	Fire	Barren	2nd 6:56 am
5 Mon 10:46 am	Taurus	Earth	Semi-fruitful	2nd
6 Tue	Taurus	Earth	Semi-fruitful	2nd
7 Wed 1:11 pm	Gemini	Air	Barren	2nd
8 Thu	Gemini	Air	Barren	2nd
9 Fri 1:14 pm	Cancer	Water	Fruitful	2nd
10 Sat	Cancer	Water	Fruitful	3rd 10:27 pm
11 Sun 12:41 pm	Leo	Fire	Barren	3rd
12 Mon	Leo	Fire	Barren	3rd
13 Tue 1:33 pm	Virgo	Earth	Barren	3rd
14 Wed	Virgo	Earth	Barren	3rd
15 Thu 5:30 pm	Libra	Air	Semi-fruitful	3rd
16 Fri	Libra	Air	Semi-fruitful	3rd
17 Sat	Libra	Air	Semi-fruitful	4th 9:46 pm
18 Sun 1:20 am	Scorpio	Water	Fruitful	4th
19 Mon	Scorpio	Water	Fruitful	4th
20 Tue 12:30 pm	Sagittarius	Fire	Barren	4th
21 Wed	Sagittarius	Fire	Barren	4th
22 Thu	Sagittarius	Fire	Barren	4th
23 Fri 1:18 am	Capricorn	Earth	Semi-fruitful	4th
24 Sat	Capricorn	Earth	Semi-fruitful	4th
25 Sun 1:56 pm	Aquarius	Air	Barren	4th
26 Mon	Aquarius	Air	Barren	1st 2:55 am
27 Tue	Aquarius	Air	Barren	1st
28 Wed 1:12 am	Pisces	Water	Fruitful	1st
29 Thu	Pisces	Water	Fruitful	1st
30 Fri 10:25 am	Aries	Fire	Barren	1st
31 Sat	Aries	Fire	Barren	1st

January Aspectarian/Favorable & Unfavorable Days

Date	Sun	Mercury	Venus	Mars	Jupiter	Saturn	Uranus	Neptune	Pluto	Aries	Taurus	Gemini	Cancer	Leo	Virgo	Libra	Scorpio	Sagittarius	Capricorn	Aquarius	Pisces
1	X			X							f	u	f		U		f	u	f		F
2						O	C				f	u	f		U		f	u	f		F
3		X			Q	X			Q		f	u	f		U		f	u	f		F
4	Q							X		F		f	u	f		U		f	u	f	
5		Q	X	T	Q				T	F		f	u	f		U		f	u	f	
6	T					T	X				F		f	u	f		U		f	u	f
7			Q		T			Q			F		f	u	f		U		f	u	f
8		T						Q		f		F		f	u	f		U		f	u
9						Q		T	O	f		F		f	u	f		U		f	u
10	O		T		O		X	T		u	f		F		f	u	f		U		f
11				O						u	f		F		f	u	f		U		f
12		O								f	u	f		F		f	u	f		U	
13								O	T	f	u	f		F		f	u	f		U	
14			O	T				O			f	u	f		F		f	u	f		U
15	T				T	C			Q		f	u	f		F		f	u	f		U
16		T		Q						U		f	u	f		F		f	u	f	
17	Q							T		U		f	u	f		F		f	u	f	
18		Q		Q					X	U		f	u	f		F		f	u	f	
19			T	X		X	T	Q			U		f	u	f		F		f	u	f
20	X	X			X						U		f	u	f		F		f	u	f
21										f		U		f	u	f		F		f	u
22			Q			Q	Q	X		f		U		f	u	f		F		f	u
23									C	f		U		f	u	f		F		f	u
24			X	C		T	X			u	f		U		f	u	f		F		f
25		C			C					u	f		U		f	u	f		F		f
26	C									f	u	f		U		f	u	f		F	
27							C			f	u	f		U		f	u	f		F	
28								X		f	u	f		U		f	u	f		F	
29		X				O	C				f	u	f		U		f	u	f		F
30			C	X	X				Q		f	u	f		U		f	u	f		F
31	X									F		f	u	f		U		f	u	f	

February Moon Table

Date	Sign	Element	Nature	Phase
1 Sun 5:08 pm	Taurus	Earth	Semi-fruitful	1st
2 Mon	Taurus	Earth	Semi-fruitful	2nd 6:13 pm
3 Tue 9:14 pm	Gemini	Air	Barren	2nd
4 Wed	Gemini	Air	Barren	2nd
5 Thu 11:05 pm	Cancer	Water	Fruitful	2nd
6 Fri	Cancer	Water	Fruitful	2nd
7 Sat 11:43 pm	Leo	Fire	Barren	2nd
8 Sun	Leo	Fire	Barren	2nd
9 Mon	Leo	Fire	Barren	3rd 9:49 am
10 Tue 12:38 am	Virgo	Earth	Barren	3rd
11 Wed	Virgo	Earth	Barren	3rd
12 Thu 3:33 am	Libra	Air	Semi-fruitful	3rd
13 Fri	Libra	Air	Semi-fruitful	3rd
14 Sat 9:50 am	Scorpio	Water	Fruitful	3rd
15 Sun	Scorpio	Water	Fruitful	3rd
16 Mon 7:53 pm	Sagittarius	Fire	Barren	4th 4:37 pm
17 Tue	Sagittarius	Fire	Barren	4th
18 Wed	Sagittarius	Fire	Barren	4th
19 Thu 8:25 am	Capricorn	Earth	Semi-fruitful	4th
20 Fri	Capricorn	Earth	Semi-fruitful	4th
21 Sat 9:06 pm	Aquarius	Air	Barren	4th
22 Sun	Aquarius	Air	Barren	4th
23 Mon	Aquarius	Air	Barren	4th
24 Tue 7:59 am	Pisces	Water	Fruitful	1st 8:35 pm
25 Wed	Pisces	Water	Fruitful	1st
26 Thu 4:24 pm	Aries	Fire	Barren	1st
27 Fri	Aries	Fire	Barren	1st
28 Sat 10:33 pm	Taurus	Earth	Semi-fruitful	1st

February Aspectarian/Favorable & Unfavorable Days

Date	Sun	Mercury	Venus	Mars	Jupiter	Saturn	Uranus	Neptune	Pluto	Aries	Taurus	Gemini	Cancer	Leo	Virgo	Libra	Scorpio	Sagittarius	Capricorn	Aquarius	Pisces
1		Q		Q				X	T		F	f	u	f			U		f	u	f
2	Q			Q							F	f	u	f			U		f	u	f
3		T	X	T		T	X	Q			F	f	u	f			U		f	u	f
4					T					f		F	f	u	f			U		f	u
5	T					Q	Q	T		f		F	f	u	f			U		f	u
6			Q						O	u	f		F	f	u	f			U		f
7		O				X	T			u	f		F	f	u	f			U		f
8			T	O	O					f	u	f		F	f	u	f			U	
9	O								O	f	u	f		F	f	u	f			U	
10									T		f	u	f		F	f	u	f			U
11		T				C	O				f	u	f		F	f	u	f			U
12			O	T	T				Q		f	u	f		F	f	u	f			U
13							T			U		f	u	f		F	f	u	f		
14	T	Q						X		U		f	u	f		F	f	u	f		
15				Q	Q					U		f	u	f		F	f	u	f		
16	Q					X	T	Q		U		f	u	f		F	f	u	f		
17		X	T	X	X						U		f	u	f		F	f	u	f	
18						Q	Q	X			U		f	u	f		F	f	u	f	
19	X								C			U		f	u	f		F	f	u	f
20			Q									U		f	u	f		F	f	u	f
21						T	X			f			U		f	u	f		F	f	u
22		C	X	C						f			U		f	u	f		F	f	u
23				C				C		u	f			U		f	u	f		F	f
24	C								X	u	f			U		f	u	f		F	f
25					O					f	u	f			U		f	u	f		F
26							C		Q	f	u	f			U		f	u	f		F
27		X	C	X						F	f	u	f			U		f	u	f	
28				X				X		F	f	u	f			U		f	u	f	

March Moon Table

Date	Sign	Element	Nature	Phase
1 Sun	Taurus	Earth	Semi-fruitful	1st
2 Mon	Taurus	Earth	Semi-fruitful	1st
3 Tue 2:59 am	Gemini	Air	Barren	1st
4 Wed	Gemini	Air	Barren	2nd 2:46 am
5 Thu 6:07 am	Cancer	Water	Fruitful	2nd
6 Fri	Cancer	Water	Fruitful	2nd
7 Sat 8:24 am	Leo	Fire	Barren	2nd
8 Sun	Leo	Fire	Barren	2nd
9 Mon 11:34 am	Virgo	Earth	Barren	2nd
10 Tue	Virgo	Earth	Barren	3rd 10:38 pm
11 Wed 2:46 pm	Libra	Air	Semi-fruitful	3rd
12 Thu	Libra	Air	Semi-fruitful	3rd
13 Fri 8:22 pm	Scorpio	Water	Fruitful	3rd
14 Sat	Scorpio	Water	Fruitful	3rd
15 Sun	Scorpio	Water	Fruitful	3rd
16 Mon 5:21 am	Sagittarius	Fire	Barren	3rd
17 Tue	Sagittarius	Fire	Barren	3rd
18 Wed 5:18 pm	Capricorn	Earth	Semi-fruitful	4th 1:47 pm
19 Thu	Capricorn	Earth	Semi-fruitful	4th
20 Fri	Capricorn	Earth	Semi-fruitful	4th
21 Sat 6:06 am	Aquarius	Air	Barren	4th
22 Sun	Aquarius	Air	Barren	4th
23 Mon 5:08 pm	Pisces	Water	Fruitful	4th
24 Tue	Pisces	Water	Fruitful	4th
25 Wed	Pisces	Water	Fruitful	4th
26 Thu 1:03 am	Aries	Fire	Barren	1st 12:06 pm
27 Fri	Aries	Fire	Barren	1st
28 Sat 6:09 am	Taurus	Earth	Semi-fruitful	1st
29 Sun	Taurus	Earth	Semi-fruitful	1st
30 Mon 9:36 am	Gemini	Air	Barren	1st
31 Tue	Gemini	Air	Barren	1st

March Aspectarian/Favorable & Unfavorable Days

Date	Sun	Mercury	Venus	Mars	Jupiter	Saturn	Uranus	Neptune	Pluto	Aries	Taurus	Gemini	Cancer	Leo	Virgo	Libra	Scorpio	Sagittarius	Capricorn	Aquarius	Pisces
1	X				Q				T		F		f	u	f		U		f	u	f
2		Q		Q		T	X	Q			F		f	u	f		U		f	u	f
3											F		f	u	f		U		f	u	f
4	Q	T	X	T	T	Q	Q		T	f		F		f	u	f		U		f	u
5									O	f		F		f	u	f		U		f	u
6	T		Q				X	T		u	f		F		f	u	f		U		f
7										u	f		F		f	u	f		U		f
8			T		O					f	u	f		F		f	u	f		U	
9		O		O				O	T	f	u	f		F		f	u	f		U	
10	O					C					f	u	f		F		f	u	f		U
11								O	Q		f	u	f		F		f	u	f		U
12			O	T						U		f	u	f		F		f	u	f	
13			T					T		U		f	u	f		F		f	u	f	
14		T							X		U		f	u	f		F		f	u	f
15	T				Q	X	T	Q			U		f	u	f		F		f	u	f
16			Q								U		f	u	f		F		f	u	f
17		Q	T		X	Q				f		U		f	u	f		F		f	u
18	Q			X			Q	X	C	f		U		f	u	f		F		f	u
19			Q							u	f		U		f	u	f		F		f
20		X				T	X			u	f		U		f	u	f		F		f
21	X									u	f		U		f	u	f		F		f
22			X		C					f	u	f		U		f	u	f		F	
23								C	X	f	u	f		U		f	u	f		F	
24			C								f	u	f		U		f	u	f		F
25						O	C				f	u	f		U		f	u	f		F
26	C	C	C						Q		f	u	f		U		f	u	f		F
27					X			X		F		f	u	f		U		f	u	f	
28									T	F		f	u	f		U		f	u	f	
29				X	Q	T	X				F		f	u	f		U		f	u	f
30			X					Q			F		f	u	f		U		f	u	f
31	X	X			Q	T	Q			f		F		f	u	f		U		f	u

April Moon Table

Date	Sign	Element	Nature	Phase
1 Wed 12:30 pm	Cancer	Water	Fruitful	1st
2 Thu	Cancer	Water	Fruitful	2nd 10:34 am
3 Fri 3:32 pm	Leo	Fire	Barren	2nd
4 Sat	Leo	Fire	Barren	2nd
5 Sun 7:01 pm	Virgo	Earth	Barren	2nd
6 Mon	Virgo	Earth	Barren	2nd
7 Tue 11:22 pm	Libra	Air	Semi-fruitful	2nd
8 Wed	Libra	Air	Semi-fruitful	2nd
9 Thu	Libra	Air	Semi-fruitful	3rd 10:56 am
10 Fri 5:23 am	Scorpio	Water	Fruitful	3rd
11 Sat	Scorpio	Water	Fruitful	3rd
12 Sun 2:00 pm	Sagittarius	Fire	Barren	3rd
13 Mon	Sagittarius	Fire	Barren	3rd
14 Tue	Sagittarius	Fire	Barren	3rd
15 Wed 1:27 am	Capricorn	Earth	Semi-fruitful	3rd
16 Thu	Capricorn	Earth	Semi-fruitful	3rd
17 Fri 2:19 pm	Aquarius	Air	Barren	4th 9:36 am
18 Sat	Aquarius	Air	Barren	4th
19 Sun	Aquarius	Air	Barren	4th
20 Mon 1:55 am	Pisces	Water	Fruitful	4th
21 Tue	Pisces	Water	Fruitful	4th
22 Wed 10:09 am	Aries	Fire	Barren	4th
23 Thu	Aries	Fire	Barren	4th
24 Fri 2:46 pm	Taurus	Earth	Semi-fruitful	1st 11:22 pm
25 Sat	Taurus	Earth	Semi-fruitful	1st
26 Sun 5:02 pm	Gemini	Air	Barren	1st
27 Mon	Gemini	Air	Barren	1st
28 Tue 6:38 pm	Cancer	Water	Fruitful	1st
29 Wed	Cancer	Water	Fruitful	1st
30 Thu 8:56 pm	Leo	Fire	Barren	1st

April Aspectarian/Favorable & Unfavorable Days

Date	Sun	Mercury	Venus	Mars	Jupiter	Saturn	Uranus	Neptune	Pluto	Aries	Taurus	Gemini	Cancer	Leo	Virgo	Libra	Scorpio	Sagittarius	Capricorn	Aquarius	Pisces
1		Q					Q	T	0	f		F		f	u	f		U		f	u
2	Q	Q		T		X				u	f		F		f	u	f		U		f
3		T					T			u	f		F		f	u	f		U		f
4	T									f	u	f		F		f	u	f		U	
5		T			0			0		f	u	f		F		f	u	f		U	
6						C		T			f	u	f		F		f	u	f		U
7			0		0						f	u	f		F		f	u	f		U
8		0							Q	U		f	u	f		F		f	u	f	
9	0					T		T		U		f	u	f		F		f	u	f	
10		0							X	U		f	u	f		F		f	u	f	
11				T	Q	X					U		f	u	f		F		f	u	f
12		T						T	Q		U		f	u	f		F		f	u	f
13						Q				f		U		f	u	f		F		f	u
14	T			Q	X		Q	X		f		U		f	u	f		F		f	u
15			Q						C	f		U		f	u	f		F		f	u
16		T						T		u	f		U		f	u	f		F		f
17	Q		X	X				X		u	f		U		f	u	f		F		f
18										f	u	f		U		f	u	f		F	
19		Q			C			C		f	u	f		U		f	u	f		F	
20	X								X	f	u	f		U		f	u	f		F	
21		X			0						f	u	f		U		f	u	f		F
22			C	C			C		Q		f	u	f		U		f	u	f		F
23										F		f	u	f		U		f	u	f	
24	C			X				X	T	F		f	u	f		U		f	u	f	
25						T					F		f	u	f		U		f	u	f
26		C	X	X	Q		X	Q			F		f	u	f		U		f	u	f
27						Q				f		F		f	u	f		U		f	u
28			Q		T		Q	T	0	f		F		f	u	f		U		f	u
29	X			Q	X					u	f		F		f	u	f		U		f
30		X					T			u	f		F		f	u	f		U		f

May Moon Table

Date	Sign	Element	Nature	Phase
1 Fri	Leo	Fire	Barren	2nd 4:44 pm
2 Sat	Leo	Fire	Barren	2nd
3 Sun 12:37 am	Virgo	Earth	Barren	2nd
4 Mon	Virgo	Earth	Barren	2nd
5 Tue 5:51 am	Libra	Air	Semi-fruitful	2nd
6 Wed	Libra	Air	Semi-fruitful	2nd
7 Thu 12:48 pm	Scorpio	Water	Fruitful	2nd
8 Fri	Scorpio	Water	Fruitful	2nd
9 Sat 9:49 pm	Sagittarius	Fire	Barren	3rd 12:01 am
10 Sun	Sagittarius	Fire	Barren	3rd
11 Mon	Sagittarius	Fire	Barren	3rd
12 Tue 9:09 am	Capricorn	Earth	Semi-fruitful	3rd
13 Wed	Capricorn	Earth	Semi-fruitful	3rd
14 Thu 10:01 pm	Aquarius	Air	Barren	3rd
15 Fri	Aquarius	Air	Barren	3rd
16 Sat	Aquarius	Air	Barren	3rd
17 Sun 10:17 am	Pisces	Water	Fruitful	4th 3:26 am
18 Mon	Pisces	Water	Fruitful	4th
19 Tue 7:30 pm	Aries	Fire	Barren	4th
20 Wed	Aries	Fire	Barren	4th
21 Thu	Aries	Fire	Barren	4th
22 Fri 12:40 am	Taurus	Earth	Semi-fruitful	4th
23 Sat	Taurus	Earth	Semi-fruitful	4th
24 Sun 2:34 am	Gemini	Air	Barren	1st 8:11 am
25 Mon	Gemini	Air	Barren	1st
26 Tue 2:58 am	Cancer	Water	Fruitful	1st
27 Wed	Cancer	Water	Fruitful	1st
28 Thu 3:44 am	Leo	Fire	Barren	1st
29 Fri	Leo	Fire	Barren	1st
30 Sat 6:17 am	Virgo	Earth	Barren	2nd 11:22 pm
31 Sun	Virgo	Earth	Barren	2nd

May Aspectarian/Favorable & Unfavorable Days

Date	Sun	Mercury	Venus	Mars	Jupiter	Saturn	Uranus	Neptune	Pluto	Aries	Taurus	Gemini	Cancer	Leo	Virgo	Libra	Scorpio	Sagittarius	Capricorn	Aquarius	Pisces
1	Q		T	T						f	u	f		F		f	u	f		U	
2					0			0		f	u	f		F		f	u	f		U	
3		Q							T	f	u	f		F		f	u	f		U	
4	T					C	0			f	u	f			F		f	u	f		U
5		T	0						Q	f	u	f			F		f	u	f		U
6				0						U		f	u	f		F		f	u	f	
7						T		T	X	U		f	u	f		F		f	u	f	
8							X				U		f	u	f		F		f	u	f
9	0			Q			T	Q			U		f	u	f		F		f	u	f
10		0	T							f		U		f	u	f		F		f	u
11				T	X	Q				f		U		f	u	f		F		f	u
12					Q	X	C			f		U		f	u	f		F		f	u
13			Q	Q		T				u	f		U		f	u	f		F		f
14	T	T					X			u	f		U		f	u	f		F		f
15			X							f	u	f		U		f	u	f		F	
16				X						f	u	f		U		f	u	f		F	
17	Q	Q				C		C	X	f	u	f		U		f	u	f		F	
18						0				f	u	f			U		f	u	f		F
19	X	X					C			f	u	f			U		f	u	f		F
20			C						Q	F		f	u	f		U		f	u	f	
21				C	X			X		F		f	u	f		U		f	u	f	
22								T		F		f	u	f		U		f	u	f	
23		C			Q	T	X	Q			F		f	u	f		U		f	u	f
24	C										F		f	u	f		U		f	u	f
25			X	X	T	Q	Q	T		f		F		f	u	f		U		f	u
26								0		f		F		f	u	f		U		f	u
27		X	Q	Q		X	T			u	f		F		f	u	f		U		f
28	X									u	f		F		f	u	f		U		f
29		Q	T							f	u	f		F		f	u	f		U	
30	Q			T	0			0	T	f	u	f		F		f	u	f		U	
31		T				C				f	u	f			F		f	u	f		U

145

June Moon Table

Date	Sign	Element	Nature	Phase
1 Mon 11:17 am	Libra	Air	Semi-fruitful	2nd
2 Tue	Libra	Air	Semi-fruitful	2nd
3 Wed 6:43 pm	Scorpio	Water	Fruitful	2nd
4 Thu	Scorpio	Water	Fruitful	2nd
5 Fri	Scorpio	Water	Fruitful	2nd
6 Sat 4:23 am	Sagittarius	Fire	Barren	2nd
7 Sun	Sagittarius	Fire	Barren	3rd 2:12 pm
8 Mon 3:59 pm	Capricorn	Earth	Semi-fruitful	3rd
9 Tue	Capricorn	Earth	Semi-fruitful	3rd
10 Wed	Capricorn	Earth	Semi-fruitful	3rd
11 Thu 4:52 am	Aquarius	Air	Barren	3rd
12 Fri	Aquarius	Air	Barren	3rd
13 Sat 5:32 pm	Pisces	Water	Fruitful	3rd
14 Sun	Pisces	Water	Fruitful	3rd
15 Mon	Pisces	Water	Fruitful	4th 6:14 pm
16 Tue 3:51 am	Aries	Fire	Barren	4th
17 Wed	Aries	Fire	Barren	4th
18 Thu 10:20 am	Taurus	Earth	Semi-fruitful	4th
19 Fri	Taurus	Earth	Semi-fruitful	4th
20 Sat 1:00 pm	Gemini	Air	Barren	4th
21 Sun	Gemini	Air	Barren	4th
22 Mon 1:12 pm	Cancer	Water	Fruitful	1st 3:35 pm
23 Tue	Cancer	Water	Fruitful	1st
24 Wed 12:50 pm	Leo	Fire	Barren	1st
25 Thu	Leo	Fire	Barren	1st
26 Fri 1:46 pm	Virgo	Earth	Barren	1st
27 Sat	Virgo	Earth	Barren	1st
28 Sun 5:24 pm	Libra	Air	Semi-fruitful	1st
29 Mon	Libra	Air	Semi-fruitful	2nd 7:28 am
30 Tue	Libra	Air	Semi-fruitful	2nd

June Aspectarian/Favorable & Unfavorable Days

Date	Sun	Mercury	Venus	Mars	Jupiter	Saturn	Uranus	Neptune	Pluto	Aries	Taurus	Gemini	Cancer	Leo	Virgo	Libra	Scorpio	Sagittarius	Capricorn	Aquarius	Pisces
1							0		Q		f	u	f		F		f	u	f		U
2	T									U		f	u	f		F		f	u	f	
3			0	0	T			T	X	U		f	u	f		F		f	u	f	
4						X					U		f	u	f		F		f	u	f
5		0			Q			T	Q		U		f	u	f		F		f	u	f
6											U		f	u	f		F		f	u	f
7	0					Q				f		U		f	u	f		F		f	u
8			T		X		Q	X	C	f		U		f	u	f		F		f	u
9				T		T				u	f		U		f	u	f		F		f
10		T						X		u	f		U		f	u	f		F		f
11			Q	Q						u	f		U		f	u	f		F		f
12										f	u	f		U		f	u	f		F	
13	T	Q				C		C	X	f	u	f		U		f	u	f		F	
14			X	X							f	u	f		U		f	u	f		F
15	Q						0	C			f	u	f		U		f	u	f		F
16		X							Q		f	u	f		U		f	u	f		F
17										F		f	u	f		U		f	u	f	
18	X				X			X	T	F		f	u	f		U		f	u	f	
19			C	C		T					F		f	u	f		U		f	u	f
20					Q			X	Q		F		f	u	f		U		f	u	f
21		C				Q				f		F		f	u	f		U		f	u
22	C				T		Q	T	0	f		F		f	u	f		U		f	u
23			X	X	X					u	f		F		f	u	f		U		f
24						T				u	f		F		f	u	f		U		f
25		X	Q	Q						f	u	f		F		f	u	f		U	
26	X				0			0	T	f	u	f		F		f	u	f		U	
27		Q		T		C					f	u	f		F		f	u	f		U
28			T					0	Q		f	u	f		F		f	u	f		U
29	Q									U		f	u	f		F		f	u	f	
30		T			T			T		U		f	u	f		F		f	u	f	

July Moon Table

Date	Sign	Element	Nature	Phase
1 Wed 12:18 am	Scorpio	Water	Fruitful	2nd
2 Thu	Scorpio	Water	Fruitful	2nd
3 Fri 10:10 am	Sagittarius	Fire	Barren	2nd
4 Sat	Sagittarius	Fire	Barren	2nd
5 Sun 10:07 pm	Capricorn	Earth	Semi-fruitful	2nd
6 Mon	Capricorn	Earth	Semi-fruitful	2nd
7 Tue	Capricorn	Earth	Semi-fruitful	3rd 5:21 am
8 Wed 11:03 am	Aquarius	Air	Barren	3rd
9 Thu	Aquarius	Air	Barren	3rd
10 Fri 11:44 pm	Pisces	Water	Fruitful	3rd
11 Sat	Pisces	Water	Fruitful	3rd
12 Sun	Pisces	Water	Fruitful	3rd
13 Mon 10:40 am	Aries	Fire	Barren	3rd
14 Tue	Aries	Fire	Barren	3rd
15 Wed 6:30 pm	Taurus	Earth	Semi-fruitful	4th 5:53 am
16 Thu	Taurus	Earth	Semi-fruitful	4th
17 Fri 10:41 pm	Gemini	Air	Barren	4th
18 Sat	Gemini	Air	Barren	4th
19 Sun 11:51 pm	Cancer	Water	Fruitful	4th
20 Mon	Cancer	Water	Fruitful	4th
21 Tue 11:27 pm	Leo	Fire	Barren	1st 10:34 pm
22 Wed	Leo	Fire	Barren	1st
23 Thu 11:22 pm	Virgo	Earth	Barren	1st
24 Fri	Virgo	Earth	Barren	1st
25 Sat	Virgo	Earth	Barren	1st
26 Sun 1:25 am	Libra	Air	Semi-fruitful	1st
27 Mon	Libra	Air	Semi-fruitful	1st
28 Tue 6:56 am	Scorpio	Water	Fruitful	2nd 6:00 pm
29 Wed	Scorpio	Water	Fruitful	2nd
30 Thu 4:10 pm	Sagittarius	Fire	Barren	2nd
31 Fri	Sagittarius	Fire	Barren	2nd

July Aspectarian/Favorable & Unfavorable Days

Date	Sun	Mercury	Venus	Mars	Jupiter	Saturn	Uranus	Neptune	Pluto	Aries	Taurus	Gemini	Cancer	Leo	Virgo	Libra	Scorpio	Sagittarus	Capricorn	Aquarius	Pisces
1	T								X	U		f	u	f		F		f	u	f	
2				0		X					U		f	u	f		F		f	u	f
3			0		Q			T	Q		U		f	u	f		F		f	u	f
4						Q				f		U		f	u	f		F		f	u
5						X		Q	X	f		U		f	u	f		F		f	u
6		0							C	u	f		U		f	u	f		F		f
7	0					T				u	f		U		f	u	f		F		f
8			T	T				X		u	f		U		f	u	f		F		f
9										f	u	f		U		f	u	f		F	
10				Q	C			C		f	u	f		U		f	u	f		F	
11			Q						X		f	u	f		U		f	u	f		F
12	T	T				0					f	u	f		U		f	u	f		F
13				X			C		Q		f	u	f		U		f	u	f		F
14			X							F		f	u	f		U		f	u	f	
15	Q	Q				X		X	T	F		f	u	f		U		f	u	f	
16											F		f	u	f		U		f	u	f
17	X	X				Q	T	X	Q		F		f	u	f		U		f	u	f
18			C							f		F		f	u	f		U		f	u
19			C		T	Q	Q	T		f		F		f	u	f		U		f	u
20									0	u	f		F		f	u	f		U		f
21	C					X	T			u	f		F		f	u	f		U		f
22		C		X						f	u	f		F		f	u	f		U	
23			X		0			0		f	u	f		F		f	u	f		U	
24				Q					T		f	u	f		F		f	u	f		U
25			Q			C	0				f	u	f		F		f	u	f		U
26	X			T					Q		f	u	f		F		f	u	f		U
27		X	T		T			T		U		f	u	f		F		f	u	f	
28	Q								X	U		f	u	f		F		f	u	f	
29						X					U		f	u	f		F		f	u	f
30		Q			Q			T	Q		U		f	u	f		F		f	u	f
31	T			0						f		U		f	u	f		F		f	u

August Moon Table

Date	Sign	Element	Nature	Phase
1 Sat	Sagittarius	Fire	Barren	2nd
2 Sun 4:08 am	Capricorn	Earth	Semi-fruitful	2nd
3 Mon	Capricorn	Earth	Semi-fruitful	2nd
4 Tue 5:08 pm	Aquarius	Air	Barren	2nd
5 Wed	Aquarius	Air	Barren	3rd 8:55 pm
6 Thu	Aquarius	Air	Barren	3rd
7 Fri 5:34 am	Pisces	Water	Fruitful	3rd
8 Sat	Pisces	Water	Fruitful	3rd
9 Sun 4:23 pm	Aries	Fire	Barren	3rd
10 Mon	Aries	Fire	Barren	3rd
11 Tue	Aries	Fire	Barren	3rd
12 Wed 12:49 am	Taurus	Earth	Semi-fruitful	3rd
13 Thu	Taurus	Earth	Semi-fruitful	4th 2:55 pm
14 Fri 6:25 am	Gemini	Air	Barren	4th
15 Sat	Gemini	Air	Barren	4th
16 Sun 9:13 am	Cancer	Water	Fruitful	4th
17 Mon	Cancer	Water	Fruitful	4th
18 Tue 9:56 am	Leo	Fire	Barren	4th
19 Wed	Leo	Fire	Barren	4th
20 Thu 10:00 am	Virgo	Earth	Barren	1st 6:01 am
21 Fri	Virgo	Earth	Barren	1st
22 Sat 11:12 am	Libra	Air	Semi-fruitful	1st
23 Sun	Libra	Air	Semi-fruitful	1st
24 Mon 3:16 pm	Scorpio	Water	Fruitful	1st
25 Tue	Scorpio	Water	Fruitful	1st
26 Wed 11:16 pm	Sagittarius	Fire	Barren	1st
27 Thu	Sagittarius	Fire	Barren	2nd 7:42 am
28 Fri	Sagittarius	Fire	Barren	2nd
29 Sat 10:44 am	Capricorn	Earth	Semi-fruitful	2nd
30 Sun	Capricorn	Earth	Semi-fruitful	2nd
31 Mon 11:43 pm	Aquarius	Air	Barren	2nd

August Aspectarian/Favorable & Unfavorable Days

Date	Sun	Mercury	Venus	Mars	Jupiter	Saturn	Uranus	Neptune	Pluto	Aries	Taurus	Gemini	Cancer	Leo	Virgo	Libra	Scorpio	Sagittarius	Capricorn	Aquarius	Pisces
1					X	Q	Q	X		u	f		U		f	u	f		F		f
2		T	O						C	u	f		U		f	u	f		F		f
3						T				u	f		U		f	u	f		F		f
4							X			f	u	f		U		f	u	f		F	
5	O									f	u	f		U		f	u	f		F	
6				T	C			C		f	u	f		U		f	u	f		F	
7		O	T						X		f	u	f		U		f	u	f		F
8			Q		O						f	u	f		U		f	u	f		F
9							C		Q		f	u	f		U		f	u	f		F
10		Q								F		f	u	f		U		f	u	f	
11	T			X	X			X		F		f	u	f		U		f	u	f	
12								T		F		f	u	f		U		f	u	f	
13	Q	T	X		Q	T	X	Q			F		f	u	f		U		f	u	f
14											F		f	u	f		U		f	u	f
15	X	Q		C	T	Q				f		F		f	u	f		U		f	u
16						Q	T	O		f		F		f	u	f		U		f	u
17		X	C		X					u	f		F		f	u	f		U		f
18						T				u	f		F		f	u	f		U		f
19					O					f	u	f		F		f	u	f		U	
20	C			X				O	T	f	u	f		F		f	u	f		U	
21					C						f	u	f		F		f	u	f		U
22		C	X	Q		O			Q		f	u	f		F		f	u	f		U
23					T					U		f	u	f		F		f	u	f	
24	X		Q	T				T	X	U		f	u	f		F		f	u	f	
25											U		f	u	f		F		f	u	f
26					Q	X	T	Q			U		f	u	f		F		f	u	f
27	Q	X	T							f		U		f	u	f		F		f	u
28				X	Q					f		U		f	u	f		F		f	u
29		Q		O			Q	X	C	f		U		f	u	f		F		f	u
30	T									u	f		U		f	u	f		F		f
31						T	X			u	f		U		f	u	f		F		f

September Moon Table

Date	Sign	Element	Nature	Phase
1 Tue	Aquarius	Air	Barren	2nd
2 Wed	Aquarius	Air	Barren	2nd
3 Thu 11:58 am	Pisces	Water	Fruitful	2nd
4 Fri	Pisces	Water	Fruitful	3rd 12:02 pm
5 Sat 10:14 pm	Aries	Fire	Barren	3rd
6 Sun	Aries	Fire	Barren	3rd
7 Mon	Aries	Fire	Barren	3rd
8 Tue 6:17 am	Taurus	Earth	Semi-fruitful	3rd
9 Wed	Taurus	Earth	Semi-fruitful	3rd
10 Thu 12:17 pm	Gemini	Air	Barren	3rd
11 Fri	Gemini	Air	Barren	4th 10:16 pm
12 Sat 4:19 pm	Cancer	Water	Fruitful	4th
13 Sun	Cancer	Water	Fruitful	4th
14 Mon 6:39 pm	Leo	Fire	Barren	4th
15 Tue	Leo	Fire	Barren	4th
16 Wed 7:56 pm	Virgo	Earth	Barren	4th
17 Thu	Virgo	Earth	Barren	4th
18 Fri 9:26 pm	Libra	Air	Semi-fruitful	1st 2:44 pm
19 Sat	Libra	Air	Semi-fruitful	1st
20 Sun	Libra	Air	Semi-fruitful	1st
21 Mon 12:52 am	Scorpio	Water	Fruitful	1st
22 Tue	Scorpio	Water	Fruitful	1st
23 Wed 7:43 am	Sagittarius	Fire	Barren	1st
24 Thu	Sagittarius	Fire	Barren	1st
25 Fri 6:19 pm	Capricorn	Earth	Semi-fruitful	1st
26 Sat	Capricorn	Earth	Semi-fruitful	2nd 12:50 am
27 Sun	Capricorn	Earth	Semi-fruitful	2nd
28 Mon 7:06 am	Aquarius	Air	Barren	2nd
29 Tue	Aquarius	Air	Barren	2nd
30 Wed 7:26 pm	Pisces	Water	Fruitful	2nd

September Aspectarian/Favorable & Unfavorable Days

Date	Sun	Mercury	Venus	Mars	Jupiter	Saturn	Uranus	Neptune	Pluto	Aries	Taurus	Gemini	Cancer	Leo	Virgo	Libra	Scorpio	Sagittarus	Capricorn	Aquarius	Pisces
1		T	0							f	u	f		U		f	u	f		F	
2					C					f	u	f		U		f	u	f		F	
3				T				C	X	f	u	f		U		f	u	f		F	
4	0										f	u	f		U		f	u	f			F
5						0	C		Q		f	u	f		U		f	u	f			F
6		0		Q						F		f	u	f		U		f	u	f	
7			T		X			X		F		f	u	f		U		f	u	f	
8				X					T	F		f	u	f		U		f	u	f	
9	T		Q		Q						F		f	u	f		U		f	u	f
10		T				T	X	Q			F		f	u	f		U		f	u	f
11	Q		X		T					f		F		f	u	f		U		f	u
12		Q				Q	Q	T	0	f		F		f	u	f		U		f	u
13				C						u	f		F		f	u	f		U		f
14	X	X				X	T			u	f		F		f	u	f		U		f
15										f	u	f		F		f	u	f		U	
16			C		0			0	T	f	u	f		F		f	u	f		U	
17				X						f	u	f		F		f	u	f			U
18	C	C				C	0		Q	f	u	f		F		f	u	f			U
19				Q						U		f	u	f		F		f	u	f	
20					T			T		U		f	u	f		F		f	u	f	
21			X						X	U		f	u	f		F		f	u	f	
22		X			T	Q	X	T	Q		U		f	u	f		F		f	u	f
23	X		Q								U		f	u	f		F		f	u	f
24				X						f		U		f	u	f		F		f	u
25		Q				Q	Q	X	C	f		U		f	u	f		F		f	u
26	Q		T							u	f		U		f	u	f		F		f
27		T		0		T	X			u	f		U		f	u	f		F		f
28	T									u	f		U		f	u	f		F		f
29					C					f	u	f		U		f	u	f		F	
30								C	X	f	u	f		U		f	u	f		F	

October Moon Table

Date	Sign	Element	Nature	Phase
1 Thu	Pisces	Water	Fruitful	2nd
2 Fri	Pisces	Water	Fruitful	2nd
3 Sat 5:20 am	Aries	Fire	Barren	2nd
4 Sun	Aries	Fire	Barren	3rd 2:10 am
5 Mon 12:33 pm	Taurus	Earth	Semi-fruitful	3rd
6 Tue	Taurus	Earth	Semi-fruitful	3rd
7 Wed 5:46 pm	Gemini	Air	Barren	3rd
8 Thu	Gemini	Air	Barren	3rd
9 Fri 9:48 pm	Cancer	Water	Fruitful	3rd
10 Sat	Cancer	Water	Fruitful	3rd
11 Sun	Cancer	Water	Fruitful	4th 4:56 am
12 Mon 1:02 am	Leo	Fire	Barren	4th
13 Tue	Leo	Fire	Barren	4th
14 Wed 3:45 am	Virgo	Earth	Barren	4th
15 Thu	Virgo	Earth	Barren	4th
16 Fri 6:29 am	Libra	Air	Semi-fruitful	4th
17 Sat	Libra	Air	Semi-fruitful	4th
18 Sun 10:22 am	Scorpio	Water	Fruitful	1st 1:33 am
19 Mon	Scorpio	Water	Fruitful	1st
20 Tue 4:49 pm	Sagittarius	Fire	Barren	1st
21 Wed	Sagittarius	Fire	Barren	1st
22 Thu	Sagittarius	Fire	Barren	1st
23 Fri 2:39 am	Capricorn	Earth	Semi-fruitful	1st
24 Sat	Capricorn	Earth	Semi-fruitful	1st
25 Sun 3:08 pm	Aquarius	Air	Barren	2nd 8:42 pm
26 Mon	Aquarius	Air	Barren	2nd
27 Tue	Aquarius	Air	Barren	2nd
28 Wed 3:45 am	Pisces	Water	Fruitful	2nd
29 Thu	Pisces	Water	Fruitful	2nd
30 Fri 1:56 pm	Aries	Fire	Barren	2nd
31 Sat	Aries	Fire	Barren	2nd

October Aspectarian/Favorable & Unfavorable Days

Date	Sun	Mercury	Venus	Mars	Jupiter	Saturn	Uranus	Neptune	Pluto	Aries	Taurus	Gemini	Cancer	Leo	Virgo	Libra	Scorpio	Sagittarius	Capricorn	Aquarius	Pisces
1			0								f	u	f		U		f	u	f		F
2		0		T		0	C				f	u	f		U		f	u	f		F
3									Q		f	u	f		U		f	u	f		F
4	0				X					F		f	u	f		U		f	u	f	
5			Q					X	T	F		f	u	f		U		f	u	f	
6					Q						F		f	u	f		U		f	u	f
7		T	T	X		T	X	Q			F		f	u	f		U		f	u	f
8	T				T					f		F		f	u	f		U		f	u
9		Q	Q			Q	Q	T	0	f		F		f	u	f		U		f	u
10										u	f		F		f	u	f		U		f
11	Q		X	C		X	T			u	f		F		f	u	f		U		f
12		X								u	f		F		f	u	f		U		f
13	X				0			0		f	u	f		F		f	u	f		U	
14								T		f	u	f		F		f	u	f		U	
15						0					f	u	f		F		f	u	f		U
16			C	X	C				Q		f	u	f		F		f	u	f		U
17		C			T			T		U		f	u	f		F		f	u	f	
18	C		Q						X	U		f	u	f		F		f	u	f	
19				Q							U		f	u	f		F		f	u	f
20				T	X	T	Q				U		f	u	f		F		f	u	f
21			X							f		U		f	u	f		F		f	u
22		X			X	Q	X			f		U		f	u	f		F		f	u
23	X				Q				C	f		U		f	u	f		F		f	u
24			Q							u	f		U		f	u	f		F		f
25	Q	Q				T	X			u	f		U		f	u	f		F		f
26			T	0						f	u	f		U		f	u	f		F	
27					C			C		f	u	f		U		f	u	f		F	
28	T	T							X	f	u	f		U		f	u	f		F	
29											f	u	f		U		f	u	f		F
30						0	C		Q		f	u	f		U		f	u	f		F
31				T	X					F		f	u	f		U		f	u	f	

November Moon Table

Date	Sign	Element	Nature	Phase
1 Sun 7:44 pm	Taurus	Earth	Semi-fruitful	2nd
2 Mon	Taurus	Earth	Semi-fruitful	3rd 2:14 pm
3 Tue	Gemini	Air	Barren	3rd
4 Wed 11:53 pm	Gemini	Air	Barren	3rd
5 Thu	Gemini	Air	Barren	3rd
6 Fri 2:42 am	Cancer	Water	Fruitful	3rd
7 Sat	Cancer	Water	Fruitful	3rd
8 Sun 5:23 am	Leo	Fire	Barren	3rd
9 Mon	Leo	Fire	Barren	4th 10:56 am
10 Tue 8:30 am	Virgo	Earth	Barren	4th
11 Wed	Virgo	Earth	Barren	4th
12 Thu 12:22 pm	Libra	Air	Semi-fruitful	4th
13 Fri	Libra	Air	Semi-fruitful	4th
14 Sat 5:24 pm	Scorpio	Water	Fruitful	4th
15 Sun	Scorpio	Water	Fruitful	4th
16 Mon	Scorpio	Water	Fruitful	1st 2:14 pm
17 Tue 12:22 am	Sagittarius	Fire	Barren	1st
18 Wed	Sagittarius	Fire	Barren	1st
19 Thu 10:00 am	Capricorn	Earth	Semi-fruitful	1st
20 Fri	Capricorn	Earth	Semi-fruitful	1st
21 Sat 10:11 pm	Aquarius	Air	Barren	1st
22 Sun	Aquarius	Air	Barren	1st
23 Mon	Aquarius	Air	Barren	1st
24 Tue 11:07 am	Pisces	Water	Fruitful	2nd 4:39 pm
25 Wed	Pisces	Water	Fruitful	2nd
26 Thu 10:10 pm	Aries	Fire	Barren	2nd
27 Fri	Aries	Fire	Barren	2nd
28 Sat	Aries	Fire	Barren	2nd
29 Sun 5:34 am	Taurus	Earth	Semi-fruitful	2nd
30 Mon	Taurus	Earth	Semi-fruitful	2nd

November Aspectarian/Favorable & Unfavorable Days

Date	Sun	Mercury	Venus	Mars	Jupiter	Saturn	Uranus	Neptune	Pluto	Aries	Taurus	Gemini	Cancer	Leo	Virgo	Libra	Scorpio	Sagittarius	Capricorn	Aquarius	Pisces
1			0					X	T	F		f	u	f		U		f	u	f	
2	0	0		Q							F	f	u	f		U		f	u	f	
3			Q				X	Q			F	f	u	f		U		f	u	f	
4				X		T				f		F		f	u	f		U		f	u
5		T				T		Q	T	f		F		f	u	f		U		f	u
6						Q			0	f		F		f	u	f		U		f	u
7	T	T					T			u	f		F		f	u	f		U		f
8			Q	C		X				u	f		F		f	u	f		U		f
9	Q	Q			0				0	f	u	f		F		f	u	f		U	
10			X					T		f	u	f		F		f	u	f		U	
11	X						0				f	u	f		F		f	u	f		U
12		X			C			Q			f	u	f		F		f	u	f		U
13				X	T					U		f	u	f		F		f	u	f	
14								T	X	U		f	u	f		F		f	u	f	
15			C	Q							U		f	u	f		F		f	u	f
16	C				Q		T	Q			U		f	u	f		F		f	u	f
17		C				X					U		f	u	f		F		f	u	f
18				T	X		Q	X		f		U		f	u	f		F		f	u
19					Q				C	f		U		f	u	f		F		f	u
20			X							u	f		U		f	u	f		F		f
21	X						X			u	f		U		f	u	f		F		f
22		X			T					f	u	f		U		f	u	f		F	
23			Q	0	C			C		f	u	f		U		f	u	f		F	
24	Q							X		f	u	f		U		f	u	f		F	
25		Q									f	u	f		U		f	u	f		F
26			T			C					f	u	f		U		f	u	f		F
27	T				0				Q	F		f	u	f		U		f	u	f	
28		T		T	X			X		F		f	u	f		U		f	u	f	
29									T	F		f	u	f		U		f	u	f	
30				Q	Q		X	Q			F		f	u	f		U		f	u	f

December Moon Table

Date	Sign	Element	Nature	Phase
1 Tue 9:23 am	Gemini	Air	Barren	2nd
2 Wed	Gemini	Air	Barren	3rd 2:30 am
3 Thu 11:00 am	Cancer	Water	Fruitful	3rd
4 Fri	Cancer	Water	Fruitful	3rd
5 Sat 12:07 pm	Leo	Fire	Barren	3rd
6 Sun	Leo	Fire	Barren	3rd
7 Mon 2:05 pm	Virgo	Earth	Barren	3rd
8 Tue	Virgo	Earth	Barren	4th 7:13 pm
9 Wed 5:47 pm	Libra	Air	Semi-fruitful	4th
10 Thu	Libra	Air	Semi-fruitful	4th
11 Fri 11:31 pm	Scorpio	Water	Fruitful	4th
12 Sat	Scorpio	Water	Fruitful	4th
13 Sun	Scorpio	Water	Fruitful	4th
14 Mon 7:25 am	Sagittarius	Fire	Barren	4th
15 Tue	Sagittarius	Fire	Barren	4th
16 Wed 5:32 pm	Capricorn	Earth	Semi-fruitful	1st 7:02 am
17 Thu	Capricorn	Earth	Semi-fruitful	1st
18 Fri	Capricorn	Earth	Semi-fruitful	1st
19 Sat 5:38 am	Aquarius	Air	Barren	1st
20 Sun	Aquarius	Air	Barren	1st
21 Mon 6:42 pm	Pisces	Water	Fruitful	1st
22 Tue	Pisces	Water	Fruitful	1st
23 Wed	Pisces	Water	Fruitful	1st
24 Thu 6:39 am	Aries	Fire	Barren	2nd 12:36 pm
25 Fri	Aries	Fire	Barren	2nd
26 Sat 3:26 pm	Taurus	Earth	Semi-fruitful	2nd
27 Sun	Taurus	Earth	Semi-fruitful	2nd
28 Mon 8:13 pm	Gemini	Air	Barren	2nd
29 Tue	Gemini	Air	Barren	2nd
30 Wed 9:45 pm	Cancer	Water	Fruitful	2nd
31 Thu	Cancer	Water	Fruitful	3rd 2:13 pm

December Aspectarian/Favorable & Unfavorable Days

Date	Sun	Mercury	Venus	Mars	Jupiter	Saturn	Uranus	Neptune	Pluto	Aries	Taurus	Gemini	Cancer	Leo	Virgo	Libra	Scorpio	Sagittarus	Capricorn	Aquarius	Pisces
1			O			T					F		f	u	f		U		f	u	f
2	O			X	T		Q			f		F		f	u	f		U		f	u
3		O				Q		T	O	f		F		f	u	f		U		f	u
4										u	f		F		f	u	f		U		f
5			T			X	T			u	f		F		f	u	f		U		f
6	T			C						f	u	f		F		f	u	f		U	
7		T			O			O	T	f	u	f		F		f	u	f		U	
8	Q		Q								f	u	f		F		f	u	f		U
9								O	Q		f	u	f		F		f	u	f		U
10		Q	X			C				U		f	u	f		F		f	u	f	
11	X			X	T			T		U		f	u	f		F		f	u	f	
12		X							X		U		f	u	f		F		f	u	f
13				Q	Q			T	Q		U		f	u	f		F		f	u	f
14					X						U		f	u	f		F		f	u	f
15			C	T						f		U		f	u	f		F		f	u
16	C			X		Q	X	C		f		U		f	u	f		F		f	u
17					Q					u	f		U		f	u	f		F		f
18		C					X			u	f		U		f	u	f		F		f
19					T					u	f		U		f	u	f		F		f
20				O						f	u	f		U		f	u	f		F	
21	X		X		C			C		f	u	f		U		f	u	f		F	
22									X		f	u	f		U		f	u	f		F
23		X				C					f	u	f		U		f	u	f		F
24	Q		Q		O				Q		f	u	f		U		f	u	f		F
25				T						F		f	u	f		U		f	u	f	
26		Q	T		X			X	T	F		f	u	f		U		f	u	f	
27	T										F		f	u	f		U		f	u	f
28		T		Q	Q			X	Q		F		f	u	f		U		f	u	f
29						T				f		F		f	u	f		U		f	u
30				X	T			Q	T	f		F		f	u	f		U		f	u
31	O		O			Q			O	u	f		F		f	u	f		U		f

2009 Retrograde Planets

Planet	Begin	Eastern	Pacific	End	Eastern	Pacific
Saturn	12/31/08	1:08 pm	**10:08 am**	05/16/09	10:06 pm	**7:06 pm**
Mercury	01/11/09	11:43 am	**8:43 am**	01/31/09		**11:10 pm**
				02/01/09	2:10 am	
Venus	03/06/09	12:17 pm	**9:17 am**	04/17/09	3:24 pm	**12:24 pm**
Pluto	04/04/09	1:35 pm	**10:35 am**	09/11/09	12:57 pm	**9:57 am**
Mercury	05/06/09		**10:00 pm**	05/30/09	9:22 pm	**6:22 pm**
	05/07/09	1:00 am		05/30/09		
Neptune	05/28/09		**9:30 pm**	11/04/09	1:10 pm	**10:10 am**
	05/29/09	12:30 am				
Jupiter	06/15/09	3:50 am	**12:50 am**	10/12/09		**9:34 pm**
				10/13/09	12:34 am	
Uranus	07/01/09	3:37 am	**12:37 am**	12/01/09	3:27 pm	**12:27 pm**
Mercury	09/06/09		**9:45 pm**	09/29/09	9:14 am	**6:14 am**
	09/07/09	12:45 am				
Mars	12/20/09	8:27 am	**5:27 am**	03/10/10	12:10 pm	**9:10 am**
Mercury	12/26/09	9:38 am	**6:38 am**	01/15/10	11:52 am	**8:52 am**

Eastern Time in plain type, **Pacific Time in bold type**

Egg-setting Dates

To Have Eggs by this Date	Sign	Qtr.	Date to Set Eggs
Jan 5, 10:46 am–Jan 7, 1:11 pm	Taurus	1st	Dec 17, 2008
Jan 9, 1:14 pm–Jan 10, 10:27 pm	Cancer	1st	Dec 21, 2008
Jan 28, 1:12 am–Jan 30, 10:25 am	Pisces	1st	Jan 7, 2009
Feb 1, 5:08 pm–Feb 3, 9:14 pm	Taurus	1st	Jan 12
Feb 5, 11:05 pm–Feb 7, 11:43 pm	Cancer	1st	Jan 16
Feb 24, 8:35 pm–Feb 26, 4:24 pm	Pisces	1st	Feb 3
Feb 28, 10:33 pm–Mar 3, 2:59 am	Taurus	1st	Feb 6
Mar 5, 6:07 am–Mar 7, 8:24 am	Cancer	1st	Feb 13
Mar 28, 5:09 am–Mar 30, 8:36 am	Taurus	1st	Mar 7
Apr 1, 11:30 am–Apr 3, 2:32 pm	Cancer	1st	Mar 11
Apr 7, 11:22 pm–Apr 9, 10:56 am	Libra	1st	Mar 18
Apr 24, 11:22 pm–Apr 26, 5:02 pm	Taurus	1st	Apr 3
Apr 28, 6:38 pm–Apr 30, 8:56 pm	Cancer	1st	Apr 8
May 5, 5:51 am–May 7, 12:48 pm	Libra	1st	Apr 14
May 26, 2:58 am–May 28, 3:44 am	Cancer	1st	May 5
Jun 1, 11:17 am–Jun 3, 6:43 pm	Libra	1st	May 11
Jun 22, 3:35 pm–Jun 24, 12:50 pm	Cancer	1st	Jun 1
Jun 28, 5:24 pm–Jul 1, 12:18 am	Libra	1st	Jun 7
Jul 21, 10:34 pm–Jul 21, 11:27 pm	Cancer	1st	Jul 1
Jul 26, 1:25 am–Jul 28, 6:56 am	Libra	1st	Jul 5
Aug 22, 11:12 am–Aug 24, 3:16 pm	Libra	1st	Aug 2
Sep 3, 11:58 am–Sep 4, 12:02 pm	Pisces	1st	Aug 13
Sep 18, 9:26 pm–Sep 21, 12:52 am	Libra	1st	Aug 28
Sep 30, 7:26 pm–Oct 3, 5:20 am	Pisces	1st	Sep 9
Oct 18, 1:33 am–Oct 18, 10:22 am	Libra	1st	Sep 27
Oct 28, 3:45 am–Oct 30, 1:56 pm	Pisces	1st	Oct 8
Nov 1, 8:44 pm–Nov 2, 3:14 pm	Taurus	1st	Oct 11
Nov 24, 11:07 am–Nov 26, 10:10 pm	Pisces	1st	Nov 4
Nov 29, 5:34 am–Dec 1, 9:23 am	Taurus	1st	Nov 8
Dec 21, 6:42 pm–Dec 24, 6:39 am	Pisces	1st	Nov 30
Dec 26, 3:26 pm–Dec 28, 8:13 pm	Taurus	1st	Dec 6
Dec 30, 9:45 pm–Dec 31, 2:13 pm	Cancer	1st	Dec 9

Dates to Hunt and Fish

Date	Quarter	Sign
Jan 9, 1:14 pm–Jan 11, 12:41 pm	2nd	Cancer
Jan 18, 1:20 am–Jan 20, 12:30 pm	4th	Scorpio
Jan 28, 1:12 am–Jan 30, 10:25 am	1st	Pisces
Feb 5, 11:05 pm–Feb 7, 11:43 pm	2nd	Cancer
Feb 14, 9:50 am–Feb 16, 7:53 pm	3rd	Scorpio
Feb 24, 7:59 am–Feb 26, 4:24 pm	4th	Pisces
Mar 5, 6:07 am–Mar 7, 8:24 am	2nd	Cancer
Mar 13, 7:22 am–Mar 16, 4:21 am	3rd	Scorpio
Mar 16, 4:21 am–Mar 18, 4:18 pm	3rd	Sagittarius
Mar 23, 4:08 pm–Mar 26, 12:03 am	4th	Pisces
Apr 1, 11:30 am–Apr 3, 2:32 pm	1st	Cancer
Apr 10, 5:23 am–Apr 12, 2:00 pm	3rd	Scorpio
Apr 12, 2:00 pm–Apr 15, 1:27 am	3rd	Sagittarius
Apr 20, 1:55 am–Apr 22, 10:09 am	4th	Pisces
Apr 28, 6:38 pm–Apr 30, 8:56 pm	1st	Cancer
May 7, 12:48 pm–May 9, 9:49 pm	2nd	Scorpio
May 9, 9:49 pm–May 12, 9:09 am	3rd	Sagittarius
May 17, 10:17 am–May 19, 7:30 pm	4th	Pisces
May 26, 2:58 am–May 28, 3:44 am	1st	Cancer
Jun 3, 6:43 pm–Jun 6, 4:23 am	2nd	Scorpio
Jun 6, 4:23 am–Jun 8, 3:59 pm	2nd	Sagittarius
Jun 13, 5:32 pm–Jun 16, 3:51 am	3rd	Pisces
Jun 22, 1:12 pm–Jun 24, 12:50 pm	4th	Cancer
Jul 1, 12:18 am–Jul 3, 10:10 am	2nd	Scorpio
Jul 3, 10:10 am–Jul 5, 10:07 pm	2nd	Sagittarius
Jul 10, 11:44 pm–Jul 13, 10:40 am	3rd	Pisces
Jul 13, 10:40 am–Jul 15, 6:30 pm	3rd	Aries
Jul 19, 11:51 am–Jul 21, 11:27 pm	4th	Cancer
Jul 28, 6:56 am–Jul 30, 4:10 pm	1st	Scorpio
Jul 30, 4:10 pm–Aug 2, 4:08 am	2nd	Sagittarius
Aug 7, 5:34 am–Aug 9, 4:23 pm	3rd	Pisces
Aug 9, 4:23 pm–Aug 12, 12:49 am	3rd	Aries
Aug 16, 9:13 am–Aug 18, 9:56 am	4th	Cancer
Aug 24, 3:16 pm–Aug 26, 11:16 pm	1st	Scorpio
Sep 3, 11:58 am–Sep 5, 10:14 pm	2nd	Pisces
Sep 5, 10:14 pm–Sep 8, 6:17 am	3rd	Aries
Sep 12, 4:19 pm–Sep 14, 6:39 pm	4th	Cancer
Sep 21, 12:52 am–Sep 23, 7:43 am	1st	Scorpio
Sep 30, 7:26 pm–Oct 3, 5:20 am	2nd	Pisces
Oct 3, 5:20 am–Oct 5, 12:33 pm	2nd	Aries
Oct 9, 9:48 pm–Oct 12, 1:02 am	3rd	Cancer
Oct 18, 10:22 am–Oct 20, 4:49 pm	1st	Scorpio
Oct 28, 3:45 am–Oct 30, 1:56 pm	2nd	Pisces
Oct 30, 1:56 pm–Nov 1, 8:44 pm	2nd	Aries
Nov 6, 3:42 am–Nov 8, 5:23 am	3rd	Cancer
Nov 14, 5:24 pm–Nov 17, 12:22 am	4th	Scorpio
Nov 24, 11:07 am–Nov 26, 10:10 pm	1st	Pisces
Nov 26, 10:10 pm–Nov 29, 5:34 am	2nd	Aries
Dec 3, 11:00 am–Dec 5, 12:07 pm	3rd	Cancer
Dec 11, 11:31 pm–Dec 14, 7:25 am	4th	Scorpio
Dec 21, 6:42 pm–Dec 24, 6:39 am	1st	Pisces
Dec 30, 9:45 pm–Jan 1, 9:41 pm	2nd	Cancer

Dates to Destroy Weeds and Pests

From		To		Sign	Qtr.
Jan 11	12:41 pm	Jan 13	1:33 pm	Leo	3rd
Jan 13	1:33 pm	Jan 15	5:30 pm	Virgo	3rd
Jan 20	12:30 pm	Jan 23	1:18 am	Sagittarius	4th
Jan 25	1:56 pm	Jan 26	2:55 am	Aquarius	4th
Feb 9	9:49 am	Feb 10	12:38 am	Leo	3rd
Feb 10	12:38 am	Feb 12	3:33 am	Virgo	3rd
Feb 16	7:53 pm	Feb 19	8:25 am	Sagittarius	4th
Feb 21	9:06 pm	Feb 24	7:59 am	Aquarius	4th
Mar 10	9:38 pm	Mar 11	1:46 pm	Virgo	3rd
Mar 16	4:21 am	Mar 18	12:47 pm	Sagittarius	3rd
Mar 18	12:47 pm	Mar 18	4:18 pm	Sagittarius	4th
Mar 21	5:06 am	Mar 23	4:08 pm	Aquarius	4th
Mar 26	12:03 am	Mar 26	11:06 am	Aries	4th
Apr 12	2:00 pm	Apr 15	1:27 am	Sagittarius	3rd
Apr 17	2:19 pm	Apr 19	6:44 pm	Aquarius	4th
Apr 19	6:44 pm	Apr 20	1:55 am	Aquarius	4th
Apr 22	10:09 am	Apr 24	2:46 pm	Aries	4th
May 9	9:49 pm	May 12	9:09 am	Sagittarius	3rd
May 14	10:01 pm	May 17	3:26 am	Aquarius	3rd
May 17	3:26 am	May 17	10:17 am	Aquarius	4th
May 19	7:30 pm	May 22	12:40 am	Aries	4th
May 24	2:34 am	May 24	8:11 am	Gemini	4th
Jun 7	2:12 pm	Jun 8	3:59 pm	Sagittarius	3rd
Jun 11	4:52 am	Jun 13	5:32 pm	Aquarius	3rd
Jun 16	3:51 am	Jun 18	10:20 am	Aries	4th
Jun 20	1:00 pm	Jun 22	1:12 pm	Gemini	4th
Jul 8	11:03 am	Jul 10	11:44 pm	Aquarius	3rd
Jul 13	10:40 am	Jul 15	5:53 am	Aries	3rd
Jul 15	5:53 am	Jul 15	6:30 pm	Aries	4th
Jul 17	10:41 pm	Jul 19	11:51 pm	Gemini	4th
Aug 5	8:55 pm	Aug 7	5:34 am	Aquarius	3rd
Aug 9	4:23 pm	Aug 12	12:49 am	Aries	3rd
Aug 14	6:25 am	Aug 16	9:13 am	Gemini	4th
Aug 18	9:56 am	Aug 20	6:01 am	Leo	4th
Sep 5	10:14 pm	Sep 8	6:17 am	Aries	3rd
Sep 10	12:17 pm	Sep 11	10:16 pm	Gemini	3rd
Sep 11	10:16 pm	Sep 12	4:19 pm	Gemini	4th
Sep 14	6:39 pm	Sep 16	7:56 pm	Leo	4th
Sep 16	7:56 pm	Sep 18	2:44 pm	Virgo	4th
Oct 4	2:10 am	Oct 5	12:33 pm	Aries	3rd
Oct 7	5:46 pm	Oct 9	9:48 pm	Gemini	3rd
Oct 12	1:02 am	Oct 14	3:45 am	Leo	4th
Oct 14	3:45 am	Oct 16	6:29 am	Virgo	4th
Nov 4	12:53 pm	Nov 6	3:42 am	Gemini	3rd
Nov 8	5:23 am	Nov 9	10:56 am	Leo	3rd
Nov 9	10:56 am	Nov 10	8:30 am	Leo	4th
Nov 10	8:30 am	Nov 12	12:22 pm	Virgo	4th
Dec 2	2:30 am	Dec 3	11:00 am	Gemini	3rd
Dec 5	12:07 pm	Dec 7	2:05 pm	Leo	3rd
Dec 7	2:05 pm	Dec 8	7:13 pm	Virgo	3rd
Dec 8	7:13 pm	Dec 9	5:47 pm	Virgo	4th
Dec 14	7:25 am	Dec 16	7:02 am	Sagittarius	4th

Time Zone Map

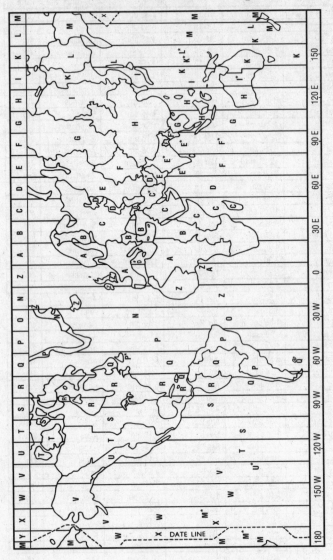

Time Zone Conversions

(R) EST—Used in book
(S) CST—Subtract 1 hour
(T) MST—Subtract 2 hours
(U) PST—Subtract 3 hours
(V) Subtract 4 hours
(V*) Subtract 4½ hours
(U*) Subtract 3½ hours
(W) Subtract 5 hours
(X) Subtract 6 hours
(Y) Subtract 7 hours
(Q) Add 1 hour
(P) Add 2 hours
(P*) Add 2½ hours
(O) Add 3 hours
(N) Add 4 hours
(Z) Add 5 hours
(A) Add 6 hours
(B) Add 7 hours
(C) Add 8 hours
(C*) Add 8½ hours

(D) Add 9 hours
(D*) Add 9½ hours
(E) Add 10 hours
(E*) Add 10½ hours
(F) Add 11 hours
(F*) Add 11½ hours
(G) Add 12 hours
(H) Add 13 hours
(I) Add 14 hours
(I*) Add 14½ hours
(K) Add 15 hours
(K*) Add 15½ hours
(L) Add 16 hours
(L*) Add 16½ hours
(M) Add 17 hours
(M*) Add 18 hours
(P*) Add 2½ hours

Important!

All times given in the *Moon Sign Book* are set in Eastern Time. The conversions shown here are for standard times only. Use the time zone conversions map and table to calculate the difference in your time zone. You must make the adjustment for your time zone and adjust for Daylight Saving Time where applicable.

Weather, Economic, & Lunar Forecasts

Forecasting the Weather

By Kris Brandt Riske

Astrometeorology—astrological weather forecasting—reveals seasonal and weekly weather trends based on the cardinal ingresses (Summer and Winter Solstices, and Spring and Autumn Equinoxes) and the four monthly lunar phases. The planetary alignments and the longitudes and latitudes they influence have the strongest effect, but the zodiacal signs are also involved in creating weather conditions.

The components of a thunderstorm, for example, are heat, wind, and electricity. A Mars-Jupiter configuration generates the necessary heat and Mercury adds wind and electricity. A severe thunderstorm, and those that produce tornados, usually involve Mercury, Mars, Uranus, or Neptune. The zodiacal signs add their energy to the planetary mix to increase or decrease the chance of weather phenomena and their severity.

In general, the fire signs (Aries, Leo, Sagittarius) indicate heat and dryness, both of which peak when Mars, the planet with a similar nature, is in these signs. Water signs (Cancer, Scorpio, Pisces) are conducive to precipitation, and air signs (Gemini, Libra, Aquarius) to cool temperatures and wind. Earth signs (Taurus, Virgo, Capricorn) vary from wet to dry, heat to cold. The signs and their prevailing weather conditions are listed here:

Aries: Heat, dry, wind
Taurus: Moderate temperatures, precipitation
Gemini: Cool temperatures, wind, dry
Cancer: Cold, steady precipitation
Leo: Heat, dry, lightning
Virgo: Cold, dry, windy
Libra: Cool, windy, fair
Scorpio: Extreme temperatures, abundant precipitation
Sagittarius: Warm, fair, moderate wind
Capricorn: Cold, wet, damp
Aquarius: Cold, dry, high pressure, lightning
Pisces: Wet, cool, low pressure

Take note of the Moon's sign at each lunar phase. It reveals the prevailing weather conditions for the next six to seven days. The same is true of Mercury and Venus. These two influential weather planets transit the entire zodiac each year, unless retrograde patterns add their influence.

Planetary Influences

People relied on astrology to forecast weather for thousands of years. They were able to predict drought, floods, and temperature variations through interpreting planetary alignments. In recent years there has been a renewed interest in astrometeorology. A weather forecast can be composed for any date—tomorrow, next week, or a thousand years in the future. According to astrometeorology, each planet governs certain weather phenomena. When certain planets are aligned with other planets, weather—precipitation, cloudy or clear skies, tornados, hurricanes, and other conditions—are generated.

Sun and Moon

The Sun governs the constitution of the weather and, like the Moon, it serves as a trigger for other planetary configurations that result in weather events. When the Sun is prominent in a cardinal ingress or lunar phase chart, the area is often warm and sunny. The Moon can bring or withhold moisture, depending upon its sign placement.

Mercury

Mercury is also a triggering planet, but its main influence is wind direction and velocity. In its stationary periods, Mercury reflects high winds, and its influence is always prominent in major weather events, such as hurricanes and tornados, when it tends to lower the temperature.

Venus

Venus governs moisture, clouds, and humidity. It brings warming trends that produce sunny, pleasant weather if in positive aspect to other planets. In some signs—Libra, Virgo, Gemini, Sagittarius—Venus is drier. It is at its wettest when placed in Cancer, Scorpio, Pisces, or Taurus.

Mars

Mars is associated with heat, drought, and wind, and can raise the temperature to record-setting levels when in a fire sign (Aries, Leo, Sagittarius). Mars also provides the spark that generates thunderstorms and is prominent in tornado and hurricane configurations.

Jupiter

Jupiter, a fair-weather planet, tends toward higher temperatures when in Aries, Leo, or Sagittarius. It is associated with high-pressure systems and is a contributing factor at times to dryness. Storms are often amplified by Jupiter.

Saturn

Saturn is associated with low-pressure systems, cloudy to overcast skies, and excessive precipitation. Temperatures drop when Saturn is involved. Major winter storms always have a strong Saturn influence, as do storms that produce a slow, steady downpour for hours or days.

Uranus

Like Jupiter, Uranus indicates high-pressure systems. It reflects descending cold air and, when prominent, is responsible for a jet stream that extends far south. Uranus can bring drought in winter, and it is involved in thunderstorms, tornados, and hurricanes.

Neptune

Neptune is the wettest planet. It signals low-pressure systems and is dominant when hurricanes are in the forecast. When Neptune is strongly placed, flood danger is high. It's often associated with winter thaws. Temperatures, humidity, and cloudiness increase where Neptune influences weather.

Pluto

Pluto is associated with weather extremes, as well as unseasonably warm temperatures and drought. It reflects the high winds involved in major hurricanes, storms, and tornados.

Climate Change is Our Future

By Bruce Scofield

When Hurricane Katrina hit the city of New Orleans a few years ago, the possible effects of climate change were brought to the public in a way that was not previously possible. But climate change was not a new issue. Scientists had talked about it long ago, and by the 1980s many of them had become extremely concerned and made public statements about what our carbon-burning lifestyles were doing to the Earth. Corporations, and politicians beholden to them, ignored these warnings and some even hired scientists to argue the contrary—that humans were not affecting the climate. Even the president was denying that anything was happening. But then came Katrina. When people see other people in life-threatening situations right on their own television sets—well, that can get to you. Since then climate change has been getting a lot more attention and slowly, the doubters are coming around.

"Warm" in One Place Means "HOT" Somewhere Else

Climate change is a better label for what's happening to us than global warming. For years, many people thought global warming would be a good thing, like going to Florida for a vacation, and didn't see any reason to do anything to prevent it. Because most people are clueless about the interconnectedness of nature and the complexities of the climate system, they never thought that warming here might mean frying somewhere else. Some concerned scientists, like James Lovelock, the author of *Gaia Theory*, describe what's happening to the Earth in more extreme terms —he prefers "global heating." It's still not that simple, however, and climate change could cause regional cooling in some places as the planet adjusts to a new climate system. New England and the countries bordering the North Atlantic in Europe may become quite cold for a time if certain ocean currents slow due to warming in the tropics.

Some corporate scientists have pointed out, correctly, that climate change has always been working on the Earth and that we should look at what's happening to us as perfectly natural. It is true that the climate has changed many times in Earth's history, and we'll take a look at that below. These same scientists have also expressed doubts that humans are creating climate change. Contrast this view with climate scientists who are not beholden to certain corporations. Nearly all of them tell us that humans are indeed aggravating the climate system and are pushing it along much faster than it normally would change. If these scientists are right, and most of the evidence supports them, it appears that humanity has backed itself into a corner. What is convenient for us today, lifestyle wise, will make our future very inconvenient if we don't change our careless habits immediately.

Let's look at great climate changes of the past. The critics say we shouldn't be shocked by the prospect of a warmer Earth

because the Earth was plenty warm for most of the past 200 million years. That's true. Back in the Mesozoic Era, the time of the dinosaurs, the Earth was downright hot. The tropics ranged much farther north and south of the equator than they do now and there were even dinosaurs living in the polar regions where temperatures were temperate. Easy living on Antarctica? Maybe, but the price was a lot less land all over the world. When you have warm temperatures, you don't get water stored as ice caps on the land masses near the poles. No ice on Greenland or Antarctica means sea levels were higher by 300 or more feet. That's a lot of water and huge sections of the continents, like the inland areas of North America and all major river valleys, were flooded.

Higher sea levels made the continents smaller and the amount of coastline was likewise reduced. This sort of thing is a formula for disaster: higher global temperatures = ice cap melting = sea level rise = less land mass = displacement of people = more people on less land. This is not good.

At the end of the Mesozoic, sixty-five million years ago, a big asteroid crashed into the Earth near Yucatan, Mexico. Recent evidence shows that climate was changing even before that time, but the Earth did take quite a hit and after the impact it cooled down a bit. Then, about fifty-five million years ago, another climate change event, called the Paleocene-Eocene Thermal Maximum (PETM), occurred. In a very short time, by geological standards, the Earth heated up again. Now this very short time is not known with precision, but many think it took about a thousand to ten thousand years. It's not known exactly why this rapid global warming occurred, but it may have had something to do with geological changes like the shifting of the continents (plate tectonics) that caused changes in the ocean currents.

When ocean currents change, heat is moved around the planet in different ways and this alone can create imbalances in the climate system, including the generation of strong storms like Katrina. One hypothesis says that warm currents flowing over cold coastlines can destabilize methane (from bacteria) trapped in the sea bed. This methane then bubbles up and enters the atmosphere where it acts as a powerful greenhouse gas, twenty-two times more powerful than carbon dioxide. Methane is not as stable as carbon dioxide, however, and after about ten years it will break down into carbon dioxide, another powerful greenhouse gas. It is very possible that the PETM was a case of global warming due to rapid greenhouse gas emissions, and because of this similarity to our world today, it is being studied intensely by climate scientists.

After the PETM a lot changed. Habitats were transformed and organisms struggled to adapt. Nearly all major forms of modern mammals began to evolve following this event including rodents, whales and primates. New kinds of plants evolved and life in the sea changed. That big spike in temperature at the PETM sent the Earth reeling and, over the next twenty million years, a gradual cooling set in. Then about fifteen million years ago the cooling trend became steeper. First, ice began to accumulate on Antarctica and about seven million years ago the first ice began to build up on Greenland. The Earth was certainly getting colder, but this was not such a bad thing for life. Colder waters are good for marine life—the most biologically productive seas are those near the poles. Cold can also be good for land dwellers. Ice on land means less water in the seas—and this means more land is exposed.

Earth Cools Down

As the Earth cooled down the climate system began to respond strongly to astronomical cycles. The Earth orbits the sun in an ellipse, not in a perfect circle. The other planets tug on the Earth and this modulates the shape of its orbit. The effect is that over a period of about 100,000 years the Earth's orbit varies from being more round to being more elongated—and this affects the amount of solar energy reaching the Earth. About two million years ago the Earth's climate system began to respond strongly to the 100,000-year cycle and a series of ice ages began. For about 90,000 years the Earth would cool down and ice would advance in the northern hemisphere (where there is more land mass). Just when things got really cold, there would be a sudden warming and the ice would retreat. Then the cycle would begin again.

Drilling into the ice sheets on Greenland and Antarctica for samples of ancient ice have shown that these warmings at the end of the ice age were very rapid, maybe taking only a few thousand years or less, and were coincident with a steep increase in greenhouse gases. The warmings that occurred, called interglacials, lasted about 10,000 years on average and then the Earth would slowly slip into another deep cooling. Now the last interglacial period began about 10,000 years ago, so it would seem logical that we are moving into another gradual cooling and that maximum cold will come eight to ninety thousand years after that. But maybe not. Astronomical calculations show that the variations of the Earth's orbit that have pushed the ice ages along are changing themselves and that we may be entering a long period of relative climate stability—or at least the cooling over the next cycle will be minimal. Still, it doesn't follow that we should be heating up right now. So what is happening?

Let's consider greenhouse gases. Carbon dioxide is the by-product of burning fossil fuels. Fossil fuels, oil for cars and coal for electricity, are actually the buried remains of plants, algae and bacteria that lived millions of years ago. Plants, algae and cyanobacteria need carbon dioxide to make their bodies and they pull it out of the air—they draw-down the most important greenhouse gas. When they die, they are often buried and over time large amounts of biotic material is compressed to form coal or oil. A few hundred million years ago, in the Carboniferous era, the Earth was loaded with plants that became our coal deposits. It took millions of years for the plants and other life to be buried and turned to coal, but we are now burning it up and pumping it back into the atmosphere in just decades. On top of that, we are cutting down the forests that we need desperately now to draw down the greenhouse gases we are adding to the atmosphere. The Earth is being exploited—raped some would say. Some people are getting rich from it, but others are getting boxed in by rising fuel costs. We will all pay the price if we keep going like this.

And Earth Warms Up

According to the vast majority of scientists, greenhouse gases are the culprits behind global warming. We know that greenhouse gases like carbon dioxide and methane hold in the heat like a warm blanket. We know that these gases can be released naturally and that they have probably caused global warming in the distant past. But the changes were slow in terms of our lifetimes. A rise of only a few degrees centigrade worldwide for a thousand years, which might be like what happened at the PETM or at the end of a glaciation, would be experienced over the course of 50 generations of people. That rate of change might be manageable. What may be happening now, however, is a warming that is occurring ten times as fast.

Another cause of warming, and one cited by opponents of global warming, is the sun. The sun is very steady and it radiates energy very predictably. But over long periods of time its output varies a small amount. Around 800 years ago it was hot, maybe as hot as it is today. But roughly between 1550 and 1850 it was cooler, not a lot cooler, but enough for a portion of this 300-year period to be called the "Little Ice Age." Records of solar activity do show that the sun has warmed up somewhat in the last fifty years, but this increase cannot account for global warming by itself. Something else is increasing global temperatures and the facts show that greenhouse gas levels are going up rapidly. We just have to point the finger at ourselves because humans are burning fossil fuels. So in thinking critically about climate change, we must consider at least two sources of recent warming—the sun and greenhouse gases—and that we are responsible for the latter.

How Concerned Should We Be?

So how concerned should we be about all of this? I think we should be very concerned. First, right now—immediately—we should all do what we can to lessen our impact on the Earth. Never underestimate the power of conservation. It may not be "cool" for someone to drive a "wimpy" fuel-efficient car, but it's smart and considerate of others who share the planet with us. We have to get over our general tendency to seek power and be swayed by commercials that show handsome people in powerful gas-guzzling SUV's climbing mountains. Second, people need to be educated about climate change. We can't trust all politicians on this matter—many have already let us down. Leadership at the top on climate change has been pathetic, if not manipulative and downright dishonest. We all need to understand more about how our planet works and not let other people do our thinking for us.

Can Technology Help?

Maybe technology will come to the rescue. Many think that some new invention will solve our problems and allow us to continue living extravagantly. This may be wishful thinking if climate change occurs at a rapid pace. Hydrogen fuel is thought by many to be a solution, but it will take a long time before it becomes readily available. Other proposed solutions, like seeding the oceans with iron to enhance the growth of algae that draw down carbon dioxide, or building a screen in space to limit sunlight reaching the planet are either unproven or too costly. Nuclear energy, which doesn't produce greenhouse gases, can generate enough power to keep the world running the way we like it. There are drawbacks, as in disposal of radioactive waste, but compared to the enormity of climate change these are minor problems and going nuclear may be a very realistic solution to our dilemma. The truth is that there may not always be an easy technological solution to every technologically-caused problem. And we should be aware that some technological solutions could make the situation worse. We're all in this together and we've got a real problem on our hands. It's an ethical problem, too—we have to learn to be

more concerned and respectful of our planet and our fellow travelers on this planet, including other species. Sometimes people just have to change their habits.

The Earth is Our Only Home

Climate change is with us now and it is a lesson for humanity that goes far beyond anything we've encountered before. The Earth is our only home and we have been trashing it. We can all do our part by conserving, but many need enlightened leadership as well. Politicians have been ridiculously slow to become engaged in the problem, as most of them are only concerned with their next election. One might think that the great religious institutions of our cultures would recognize the seriousness of the problem, but, except for pagans, they are essentially anthropocentric and will have to rise above that in order to rally the faithful and make a difference. To their credit, a few thoughtful and brave celebrities have stepped to the plate and drawn attention to the problem.

The message of climate change has been tacked on the bulletin board, but we need an emergency siren to get the world's attention. It may just take another disaster like Katrina to make this happen.

About the Author
Bruce Scofield, a professional astrologer with a worldwide clientele, specializes in both psychological and electional astrology. He is the author of thirteen books and is on the faculty of Kepler College.

2009 Severe Weather Forecast

By Kris Brandt Riske

Winter

Northern areas of the West Coast can expect wet winter weather with abundant downfall as maritime polar air masses trigger low-pressure systems. Areas from southern California to northwestern Utah to northeastern Montana will see some storms that bring abundant precipitation, but moisture will be below normal in areas east and west of that line.

The central Plains are the site of the season's major storm and blizzard potential in areas from mid-North Dakota south to mid-Texas. In addition to cloudy skies and periods of abundant downfall, these areas are prone to chilling cold when the jet stream drives continental polar air masses south. The Mississippi River Valley will also experience frigid weather and major storms.

Periods of abundant precipitation can be expected from eastern Ohio/western Pennsyvlania south, and conditions are ripe for mid-latitude low-pressure systems to form over Tennessee and Kentucky, bringing heavy snow east and north of there.

Significant weather events include:

Stormy conditions in the Northwest and in the Plains in mid-January advance into eastern parts of the United States.

Much of the United States will see cold weather in mid-February and again in early March.

Cold temperatures will accompany significant precipitation across the Plains in mid-March.

Spring

The spring season has high potential for severe thunderstorms and tornados, especially in areas from eastern Texas through western Missouri, and from Indiana south to Alabama. The Mississippi River Valley is also at risk. Wet weather will continue to be the norm in the northwestern United States, which has high flood potential, and the western states from Arizona to Utah to Montana and western North Dakota will be dry with temperatures above normal. Areas from the central Plains to Indiana and south to Alabama will experience periods of cold weather as the Jet Stream dips south. The East coast will be drier than average.

Significant weather events include:

The third week of March will bring severe thunderstorms with tornado potential across the Plains and into eastern areas.

Severe thunderstorms with tornado potential in the mid-Atlantic states and areas to the south are in the forecast for early April.

Much of the eastern third of the United States will see severe thunderstorms with tornado potential the last week of March and the first week of May, when the Plains will also experience stormy weather.

Mid-May will also feature thunderstorms with tornado potential in much of the eastern third of the country.

Summer

The Northwest continues to be wet, with significant precipitation and flooding potential throughout the summer as low-pressure systems form over the area. Although areas from eastern Arizona to mid-North Dakota can expect average precipitation early in the season, it will be followed by less rainfall but high humidity. Cool, cloudy conditions will prevail from the eastern Plains to the Mississippi River Valley to areas from Michigan to Alabama, which will have fewer typical summer days. Hot, dry weather will prevail in much of the eastern United States. Summer hurricane potential will be strongest in the Gulf states from eastern Texas to Alabama and northwestern Florida.

Significant weather events include:

The Plains and areas from Ohio south will see severe thunderstorms with tornado potential the first two weeks of July, and a tropical storm is possible in the Gulf.

Temperatures will rise across much of the country in late July and early August, sparking strong thunderstorms with tornado potential in the Plains, and a tropical storm could bring severe weather to the Gulf states.

High temperatures in mid-August will trigger severe thunderstorms in the West, the Plains and eastern areas, along with tornado potential, and the eastern United States could see heavy precipitation from a tropical storm.

A tropical storm or hurricane is possible in the Gulf in mid-September.

Autumn

Major low-pressure systems will target the Northwest throughout the season, along with chilly temperatures, which will prevail throughout much of the West and across the Plains. Western areas will see more precipitation to ease summer dryness. The heaviest precipitation, however, will occur in the Mississippi River Valley and in surrounding areas. Some eastern coastal and New England locations will also see significant precipitation from low-pressure systems.

Significant weather events include:

Cold weather prevails across the country's mid-section in late October.

Western parts of the United States will be stormy as a major storm arrives in late November, and continues into the Plains in early December.

Cold temperatures will dip far south in mid-December, when a Nor'easter is also possible.

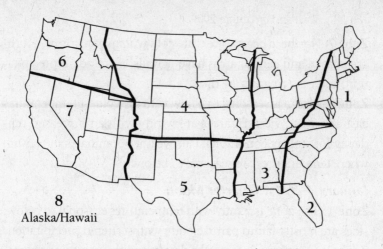

Alaska/Hawaii

Weather Forecast for 2009

By Kris Brandt Riske

Winter 2009

Zone 1: Temperatures across the zone are seasonal with average to below normal precipitation.

Zone 2: Average to below precipitation and seasonal temperatures.

Zone 3: Temperatures range from seasonal to below, with major storms west. Conditions are drier in the central and eastern areas with average to below precipitation levels.

Zone 4: Temperatures are seasonal to below across the zone, with major storms and high winds, especially in western areas, where it is also the coldest.

Zone 5: Cold temperatures dip far south, especially in central and western areas; central and eastern parts of the zone see the heaviest precipitation from major storms.

Zone 6: Western areas are cold with abundant precipitation and flood potential, while central parts of the zone are cold and windy with major storms. Eastern areas are mostly seasonal.

Zone 7: Northern coastal areas are cold with major storms, southern coastal and central areas have periods of abundant precipitation, and eastern areas are dry.

Zone 8: Alaska is seasonal to below with the coldest temperatures east and west; western areas are windy with an increased tendency for stormy conditions. Fair weather dominates in Hawaii, where temperatures are seasonal to below.

January 4–9, 1st Quarter Moon

Zone 1: The zone is windy with temperatures seasonal to below; skies are mostly fair to partly cloudy with scattered precipitation.

Zone 2: Skies are fair to partly cloudy and temperatures are seasonal to above. Conditions in eastern part of zone are windy.

Zone 3: Western and central areas are cold and windy with scattered precipitation, while eastern parts of the zone are fair to partly cloudy and more seasonal.

Zone 4: Northwestern areas are fair with increasing clouds and precipitation later in the week, central areas are fair and windy, while eastern parts of the zone are windy, cloudy, and more seasonal with precipitation.

Zone 5: Temperatures range from seasonal to below and conditions are windy across the zone, with cloudy skies central and east as a front advances; western areas are fair.

Zone 6: Overcast skies bring precipitation to western areas later in the week, central parts of the zone are fair to partly cloudy, and eastern areas are cold, overcast, windy, and stormy with abundant precipitation in some areas.

Zone 7: Southeastern parts of the zone are fair and windy, central and northeastern areas are stormy, and coastal areas are fair to partly cloudy with scattered precipitation.

Zone 8: Alaska is cold and mostly cloudy, wet, and windy, with abundant precipitation east. Temperatures in Hawaii are seasonal to below. Conditions are very windy with precipitation across the zone as a front advances, followed by clearing.

January 10–16, Full Moon

Zone 1: Northern areas are very cold and windy, while skies are fair to partly cloudy and temperatures more seasonal to the south.

Zone 2: Temperatures are seasonal to below with fair skies north; cloudy, stormy conditions prevail in central and southern areas.

Zone 3: Skies are fair to partly cloudy west with precipitation later in the week, and central and eastern parts of the zone are cloudy with precipitation, some abundant, and cold temperatures.

Zone 4: Cloudy skies bring precipitation to central and eastern areas, where stormy conditions bring heavy downfall, while western parts of the zone are fair to partly cloudy; temperatures across the zone are seasonal to below.

Zone 5: Seasonal temperatures accompany fair skies west and central, while eastern areas are windy and cloudy with precipitation.

Zone 6: Western areas are windy with abundant precipitation in some areas, increasing wind and cloudiness brings precipitation to central areas at week's end, and eastern areas are cloudy and cold with precipitation—some abundant.

Zone 7: Northern coastal and eastern areas are windy with precipitation—some abundant, and much of the rest of the zone is fair to partly cloudy; temperatures are seasonal to below, and cold in the central mountain area.

Zone 8: Eastern Alaska is seasonal, while western and central areas are windy and cold as a front advances. Hawaii is fair to partly cloudy with scattered precipitation and temperatures ranging from seasonal to below.

January 17–24, 3rd Quarter Moon

Zone 1: Northern areas are mostly fair and cold, while southern areas are also cold and cloudy with precipitation later in the week.

Zone 2: The zone is stormy and cold with abundant precipitation in many areas.

Zone 3: Central and eastern areas are windy, stormy, and cold with abundant precipitation in some locations; conditions in western parts of the zone are fair and seasonal to below.

Zone 4: Western skies are cloudy with precipitation, mostly north; central and eastern areas of the zone are mostly fair, windy, and seasonal.

Zone 5: The zone is mostly fair, windy, and seasonal.

Zone 6: Wind and cloudy skies bring precipitation to western areas, while central and eastern areas experience windy conditions and variably cloudiness with scattered precipitation later in the week; temperatures are seasonal to below.

Zone 7: Northern coastal areas see precipitation, some abundant, later in the week; skies in southern coastal and central parts of the zone are fair to partly cloudy; and eastern areas are cloudy with precipitation, some abundant.

Zone 8: Alaska is stormy west with abundant downfall, and fair and windy central and east. Conditions in Hawaii are fair, windy, and seasonal.

January 25–February 1, New Moon

Zone 1: The zone is cold, cloudy, and windy with precipitation north as a front moves through the area.

Zone 2: Colder temperatures, wind, and precipitation prevail to the north, while much of the rest of the zone is fair and seasonal.

Zone 3: Western and central areas are seasonal, while eastern parts of the zone are colder and variably cloudy.

Zone 4: The zone is seasonal to below with possible abundant precipitation in the western Plains; cloudy skies east with scattered precipitation.

Zone 5: Western skies are fair, while central and eastern areas are cloudy with the potential for abundant precipitation; temperatures are below normal.

Zone 6: Temperatures range from seasonal to below with the coldest readings in central areas; western parts of the zone see precipitation later in the week.

Zone 7: Conditions are mostly fair with temperatures ranging from seasonal to below; eastern areas can expect variable cloudiness and scattered precipitation.

Zone 8: Central and eastern areas in Alaska are very cold, but temperatures are more seasonal west, with precipitation west and central. Hawaii is windy and temperatures are seasonal to below; western and central areas will see precipitation later in the week.

February 2–8, 1st Quarter Moon

Zone 1: The zone is overcast and windy with precipitation, some abundant; temperatures are colder north.

Zone 2: Cold temperatures accompany cloudy skies and precipitation in areas to the north, while southern areas are more seasonal and fair to partly cloudy with scattered precipitation.

Zone 3: Western and central areas are windy where variable cloudiness brings scattered precipitation; eastern areas are colder and cloudy with precipitation.

Zone 4: Temperatures across the zone are seasonal to below. Skies are fair to partly cloudy west; central areas are windy with scattered precipitation; and eastern areas are cloudy with precipitation.

Zone 5: The zone is windy and seasonal with fair skies west; variable cloudiness prevails in the central and eastern parts of zone, with scattered precipitation east.

Zone 6: Western areas see precipitation and then clearing with colder temperatures; windy conditions and cloudy skies bring heavy precipitation and colder temperatures to central areas at week's end; and eastern areas are mostly fair and seasonal.

Zone 7: Coastal parts of the zone, especially to the south, see precipitation, as do the central mountains, while eastern areas are fair to partly cloudy; temperatures across the zone are seasonal to below.

Zone 8: Alaska is seasonal, with mostly fair in eastern and western areas, and cloudiness with precipitation in central areas. Hawaii is fair and seasonal, with increasing cloudiness and precipitation in central areas midweek.

February 9–15, Full Moon

Zone 1: Temperatures are seasonal to below with cloudy skies north and fair to partly cloudy skies south.

Zone 2: Variably cloudiness across the zone increases in the south later in the week, bringing precipitation.

Zone 3: Weather is fair to partly cloudy and cold west, while central areas see precipitation, and eastern parts of the zone are cloudy; temperatures are seasonal to below.

Zone 4: Skies are overcast west with precipitation, some abundant; eastern areas are mostly fair; cold temperatures dominate.

Zone 5: Western and eastern parts of the zone are cloudy and stormy, while eastern skies are fair.

Zone 6: The zone is mostly fair and seasonal, with variably cloudiness, scattered precipitation, and cooler temperatures west; and with more precipitation east.

Zone 7: Fair skies and seasonal temperatures dominate across the zone, with some precipitation in the south central mountain area.

Zone 8: Alaska is windy and stormy central and east as a front moves through the areas; western skies are mostly fair. Hawaii is fair to partly cloudy, windy, and cooler as the week progresses.

February 16–23, 3rd Quarter Moon

Zone 1: Stormy conditions south move into northern areas, where precipitation is heaviest; temperatures throughout the zone are seasonal.

Zone 2: The zone is windy and variably cloudy with precipitation and temperatures seasonal to below; southern areas see thunderstorms, some severe with tornado potential.

Zone 3: Western areas are windy and fair to partly cloudy. Thunderstorms, some severe with high winds, followed by colder temperatures, are possible east.

Zone 4: Windy conditions accompanies partly cloudy skies east, which is cold; scattered precipitation to the north; western and central areas are variably cloudy with precipitation.

Zone 5: Temperatures are seasonal to below throughout the zone; eastern areas are mostly fair, while western and central parts of the zone see precipitation.

Zone 6: Temperatures dip, and skies are overcast with precipitation in the west and central parts of the zone; it remains fair to partly cloudy east.

Zone 7: Much of the zone is overcast with precipitation, which is heaviest in central areas and the mountains, and in eastern areas later in the week; temperatures are seasonal to below.

Zone 8: Western and central Alaska are stormy and windy as a front moves through, far eastern areas see precipitation, and temperatures are seasonal to below. Hawaii is fair with a chance of scattered showers and temperatures ranging from seasonal to above.

February 24–March 2, New Moon

Zone 1: The zone is fair to partly cloudy with temperatures ranging from seasonal to below.

Zone 2: Southern areas are variably cloudy with scattered precipitation, northern areas are fair, and temperatures are seasonal to below across the zone.

Zone 3: Western areas are cold with fair skies; temperatures are more seasonal east with precipitation, some abundant, and central parts of the zone are windy and stormy.

Zone 4: Temperatures are seasonal to below and coldest to the east, which is mostly fair, as are central parts of the zone; western areas are cloudy with precipitation.

Zone 5: Central areas are cloudy with precipitation, and skies are mostly fair east; central and eastern parts of the zone are cold.

Zone 6: Weather is mostly fair and seasonal across the zone, and windy east with scattered precipitation.

Zone 7: Northern coastal areas see precipitation followed by clearing and fair skies, which dominate across the zone; eastern areas are windy, and temperatures are seasonal to above.

Zone 8: Alaska is fair to partly cloudy and seasonal. Hawaii is fair and seasonal.

March 3–9, 1st Quarter Moon

Zone 1: The zone is windy, with fair to partly cloudy skies south and more cloudiness north, where there is precipitation and colder temperatures.

Zone 2: Temperatures are seasonal to above and skies fair to partly cloudy, with thunderstorms, some severe, to the south.

Zone 3: The zone is cold with fair skies west; central and east are cloudy with precipitation, some abundant in eastern areas.

Zone 4: Much of the zone is fair and cold with variable cloudiness west and precipitation in some areas; central and eastern areas are windy; some eastern areas see abundant precipitation.

Zone 5: Cloudy skies and cold temperatures prevail across much of the zone, especially west, where the heaviest downfall occurs.

Zone 6: Temperatures are seasonal to below in western areas where skies are fair to partly cloudy, and eastern areas are warmer with increasing cloudiness later in the week as precipitation in central areas, some of which is abundant, moves east.

Zone 7: Eastern skies are cloudy, northern coastal areas see abundant precipitation, and much of the rest of the zone is fair; temperatures are seasonal to below.

Zone 8: Central Alaska is partly cloudy with scattered precipitation, and much of the rest of the state is fair and seasonal with cooler temperatures east. Temperatures in Hawaii are seasonal to below and skies are mostly fair.

March 10–17, Full Moon

Zone 1: The zone is fair to partly cloudy and cold with scattered precipitation north.

Zone 2: Skies are fair north and partly cloudy central and south with scattered precipitation and temperatures seasonal to below.

Zone 3: Temperatures range from seasonal to below, skies are variably cloudy but mostly fair and windy with scattered precipitation central.

Zone 4: Precipitation, some abundant, is in the forecast for cloudy western areas; central and eastern parts of the zone are fair but with increasing cloudiness as a front moves in; temperatures across the zone are seasonal to below.

Zone 5: Skies are cloudy and much of the zone sees precipitation as a front advances from west to east.

Zone 6: The zone is fair with temperatures ranging from seasonal to below, but western areas see significant precipitation later in the week as a front moves in.

Zone 7: Variably cloudy skies accompany temperatures that are seasonal to below under high pressure, eastern areas are mostly fair, and western areas are windy.

Zone 8: Central and eastern Alaska are seasonal and windy with abundant precipitation; central and western areas are mostly fair and cold. Hawaii is cloudy with some areas receiving significant precipitation, followed by clear skies and cooler temperatures.

Spring 2009

Zone 1: Temperatures are seasonal and precipitation above average, especially south.

Zone 2: Northern areas see abundant precipitation. Central and southern areas are drier, but potential exists for severe thunderstorms and tornados.

Zone 3: Western and central areas see severe thunderstorms with tornado potential, while eastern areas are cloudy with abundant precipitation; temperatures are seasonal to below.

Zone 4: Western areas are windy and seasonal with average to below precipitation. Much of the rest of the zone sees severe thunderstorms with tornado potential and chilly temperatures.

Zone 5: Temperatures are above average and conditions are dry in the west; central and eastern areas are seasonal to below with severe thunderstorms and tornado potential.

Zone 6: Western and central areas see abundant precipitation; conditions are windy and drier east, and temperatures are seasonal to below.

Zone 7: Eastern areas are dry with temperatures ranging from seasonal to above, while western and central areas are seasonal with average to above precipitation.

Zone 8: Western Alaska sees more storms, while central and eastern areas are seasonal. Hawaii is seasonal with precipitation ranging from average to below, and windy in central areas.

March 18–25, 3rd Quarter Moon

Zone 1: Temperatures ranging from seasonal to below accompany precipitation, some locally heavy, across the zone, as winds increase to the north.

Zone 2: Northern areas see precipitation, while central and southern parts of the zone are fair and windy with higher temperatures and severe thunderstorms later in the week.

Zone 3: Severe thunderstorms, some with tornado potential, are possible for much of the zone, which is windy central and east.

Zone 4: Weather is fair, seasonal, and windy west and in the western Plains, while central and eastern areas are stormy and cold with abundant precipitation and tornado potential in some southern areas.

Zone 5: Western conditions are fair with increasing cloudiness and scattered precipitation, and central and eastern areas see thunderstorms, some severe with tornado potential and abundant precipitation.

Zone 6: Weather is fair and seasonal, but colder in central areas and at higher elevations.

Zone 7: Southern coastal and central areas are mostly cloudy, as are northeastern parts of the zone; other areas are mostly fair; temperatures range from seasonal to above across the zone.

Zone 8: Western Alaska sees precipitation, while central parts of the zone are very windy; temperatures are below normal with variable cloudiness. Skies are mostly fair to partly cloudy in Hawaii with breezy conditions central and east, and precipitation west.

March 26–April 1, New Moon

Zone 1: The zone is cloudy and stormy, especially south, where some areas receive abundant precipitation.

Zone 2: Northern areas are stormy, while southern parts of the zone see variable cloudiness; severe thunderstorms are possible in central areas.

Zone 3: Thunderstorms, some severe with tornado potential, are in the forecast for central areas later in the week, while eastern areas are stormy and overcast; western parts of the zone are more seasonal with scattered precipitation.

Zone 4: Western areas are fair and seasonal with precipitation later in the week; western and central Plain areas, especially to the north, see abundant precipitation in some areas; eastern areas are fair and windy, and the zonal temperatures are seasonal to below.

Zone 5: Skies are mostly fair with a chance for precipitation west; central areas see thunderstorms, some severe with tornado potential, and eastern parts of the zone are variably cloudy; temperatures range from seasonal to below.

Zone 6: The zone is variably cloudy with scattered precipitation; temperatures are cooler central and east.

Zone 7: Western parts of the zone see precipitation with more cloudiness and cooler temperatures in northern coastal areas; fair skies prevail to the east, and central areas see scattered precipitation.

Zone 8: Alaska weather varies from windy with precipitation east, cloudy and cold west, and fair and cold in the central area. Central and eastern areas of Hawaii are windy and stormy, while western parts of the state are fair to partly cloudy and cool.

April 2–8, 1st Quarter Moon

Zone 1: The zone is seasonal and fair to partly cloudy with scattered precipitation.

Zone 2: Northern areas are mostly fair with a chance for precipitation, while central and southern parts of the zone see severe storms with tornado potential and heavy downfall.

Zone 3: Western areas are fair to partly cloudy with scattered precipitation; central and eastern parts of the zone are stormy as a front advances.

Zone 4: Areas to the west are cloudy with precipitation, central areas are fair, and eastern areas see more cloudiness with scattered precipitation, especially north, which could be stormy.

Zone 5: Weather is mostly fair, windy, and seasonal with a chance for showers.

Zone 6: Conditions are windy west with showers and then fair and seasonal as a front advances, bringing scattered showers, variable cloudiness and cooler temperatures to the rest of the zone.

Zone 7: Temperatures are seasonal across the zone; skies are mostly fair east, but cloudy with precipitation central and western areas.

Zone 8: Alaska is fair and seasonal west, and stormy with high winds central and east. Temperatures range from seasonal to below. Western skies are fair in Hawaii, while central and eastern areas are cloudy and windy with precipitation, some abundant.

April 9–16, Full Moon

Zone 1: The zone is cloudy with storms, high winds, and below normal temperatures.

Zone 2: Northern areas are stormy with high winds and heavy precipitation in some locations, while central and southern parts

of the zone see thunderstorms, some severe with tornado potential; temperatures are below normal.

Zone 3: Skies are variably cloudy west and central, but overcast and stormy east with abundant precipitation in some areas.

Zone 4: Western areas are fair with increasing winds at week's end, and eastern parts of the zone are stormy with tornado potential and abundant precipitation in some areas.

Zone 5: Much of the zone is fair, but eastern areas see heavy precipitation from thunderstorms with tornado potential.

Zone 6: Weather is fair and seasonal west, and cloudy with precipitation central and east as a front moves through bringing cooler temperatures.

Zone 7: Northwestern areas see precipitation; cloudy and windy south and central with scattered precipitation; eastern areas are mostly fair and windy with a chance for precipitation north.

Zone 8: Eastern Alaska is mostly fair, and western and central parts of the zone are cloudy with precipitation, some abundant, as temperatures range from seasonal to below. Much of Hawaii is cool, with precipitation in some areas.

April 17–23, 3rd Quarter Moon

Zone 1: The zone is fair and seasonal with scattered precipitation south.

Zone 2: Northern areas see scattered precipitation, while central and southern parts of the zone are wet, with heavy downfall and flood potential; temperatures are seasonal to below.

Zone 3: Strong thunderstorms across the zone could trigger tornados; precipitation is heaviest in central areas.

Zone 4: The zone is variably cloudy, and windy east, with strong storms to the north.

Zone 5: Western areas are fair and windy; central and eastern areas see scattered thunderstorms, with more cloudiness east.

Zone 6: Cloudy, cool conditions prevail across the zone, with rising temperatures and scattered showers east as the week progresses.

Zone 7: Much of the zone is fair with temperatures ranging from seasonal to above, while western areas are windy with a chance for precipitation.

Zone 8: Alaska is fair and seasonal west, and overcast and cold with precipitation in central and eastern areas as a storm front advances. Much of Hawaii is cloudy and cool, with abundant precipitation in some areas; temperatures are seasonal to below.

April 24–30, New Moon

Zone 1: The zone is fair and windy with seasonal temperatures.

Zone 2: Thunderstorms across the zone are strongest with tornado potential in central areas and south; temperatures are seasonal to above.

Zone 3: Temperatures range from seasonal to above, and western skies are fair. Central areas see showers and thunderstorms, some severe with high winds and tornado potential; eastern parts of the zone have scattered thunderstorms at week's end.

Zone 4: Seasonal temperatures, mostly fair skies with variable cloudiness central, and scattered precipitation prevail across the zone.

Zone 5: Central and eastern areas are cloudy with precipitation, some abundant; fair to partly cloudy in eastern parts of the zone.

Zone 6: Fair skies prevail to the west; central and eastern areas see precipitation, some heavy; temperatures are seasonal to below.

Zone 7: Precipitation, some heavy, in western and central areas, while eastern parts of the zone are windy and fair.

Zone 8: Alaska is fair and seasonal with scattered precipitation east. Hawaii is fair to partly cloudy and seasonal.

May 1–7, 1st Quarter Moon

Zone 1: Severe thunderstorms pop up across the zone, some strong with abundant precipitation.

Zone 2: Strong thunderstorms across the zone are accompanied by high winds, humidity, and abundant precipitation, especially in coastal areas; temperatures are seasonal to below.

Zone 3: Scattered thunderstorms occur across the zone, some severe with high winds and tornado potential; conditions are humid and temperatures are seasonal to below.

Zone 4: Western areas are windy and mostly fair with a chance for precipitation north. Central parts of the zone are overcast and cool, and some eastern areas see thunderstorms, some severe with tornado potential.

Zone 5: Weather is fair and windy west, and cloudy central and east with temperatures ranging from seasonal to below.

Zone 6: Western skies clear as cloudy, wet weather moves into central and eastern areas, which are cloudy with precipitation, some abundant.

Zone 7: Skies are mostly fair west with scattered showers north, central parts of the zone see precipitation, which is heavy in some locations, and eastern areas are fair, cool, and windy with a chance for precipitation.

Zone 8: Alaska is windy west with precipitation, partly cloudy central, and fair east. Hawaii is windy, fair, and seasonal.

May 9–16, Full Moon

Zone 1: Seasonal temperatures prevail. Fair conditions prevail across the zone, with scattered showers and thunderstorms.

Zone 2: Weather to the north is seasonal and partly cloudy, while southern areas are humid and variably cloudy with above normal temperatures and scattered thunderstorms, some strong.

Zone 3: Temperatures are seasonal to above across the zone, western areas are humid with scattered thunderstorms, and central and eastern parts of the zone are fair to partly cloudy with a chance for precipitation.

Zone 4: The western Plains see showers and thunderstorms with variably cloudiness, as do southeastern areas of the zone. Other areas are fair and dry.

Zone 5: The zone is windy with seasonal to above temperatures that spark thunderstorms, some severe with tornado potential; central and eastern areas are humid, and some central locations see abundant precipitation.

Zone 6: Skies are cloudy west with some abundant precipitation, and eastern and central parts of the zone are mostly fair and windy, with scattered thunderstorms central; temperatures are seasonal to below.

Zone 7: Northern coastal areas are cloudy with precipitation, while variable cloudiness prevails across the rest of the zone with scattered precipitation northeast.

Zone 8: Alaska is mostly fair, but windy east with precipitation, some abundant; temperatures are seasonal to below. Hawaii is fair, seasonal, and windy with scattered precipitation east.

May 17–23, 3rd Quarter Moon

Zone 1: Conditions are windy with scattered showers and thunderstorms, some with high winds; seasonal temperatures prevail.

Zone 2: The zone is windy and seasonal with strong scattered thunderstorms, which are more severe with tornado potential to the south.

Zone 3: Western skies are cloudy and windy with scattered precipitation; central and eastern areas are variably cloudy with scattered thunderstorms, some severe with high winds and tornado potential.

Zone 4: Western areas are windy, fair, and dry with rising temperatures midweek, while eastern areas are cloudy and seasonal with scattered precipitation.

Zone 5: Central areas are partly cloudy and humid, western areas fair and windy, and eastern areas are cloudy with scattered precipitation; temperatures are seasonal to above.

Zone 6: Western parts of the zone are windy, cool, and cloudy with scattered precipitation; central areas are fair and windy; eastern areas are stormy with abundant precipitation and flood potential.

Zone 7: Central and western parts of the zone are fair to partly cloudy and windy, while eastern areas are cloudy and windy with abundant precipitation; temperatures are seasonal to below.

Zone 8: Eastern and western Alaska are windy, with cooler temperatures scattered precipitation west, while some central parts of the state see abundant downfall. Locally heavy precipitation and windy conditions prevail in central and eastern Hawaii, and western areas are mostly fair.

May 24–29, New Moon

Zone 1: Fair skies prevail to the south, and northern areas see scattered thunderstorms.

Zone 2: Seasonal temperatures and windy conditions accompany cloudy skies across the zone, and southern areas are humid with scattered thunderstorms.

Zone 3: Western areas have a chance for precipitation, while central areas see strong thunderstorms. Eastern skies are cloudy, and temperatures are seasonal across the zone.

Zone 4: Temperatures range from seasonal to above across the zone, with high humidity and thunderstorms, some severe with tornado potential, in central areas. Western areas see abundant precipitation, and eastern areas are cooler and windy with scattered thunderstorms.

Zone 5: Western areas have a chance for showers, and some central and eastern areas see significant precipitation, high winds, and severe thunderstorms with tornado potential.

Zone 6: The zone is mostly fair and windy with seasonal temperatures, except for western areas, which see abundant precipitation in some areas.

Zone 7: Northern coastal areas are cloudy and cool with precipitation, while central areas see scattered showers. Southern coastal and eastern areas are fair to partly cloudy, and temperatures across the zone are seasonal to above.

Zone 8: Eastern Alaska is fair, central areas are windy, and western parts of the state are stormy. Hawaii is fair with windy conditions.

May 30–June 6, 1st Quarter Moon

Zone 1: The zone is cloudy with precipitation later in the week; cooler north, where precipitation is heaviest.

Zone 2: Northern areas are cloudy with precipitation, while southern parts of the zone see scattered thunderstorms, some severe with tornado potential, along with humid, windy conditions.

Zone 3: Western and central parts are humid and seasonal with thunderstorms, some severe with tornado potential; eastern areas are overcast with significant precipitation later in the week.

Zone 4: Strong scattered thunderstorms pop up in western areas and across the Plains, with temperatures that are seasonal to above; northwestern parts of the zone are cloudy with precipitation.

Zone 5: Central areas are fair to partly cloudy, western areas are windy with scattered thunderstorms, while eastern parts of the zone are humid with showers and thunderstorms; temperatures rise across the zone.

Zone 6: The zone is fair with temperatures ranging from seasonal to above; windy conditions to the east.

Zone 7: Southern coastal areas of the zone are windy, northern coastal areas are cooler with scattered precipitation, while central mountains see some cloudiness with precipitation. The desert is hot with rising humidity; fair skies prevail throughout eastern parts of the zone, which are windy.

Zone 8: Temperatures across Alaska are seasonal to below and fair except for the central part of the state, which is windy and stormy with abundant precipitation in some areas. Western Hawaii is fair, but central and eastern areas are stormy and windy with heavy precipitation.

June 7–14, Full Moon

Zone 1: Southern areas are windy with strong scattered thunderstorms, and northern areas see showers and thunderstorms; temperatures are seasonal.

Zone 2: Temperatures are seasonal to above with strong thunderstorms, some with tornado potential, across the zone.

Zone 3: Cloudy skies bring scattered showers and thunderstorms to western areas, while other parts of the zone, especially those to the east, see thunderstorms, some severe with high winds; temperatures are seasonal to above.

Zone 4: Western and eastern skies are mostly fair, while central areas of the zone are cloudy with scattered precipitation; temperatures are seasonal.

Zone 5: Skies are mostly fair west and central, with some cloudiness and scattered precipitation in central northern areas. Cloudy skies, scattered showers, and thunderstorms prevail to the east; temperatures are seasonal to above.

Zone 6: Western areas see partly cloudy skies and scattered precipitation, while central and eastern areas are windy and cloudy with some abundant precipitation as a front moves through the zone.

Zone 7: Desert areas are hot and dry, central areas see heavy precipitation, and western and northeastern parts of the zone are variably cloudy with scattered precipitation; temperatures are seasonal to above.

Zone 8: Alaska is mostly fair and seasonal with scattered precipitation east. Hawaii is fair and seasonal with scattered precipitation west.

June 15–21, 3rd Quarter Moon

Zone 1: Skies across the zone are cloudy with abundant precipitation in some areas.

Zone 2: Skies across the zone are mostly fair, with wind, humidity, with scattered thunderstorms.

Zone 3: Eastern areas are windy and mostly fair with scattered showers and thunderstorms, while western parts of the zone are humid and cloudy with locally heavy precipitation.

Zone 4: Central areas are fair and windy, western areas see showers and scattered thunderstorms, and eastern areas are cloudy and humid with showers and thunderstorms, some severe.

Zone 5: Western and central areas see thunderstorms, some severe, while eastern areas are fair to partly cloudy with scattered thunderstorms.

Zone 6: The zone is fair to partly cloudy and seasonal, but cooler to the east.

Zone 7: Fair skies prevail to the west, with more cloudiness in central and northeastern parts of the zone; desert areas are fair and windy; temperatures are seasonal.

Zone 8: Central and eastern Alaska are mostly fair and seasonal, while western areas are cloudy with significant precipitation. Eastern Hawaii is fair, cool, and humid, central parts of the state are stormy and then cooler, and western areas are mostly fair.

Summer 2009

Zone 1: Temperatures are seasonal to above average, and precipitation is normal.

Zone 2: Conditions are seasonal north; central and southern areas, although drier, see severe thunderstorms with temperatures ranging from seasonal to above average.

Zone 3: Temperatures are above average in all but eastern areas, which are cooler with average precipitation; western and central parts of the zone are drier, although with increased thunderstorm, tornado, and hurricane potential.

Zone 4: Western areas are windy and seasonal with precipitation ranging from average to below; the western and central Plains see more precipitation later in the season; and eastern areas are humid with temperatures ranging from seasonal to above.

Zone 5: Dry conditions prevail to the west, precipitation ranges from average to below in central areas, while eastern areas see more precipitation later in the season; temperatures are seasonal to above average.

Zone 6: Western and some central areas see abundant precipitation, while conditions are cooler east with precipitation ranging from average to above.

Zone 7: Northern coastal areas see abundant precipitation; southern coastal and central parts of the zone see precipitation ranging from average to below; eastern areas are windy and dry; temperatures are seasonal throughout the zone.

Zone 8: Alaska is seasonal with precipitation ranging from average to below. Fair weather prevails in Hawaii, where precipitation is average to below.

June 22–28, New Moon

Zone 1: The zone is cool and partly cloudy with showers and thunderstorms south.

Zone 2: Mostly fair skies with some scattered clouds prevail, and southern areas are humid.

Zone 3: Fair and breezy to the west, while central and eastern areas see more cloudiness with humidity and scattered thunderstorms.

Zone 4: The zone is fair to the east, with variable cloudiness in other areas and scattered precipitation central; temperatures are seasonal to below.

Zone 5: Cloudy skies produce scattered showers and thunderstorms across the zone, where temperatures are seasonal.

Zone 6: Conditions are fair and warm west and central, but cooler east with thunderstorms and high winds.

Zone 7: Northern coastal and central areas are fair and seasonal, and central, eastern, and southern coastal parts of the zone see scattered thunderstorms, some strong with high winds, and above normal temperatures.

Zone 8: Western and central Alaska sees precipitation, while eastern areas are mostly fair; temperatures are seasonal. A front brings showers and thunderstorms to western and central areas of Hawaii, some with locally heavy precipitation, and conditions are seasonal and humid.

June 29–July 6, 1st Quarter Moon

Zone 1: The zone is fair to partly cloudy and seasonal with scattered showers north.

Zone 2: The zone is seasonal and humid with scattered showers.

Zone 3: Western areas have severe thunderstorms with tornado potential; central and eastern areas see scattered precipitation; temperatures are seasonal and the zone is humid.

Zone 4: Much of the zone has strong thunderstorms, some severe with tornado potential.

Zone 5: Seasonal temperatures and humidity accompany severe thunderstorms across much of the zone; some are severe with tornado potential in central and eastern areas.

Zone 6: Western areas are cloudy with abundant precipitation as a front moves through, bringing windy conditions and strong thunderstorms to central and eastern areas later in the week.

Zone 7: Northern coastal areas see heavy precipitation and strong thunderstorms, which moves into central parts of the zone the end of the week. Southern coastal areas have a chance for showers, and eastern areas are fair.

Zone 8: Alaska is variably cloudy and seasonal with scattered precipitation. Hawaii sees scattered precipitation accompanying seasonal temperatures and fair to partly cloudy skies.

July 7–14, Full Moon

Zone 1: The zone has cloudy skies, high humidity, showers, and thunderstorms, which are strongest to the north with some heavy precipitation.

Zone 2: The zone is humid with showers and thunderstorms, some strong in southern areas. Cloudy skies prevail to the north.

Zone 3: Eastern areas are cloudy with scattered thunderstorms and locally heavy precipitation, possibly from a tropical storm; the rest of the zone is windy with variable cloudiness and precipitation in some areas.

Zone 4: The zone is variably cloudy with showers west, and high humidity and severe thunderstorms with tornado potential in the central Plains and east, where some areas see heavy precipitation.

Zone 5: Areas to the west are mostly fair with a chance for precipitation, while central and eastern parts of the zone are cloudy and humid with severe thunderstorms with tornado potential and some heavy precipitation, possibly from a tropical storm.

Zone 6: Western areas are windy with some locally heavy precipitation, central parts of the zone are cloudy with precipitation, and eastern areas are fair to partly cloudy with scattered precipitation.

Zone 7: Northern coastal areas are cloudy and windy with precipitation, and southern coastal parts of the zone are variably cloudy; central areas see precipitation, some heavy; and eastern areas are mostly fair with a chance for precipitation; temperatures are seasonal to above.

Zone 8: Central Alaska is stormy with high winds, and central and eastern areas are windy with scattered precipitation central. Hawaii is windy and variably cloudy with scattered precipitation.

July 15–20, 3rd Quarter Moon

Zone 1: The zone is humid, cloudy, and seasonal with scattered showers.

Zone 2: Much of the zone is windy with scattered thunderstorms, some severe south with heavy precipitation, high winds, and high humidity.

Zone 3: Western parts of the zone are cloudy with scattered precipitation, while central and eastern areas have high humidity and strong thunderstorms with high winds; temperatures are seasonal to above average.

Zone 4: Eastern areas are fair to partly cloudy and humid, western areas are windy with scattered thunderstorms, and the Plains are cloudy with precipitation, some locally heavy.

Zone 5: Western parts of the zone have scattered thunderstorms, while central areas see severe thunderstorms, while eastern areas are cloudy with precipitation later in the week; temperatures are seasonal.

Zone 6: Skies range from fair and windy in the west to partly cloudy central to cloudy east with scattered showers; temperatures are seasonal to above.

Zone 7: The zone is fair west and central, and humid east with more cloudiness and scattered precipitation; temperatures are seasonal to above.

Zone 8: Much of Alaska is seasonal and fair to partly cloudy with showers and cooler temperatures east. Hawaii is windy and mostly fair and seasonal.

July 21–27, New Moon

Zone 1: Conditions are windy with strong thunderstorms, and some areas see heavy precipitation.

Zone 2: Strong thunderstorms, some with heavy precipitation, prevail across the zone, possibly because of a tropical storm that moves north along the coast.

Zone 3: Scattered thunderstorms are possible to the west, which is mostly fair and hot; central and eastern areas see showers and scattered thunderstorms, with some areas receiving abundant precipitation later in the week.

Zone 4: Temperatures are seasonal to above across the zone and eastern areas are hot and humid; central and western parts of the zone see showers and thunderstorms, with locally heavy precipitation in some areas.

Zone 5: Areas to the west are cloudy with precipitation, some heavy; central areas are fair; eastern areas are humid with scattered precipitation. Temperatures are seasonal to above.

Zone 6: Western areas are windy and cloudy with showers, while central and eastern parts of the zone see scattered showers and thunderstorms; temperatures are seasonal; eastern areas are windy.

Zone 7: Showers and thunderstorms prevail across much of the zone, which is windy with seasonal temperatures and variable cloudiness; eastern areas see more clouds.

Zone 8: Western Alaska is stormy and then cooler; eastern areas are fair; central parts of the state are windy with precipitation. Hawaii is mostly fair with temperatures seasonal to above and scattered thunderstorms east.

July 28–August 4, 1st Quarter Moon

Zone 1: Much of the zone is windy and fair with temperatures ranging from seasonal to above and strong thunderstorms later in the week.

Zone 2: Areas to the south are mostly fair and dry, while northern areas see strong scattered thunderstorms and high humidity; temperatures are seasonal to above.

Zone 3: Variable cloudiness prevails in central and eastern areas with scattered showers and thunderstorms, and eastern parts of the zone see abundant precipitation in some areas and strong thunderstorms with tornado potential.

Zone 4: The Plains and eastern areas of the zone see severe thunderstorms with tornado potential; western areas are variably cloudy; temperatures are seasonal to above average.

Zone 5: Showers and cloudy skies prevail to the west, while central and eastern areas of the zone are stormy and cloudy with some abundant precipitation, possibly from a tropical storm or hurricane.

Zone 6: Areas to the west are fair and cool; central areas see scattered precipitation, and eastern portions of the zone are variably cloudy with scattered thunderstorms; temperatures are seasonal.

Zone 7: Western skies are fair, with scattered showers central, and scattered thunderstorms east; temperatures range from seasonal to above in eastern parts of the zone.

Zone 8: Alaskan skies are stormy east, and mostly fair west and central, with seasonal temperatures. Hawaii sees scattered precipitation and is mostly fair, humid, and seasonal.

August 5–12, Full Moon

Zone 1: Cloudy skies and thunderstorms prevail across the zone.

Zone 2: The zone is windy with a chance for precipitation, and southern areas are very humid.

Zone 3: Mostly fair and windy, with a chance for precipitation.

Zone 4: Western areas are fair to partly cloudy with a chance for precipitation; the central and eastern Plains see precipitation, mostly north and some locally heavy; eastern areas are mostly fair; and temperatures range from seasonal to below.

Zone 5: Temperatures are seasonal to below across the zone, western and central areas are fair to partly cloudy with scattered precipitation, and eastern parts of the zone see precipitation, some locally heavy.

Zone 6: Variable cloudiness and precipitation prevail across the zone, which is cool, and central areas see more cloudiness with strong thunderstorms.

Zone 7: Northern coastal areas are mostly fair and windy with a chance for precipitation, central areas see scattered thunderstorms, and southern coastal and eastern parts of the zone are mostly fair and dry; temperatures are seasonal to above.

Zone 8: Western and central Alaska are stormy and then much cooler, and eastern areas are mostly fair after precipitation early in the week. Hawaii is mostly fair with seasonal temperatures.

August 13–19, 3rd Quarter Moon

Zone 1: Severe thunderstorms could be the result of a tropical storm, as cloudy skies prevail and some areas see abundant precipitation.

Zone 2: Central and southern areas see scattered precipitation, and northern areas are cloudy with abundant precipitation in some areas, possibly from a tropical storm.

Zone 3: Western and central areas are mostly fair and seasonal, and eastern parts of the zone are cloudy with significant precipitation, possibly from a tropical storm.

Zone 4: The zone is variably cloudy, hot, and humid. Potential for strong thunderstorms with tornado potential and abundant precipitation in the western and central Plains; northwestern areas are seasonal and partly cloudy, and eastern parts of the zone are fair, windy, and humid.

Zone 5: Western and central areas are hot and humid, central parts of the zone see strong thunderstorms with abundant precipitation with tornado potential; eastern areas are fair to partly cloudy, humid, and cooler.

Zone 6: Western areas are fair and breezy, central areas are partly cloudy with scattered precipitation, and eastern areas see strong thunderstorms; temperatures range from seasonal to above.

Zone 7: Western and central parts of the zone are windy and fair to partly cloudy with scattered precipitation, while eastern areas see thunderstorms, some strong with high winds; temperatures are seasonal to above average.

Zone 8: Central Alaska is windy, eastern areas see scattered precipitation, and western parts of the state are stormy; temperatures are seasonal to below. Western parts of Hawaii see severe thunderstorms, possibly from a tropical storm, and temperatures range from seasonal to above across the zone.

August 20–26, New Moon

Zone 1: Southern areas are windy with thunderstorms later in the week, while northern areas are cloudy with precipitation, some abundant.

Zone 2: The zone is variably cloudy north and windy with strong thunderstorms later in the week; skies are cloudy to the south with severe thunderstorms.

Zone 3: Western areas are windy with scattered precipitation, while central and eastern areas see strong thunderstorms.

Zone 4: Central parts of the zone see precipitation, as do eastern areas later in the week, while western areas are fair and seasonal.

Zone 5: The zone is mostly fair to partly cloudy, with increasing clouds and precipitation east; central and eastern areas are humid.

Zone 6: Skies are fair to partly cloudy east with scattered precipitation; central and eastern parts of the zone are windy with strong thunderstorms as a front advances, and temperatures are seasonal to below.

Zone 7: Coastal and central areas are windy with precipitation, northern coastal areas are stormy, central parts of the zone see strong thunderstorms later in the week, and eastern areas are fair to partly cloudy with scattered precipitation north.

Zone 8: Alaska is mostly fair with scattered precipitation east. Hawaii is humid with variable cloudiness and showers central and east.

August 27–September 3, 1st Quarter Moon

Zone 1: Northern areas are cloudy and cold with precipitation; southern areas are partly cloudy and seasonal.

Zone 2: The zone is fair and seasonal with a chance for precipitation north.

Zone 3: Western areas see scattered showers and thunderstorms, and central and eastern areas are fair.

Zone 4: Windy conditions, variable cloudiness, showers, and scattered thunderstorms prevail across much of the zone, with abundant precipitation and flood potential in some areas of the Plains; eastern areas are mostly fair and warmer.

Zone 5: Western areas are windy with variable cloudiness and strong thunderstorms; central and eastern areas see cloudy skies, thunderstorms, and showers, some of which are locally heavy; eastern areas are cooler later in the week.

Zone 6: Central and eastern parts of the zone see scattered precipitation, eastern areas are windy and cooler, and western areas are fair to partly cloudy and windy.

Zone 7: Western and central areas are cloudy with precipitation, while eastern parts of the zone are very windy with scattered thunderstorms, some severe.

Zone 8: Central Alaska is stormy and cold with high winds and overcast skies, while western and eastern areas are mostly fair. Temperatures are seasonal to below in Hawaii; skies are fair in central and eastern areas, and western areas are cloudy with precipitation later in the week.

September 4–10, Full Moon

Zone 1: Conditions are fair and windy with temperatures seasonal to below across the zone.

Zone 2: Central and southern areas are fair to partly cloudy with scattered thunderstorms; northern areas see showers and thunderstorms, some with locally heavy precipitation; temperatures are seasonal to below average.

Zone 3: Showers and thunderstorms, some strong with abundant precipitation, prevail across the zone, which is windy and has seasonal to below average temperatures.

Zone 4: Western and central areas are fair to partly cloudy with scattered precipitation; eastern areas are windy with precipitation centered south; temperatures are seasonal to below average.

Zone 5: The zone is variably cloudy with temperatures ranging from seasonal to below; eastern areas are windy with an increased chance for precipitation.

Zone 6: High winds accompany a storm front that moves into western areas, while central and eastern parts of the zone are mostly fair and seasonal.

Zone 7: Increasing cloudiness in northern coastal areas brings precipitation later in the week, and the rest of the zone is fair to partly cloudy with scattered precipitation east.

Zone 8: Much of Alaska is fair to partly cloudy and seasonal, but eastern areas are windy and stormy. Hawaii is fair and seasonal with a chance for precipitation.

September 11–17, 3rd Quarter Moon

Zone 1: The zone is seasonal and fair to partly cloudy with scattered precipitation.

Zone 2: Northern areas are cloudy with precipitation, and central and southern parts of the zone are fair to partly cloudy with scattered thunderstorms.

Zone 3: Western areas are variably cloudy with scattered precipitation, central and eastern areas are fair to partly cloudy, and eastern areas are much cooler.

Zone 4: Western and central parts of the zone see strong thunderstorms, some with tornado potential, eastern areas are cloudy with scattered precipitation, and temperatures are seasonal to above.

Zone 5: Much of the zone is humid with temperatures seasonal to above and strong thunderstorms with tornado potential west and central.

Zone 6: Eastern parts of the zone are fair and windy, while western and central areas are cloudy and cool with abundant precipitation in some locations.

Zone 7: Western and central areas are cloudy with abundant precipitation, while eastern areas are fair to partly cloudy, windy, and seasonal to above.

Zone 8: Central areas are stormy with abundant precipitation; and eastern and western areas are mostly fair. Hawaii is seasonal and humid with precipitation, which is heaviest in eastern areas.

Autumn 2009

Zone 1: Temperatures are seasonal, and precipitation is average to below.

Zone 2: Precipitation is average, and temperatures are seasonal to above.

Zone 3: Some areas in western and central parts of the zone see abundant precipitation, and conditions are drier east; temperatures are seasonal to below.

Zone 4: Precipitation is average to below and temperatures cold in all but eastern areas, which are more seasonal with precipitation ranging from average to above.

Zone 5: Precipitation is average to above, with temperatures ranging from seasonal to below; western areas are colder.

Zone 6: Precipitation is average to below across zone, with significant storms accompanying high winds in the mountains; temperatures are seasonal to below.

Zone 7: Northern coastal areas are very windy with major storms, while much of the rest of the zone is dry with precipitation levels ranging from average to below; temperatures are seasonal.

Zone 8: Eastern Alaska sees above average precipitation, cold temperatures, and major storms, while central and western areas are seasonal with average precipitation. Hawaii is seasonal with average precipitation.

September 18–25, New Moon

Zone 1: The zone is windy and seasonal with variable cloudiness and scattered precipitation.

Zone 2: Northern areas see scattered precipitation, and central and southern areas are mostly fair with temperatures ranging from seasonal to above.

Zone 3: Western parts of the zone see scattered precipitation; central areas are mostly fair; eastern areas are cloudier and windy with scattered precipitation.

Zone 4: Stormy conditions prevail west and in the western Plains, while central and eastern areas are fair to partly cloudy and windy with scattered precipitation; temperatures are seasonal to below.

Zone 5: Temperatures are seasonal to below, eastern skies are fair, and western and central areas are stormy.

Zone 6: The zone is mostly fair and seasonal, with showers west later in the week.

Zone 7: Northern coastal areas see showers, some locally heavy, later in the week, and the rest of the zone is fair with temperatures ranging from seasonal to above.

Zone 8: Alaska is fair and seasonal. Temperatures are seasonal to above under fair skies in Hawaii.

September 26–October 3, 1st Quarter Moon

Zone 1: The zone is windy and fair south, and partly cloudy north with scattered precipitation; temperatures are seasonal.

Zone 2: Northern areas are fair to partly cloudy with scattered precipitation, while central and southern areas are stormy, possibly from a tropical storm; temperatures are seasonal to below.

Zone 3: Western skies are fair to partly cloudy; central parts of the zone are windy and cool with precipitation; eastern areas are fair.

Zone 4: Eastern and western areas are mostly fair with more cloudiness northwest, and central parts of the zone are windy and cool with precipitation.

Zone 5: Fair weather prevails to the west, while central and eastern areas see precipitation; temperatures are seasonal.

Zone 6: The zone is variably cloudy with scattered precipitation west and central, with increasing clouds and abundant precipitation east later in the week.

Zone 7: Eastern areas see more cloudiness with abundant precipitation in some areas, while western and central parts of the zone are mostly fair with scattered thunderstorms.

Zone 8: Western Alaska is stormy, and central and eastern parts of the state are mostly fair and seasonal. Hawaii is fair to partly cloudy, humid, and seasonal.

October 4–10, Full Moon

Zone 1: The zone is cloudy, windy, and cool with precipitation.

Zone 2: Wind and variable cloudiness bring precipitation to much of the zone.

Zone 3: The zone is fair to partly cloudy with seasonal temperatures, windy conditions central, and scattered precipitation central and east.

Zone 4: Variable cloudiness prevails across the zone; western areas are cool and windy; eastern areas see scattered precipitation; and central and eastern areas are warmer with temperatures ranging from seasonal to above.

Zone 5: The zone is fair to partly cloudy temperatures seasonal to above.

Zone 6: Western parts of the zone are windy and fair, while central areas see diminishing precipitation that moves east, where stormy conditions bring cooler temperatures.

Zone 7: Western skies are fair, while central mountains see precipitation, and eastern areas are cloudy, windy, and stormy with abundant precipitation in some areas and cool temperatures.

Zone 8: Central Alaska is cloudy with precipitation, and eastern and western areas are fair with temperatures ranging from seasonal to below. Hawaii is seasonal with variable cloudiness and scattered precipitation.

October 11–17, 3rd Quarter Moon

Zone 1: Stormy weather brings temperatures ranging from seasonal to below, and some areas receive abundant precipitation.

Zone 2: Northern areas are fair and windy, as central and southern parts of the zone experience mostly fair and windy conditions, with strong thunderstorms in some locations.

Zone 3: The zone is mostly fair and seasonal, with windy conditions in the central areas.

Zone 4: Western areas are cloudy and cool with precipitation, central parts of the zone are fair to partly cloudy, cool, and windy, and eastern areas are fair and seasonal.

Zone 5: Central parts of the zone are cloudy with some locally heavy precipitation; eastern areas are windy and fair to partly cloudy; western areas are partly cloudy with scattered precipitation.

Zone 6: Conditions are fair and windy west, while central and eastern areas are fair to partly cloudy, windy, and cooler with scattered precipitation.

Zone 7: Much of the zone sees precipitation, which is heavier east under windy, cloudy skies; temperatures are seasonal to below.

Zone 8: Central Alaska is stormy, and eastern and western areas are fair and windy. Western and central Hawaii are cloudy with precipitation, some abundant, as eastern areas parts of zone are fair and seasonal.

October 18–24, New Moon

Zone 1: The zone is windy and cool with more cloudiness north.

Zone 2: Northern areas are mostly fair with scattered precipitation later in the week, and central and southern areas are windy with more cloudiness and scattered precipitation; temperatures are seasonal to below.

Zone 3: Western areas are fair and seasonal, and central and eastern areas are cooler, windy, and cloudy.

Zone 4: Precipitation in western areas moves into the western Plains, and central and eastern areas are mostly fair and windy with scattered precipitation in some locations; temperatures are seasonal.

Zone 5: Western and central parts of the zone see showers, followed by clearing, and eastern areas are fair and windy; temperatures are seasonal to above.

Zone 6: Western skies are cloudy and windy, followed by clear weather, and central and eastern parts of the zone are cloudy, windy, and much cooler with scattered precipitation.

Zone 7: Temperatures are seasonal to below, and scattered precipitation and wind prevail across much of the zone along with variable cloudiness.

Zone 8: Eastern areas see precipitation later in the week, central parts of the state are windy and partly cloudy, and western skies are fair; temperatures are seasonal. Hawaii is breezy and fair to partly cloudy with temperatures ranging from seasonal to below.

October 25–November 1, 1st Quarter Moon

Zone 1: Southern areas are windy with scattered precipitation, and northern skies are fair to partly cloudy.

Zone 2: The zone is humid with variable cloudiness and precipitation, which is abundant in some areas.

Zone 3: Temperatures range from seasonal to below, central and western skies are partly cloudy, and some eastern areas receive abundant precipitation.

Zone 4: Western skies are windy and partly cloudy, central areas are windy with precipitation, and eastern parts of the zone are cloudy; temperatures are seasonal to below.

Zone 5: The zone is windy with variable cloudiness, precipitation central and east, and temperatures seasonal to below.

Zone 6: Western parts of the zone are fair to partly cloudy, as central and eastern areas see precipitation when a front moves through the zone; temperatures are seasonal.

Zone 7: Much of the zone sees showers, but skies are mostly partly cloudy with seasonal temperatures.

Zone 8: Central and eastern Alaska are partly cloudy, western skies are fair, and temperatures are seasonal. Hawaii is breezy, fair, and seasonal.

November 2–8, Full Moon

Zone 1: Fair skies prevail south, and northern areas are windy and cold with precipitation.

Zone 2: The zone is fair to partly cloudy with a chance for precipitation central and south.

Zone 3: Eastern skies are fair, while western and central areas are partly cloudy with scattered precipitation.

Zone 4: Central areas are cloudy with locally heavy precipitation, eastern areas are partly cloudy, and western parts of the zone see scattered precipitation; temperatures are seasonal.

Zone 5: Temperatures range from seasonal to below along with variable cloudiness and precipitation across the zone; locally heavy downfall is possible in central areas.

Zone 6: Western areas are variably cloudy with precipitation, and central and eastern parts of the zone are cloudy and windy with scattered precipitation.

Zone 7: Seasonal temperatures prevail across the zone, which is variably cloudy and windy with scattered precipitation.

Zone 8: Eastern Alaska is cloudy and cold with precipitation, and central and western areas are fair to partly cloudy and seasonal. Hawaii is mostly fair and windy, with a chance for precipitation.

November 9–15, 3rd Quarter Moon

Zone 1: The zone is windy and cold with precipitation.

Zone 2: Northern and central coastal areas see precipitation, and the rest of the zone is partly cloudy and seasonal.

Zone 3: Scattered precipitation accompanies variable cloudiness and seasonal temperatures.

Zone 4: Eastern areas are windy and partly cloudy, and central parts of the zone are cloudy and windy with precipitation, some abundant.

Zone 5: The zone is cloudy with precipitation as a front moves across the area.

Zone 6: Weather is fair and seasonal west, and cold with increasing cloudiness and precipitation central and east.

Zone 7: Central and eastern areas see precipitation, and eastern areas are fair and windy.

Zone 8: Western and central Alaska are windy, cold, and fair; eastern areas are cloudy with precipitation. Hawaii is fair with temperatures ranging from seasonal to above average.

New Moon, November 16–23

Zone 1: The zone is cloudy, cold, and stormy.

Zone 2: Cloudy skies accompany precipitation, wind, and cold temperatures.

Zone 3: Western and central areas are fair to partly cloudy and seasonal, while eastern parts of the zone are cold and cloudy with precipitation.

Zone 4: Cloudy skies prevail to the west, and central and eastern areas are fair; temperatures are seasonal to above.

Zone 5: Western areas are windy, cloudy, and cool, and central and eastern areas are fair to partly cloudy with increasing winds and scattered precipitation.

Zone 6: Precipitation is the norm across the zone, with heaviest downfall central and east under cloudy, windy skies.

Zone 7: Much of the zone sees precipitation, some locally heavy, with cloudy, windy skies and cool temperatures.

Zone 8: Western and central Alaska are stormy with abundant downfall in some areas, and eastern areas are fair. Hawaii has seasonal to below temperatures with cloudy skies and precipitation.

November 24–December 1, 1st Quarter Moon

Zone 1: The zone is windy and cloudy with precipitation, some abundant to the north.

Zone 2: Temperatures are seasonal to below with variably cloudiness and precipitation central and south, especially in coastal areas.

Zone 3: Conditions are fair to partly cloudy and seasonal, but cooler east with scattered precipitation.

Zone 4: The zone is fair to partly cloudy and windy, with cold temperatures and precipitation east.

Zone 5: Temperatures range from seasonal to below under fair to partly cloudy skies and scattered precipitation.

Zone 6: Western areas are fair to partly cloudy and cool, and central and eastern areas have major storm potential with abundant precipitation.

Zone 7: Northern coastal and central areas are cold and stormy with high winds, southern coastal areas are cloudy, and eastern skies are variably cloudy with scattered precipitation.

Zone 8: Central Alaska sees abundant precipitation, western areas are stormy, and eastern areas are cloudy and seasonal. Cool temperatures and showers, some heavy, dominate Hawaii's forecast.

December 2–7, Full Moon

Zone 1: Temperatures are seasonal and skies fair to partly cloudy with scattered precipitation across the zone.

Zone 2: The zone is partly cloudy and seasonal with scattered precipitation.

Zone 3: Western areas are cold and stormy, central parts of the zone are cloudy with precipitation, and eastern areas are windy with scattered precipitation; temperatures are seasonal to below.

Zone 4: Windy, stormy conditions west move into central and eastern parts of the zone, with cold temperatures and some abundant precipitation north.

Zone 5: Central areas are cold with precipitation, eastern areas see increasing clouds and wind as a front moves in, and western skies are partly cloudy.

Zone 6: Eastern areas are fair with a warming trend, and western and central parts of the zone see precipitation.

Zone 7: Skies are partly cloudy west, and fair central and east, with temperatures seasonal to above.

Zone 8: Alaska is fair to partly cloudy and seasonal. Hawaii is windy with precipitation west and central, and fair skies and seasonal temperatures east.

December 8–15, 3rd Quarter Moon

Zone 1: The zone is partly cloudy with increasing cloudiness south as a front brings wind and precipitation; temperatures are seasonal to below.

Zone 2: Precipitation, some abundant, accompanies cloudy, windy, and cold conditions.

Zone 3: Cold temperatures dip far south, and the zone is cloudy with the heaviest precipitation to the east.

Zone 4: Western areas are windy with precipitation north; central areas are windy with precipitation, and eastern parts of the zone are cold and cloudy with scattered precipitation.

Zone 5: Precipitation in central areas moves east, western areas are fair and windy, and temperatures are seasonal.

Zone 6: Western and central skies are stormy with some abundant precipitation, eastern areas are cloudy, and temperatures are seasonal to below.

Zone 7: Southern coastal areas are stormy with strong thunderstorms, northern coastal and central areas see abundant precipitation, and eastern parts of the zone are fair to partly cloudy with scattered precipitation north.

Zone 8: Western Alaska is windy, stormy, and cold, while central and eastern areas are seasonal. Hawaii is fair and seasonal.

December 16–23, New Moon

Zone 1: The zone sees scattered precipitation, variable cloudiness, and seasonal temperatures.

Zone 2: The zone is windy and cloudy with precipitation, some abundant, especially in coastal areas, and temperatures are seasonal to below normal.

Zone 3: Much of the zone sees precipitation, with more cloudiness central and east; stormy skies south, and temperatures seasonal to below average.

Zone 4: Northwest areas are partly cloudy, western areas are fair, and central and eastern parts of the zone see precipitation, with stormy conditions north.

Zone 5: Eastern areas are windy and cold with precipitation, and the rest of the zone is fair and seasonal.

Zone 6: Stormy conditions prevail west, central areas are windy with precipitation, some abundant, and eastern areas are cloudy and windy.

Zone 7: Western and central areas are cloudy with abundant precipitation, and eastern skies are partly cloudy and windy with increasing cloudiness that brings precipitation.

Zone 8: Central Alaska is cold with precipitation; other areas are fair and seasonal. Hawaii is windy and cool with scattered precipitation.

December 24–31, 1st Quarter Moon

Zone 1: The zone is fair to partly cloudy and windy.

Zone 2: Central areas are stormy with high winds, northern areas are fair to partly cloudy, and southern parts of the zone are variably cloudy with precipitation; temperatures are seasonal to below.

Zone 3: Western and central areas are windy and stormy, central areas are partly cloudy, and temperatures are seasonal to below.

Zone 4: Western skies are fair and seasonal, and central and eastern areas are windy with precipitation.

Zone 5: Fair skies and windy conditions prevail west and central, while eastern areas are partly cloudy; temperatures are seasonal to below normal.

Zone 6: Central and eastern areas are partly cloudy with scattered precipitation, and western parts of the zone see significant precipitation; temperatures are seasonal to below normal.

Zone 7: Northern coastal areas see abundant precipitation, southern coastal and central areas are variably cloudy with scattered precipitation, and eastern areas are fair to partly cloudy with scattered precipitation north.

Zone 8: Alaska is seasonal with precipitation in central parts of the state. Hawaii is windy with scattered precipitation, variable cloudiness, and seasonal temperatures.

About the Author

Kris Brandt Riske holds professional certification from the American Federation of Astrologers (PMAFA). She has a master's degree in journalism and has authored several books, including Llewellyn's Complete Book of Astrology: The Easy Way to Learn Astrology *(2007) and* Astrometeorology: Planetary Power in Weather Forecasting *(AFA). Kris is studying meteorology as a student enrolled in Penn State University's Certificate in Weather Forecasting Program.*

Economic Forecast for 2009

By Dorothy J. Kovach

The Party's Over, it's time to call it a day. They've burst your pretty balloon and taken the Moon away.

~BETTY COMDEN

Money doesn't go away, it just moves around a lot. What we need to do is find where that money is. However, like all things in life, there is a catch. For close to a decade the money has been flowing out of this country at a pace that should have alarmed Americans a long time, ago. For several years now, a sort of dull disconnect has existed between the people of this country and the growing economic deficits, and what that deficit means to our future. On top of that, our leaders, starting in the executive branch, created a war that appears to be lining their own pockets. We can only hope that the next administration has the fiscal interests of the United States at heart. There is something wrong when those at the very highest reaches of the administration loudly proclaim "deficits no longer matter," while at the same time they invest against our own currency by loading up their personal portfolio with Euros.

Some call our current economic state a "recession," others call it "stagflation." I just call it "bearish." When will the Fed learn, that "what goes up must come down." Placing artificial means, from starting foreign wars to allowing interest rates to remain low for too long, in order to "stimulate" the economy will only delay the inevitable. When government tries to keep the good times going for too long, what you wind up with is the Weimar Republic, where a loaf of bread takes a bushel basket of money. Recessions are necessary evils, but they are not fun.

However, armed with the ways of the stars, we can step nimbly around the puddles. We can know what is coming ahead of time and become like inside traders. The great second-century astrologer Ptolemy said, "if one became skillful in the art of astrology, that he or she may evade the effects of the stars, once he or she knows their natures, and prepares to receive their effects." In market terms, there is always a boom happening someplace. Just knowing how the forces above intermingle can make the difference between making money and losing your shirt. When we learn the ways of the stars, we are far better equipped to navigate our way around any obstacles that may lurk in troubled waters ahead.

A bear market is generally defined as one in which stocks tend to drop for a prolonged period of time. During bear markets, there is a distinct trend to sell into every rally. We stand at the end of a long era of disinflation. This kept interest rates low as merchandise and goods flowed. Unfortunately, so few goods were produced in our own country that this liquidity has stimulated mega-deficits. After such a long spending spree, with nothing coming in, something had to give.

An era of frozen wages coupled with years of very low interest rates prompted many people who were strapped for money to dig into the equity in their homes. At the same time, many banks made very risky investments. This created a bubble in our economy, and when we have a bubble, there is only one place for it to go, and that is down. Unfortunately, since so many of the new jobs created in this country, from builders to loan brokers, were suckled at the breast of the real-estate industry, there are probably still more losses to come.

The economic news is all gloom and doom, revolving around the sub-prime issues, a slowing economy, a graying population with poor health care. But with all this negativity, there is also an undercurrent of optimism in the air. It is as if we, as a nation, have been driving around for the longest time in the dark, lost in a vast suburban subdivision, and we suddenly have found a highway. We don't know if the road will get us where we are going, but there is at least hope that with a new administration at the helm, we may finally get America back on the right fiscal course.

Inauguration Chart
The winds of change are in the air.

Unless, God forbid, something out of the ordinary happens, the next inauguration will take place at approximately noon on January 20, 2009. As of the time of this writing, (in 2007) we do not even know who will be the party nominee, much less, who will run against whom. Thus, I am not venturing to say who the next president will be at this time. Since the date and time are pretty much fixed, we can get some real insights into how the next administration will be, even if we don't know who the next president will be, however.

Whether we recognize it or not, each time a new president is sworn in, the entire financial aura of the United States is changed by the moment he or she swears to uphold the Constitution. Our financial wellbeing rests upon the strength of the inauguration chart. We can only hope the new president will have the people's interests at heart. Given the strong emphasis on idealism in the sign of Aquarius, we may hear much talk about reforming the system. Let's hope it is not just more rhetoric. After years of empty promises, Americans could be compared to the Howard Beale character in the movie Network who says: "I'm mad as hell, and I'm not going to take this anymore." Many are no longer willing to sit passively by and accept the status quo, given their juxtaposition next to the rabble rousing energy of Uranus. The last administration's answer to deficits and expensive wars was to run the treasury printing presses at full speed. This course has left our currency battered and bruised, and our treasury pretty bleak. It is pretty hard to make necessary changes, without the fiscal means to do so.

The Good News

After being down for the count, it is not yet time to give up on the dollar. Once proper fiscal policies, like "pay-go," are put back in place, there is every reason to believe that we may actually see the dollar make a come back in the months and years ahead. However, don't expect that it is going to be easy for the dollar to regain strength. It is very easy to get into debt, and very difficult to get out of it. Thus, Americans must be prepared to make some serious sacrifices. The long era of liquidity is coming to a close, and money will be tighter. With our equity tapped out, it will not be as easy to live off our houses. Not only that, we can expect to receive less in the way of dividends, too. Above all, we will probably see a rise in income taxes. Although, much of the pain may be reserved for those making more than $200,000 a year, it is unlikely that those in the lower income bracket will come away unscathed.

While it won't be a bed of roses for the new president, the people of the United States are so yearning for change that any new ideas will be welcomed. People are restless, and many are skeptical and more than a few are skeptical anybody in elected office even cares. Everything seems to hinge on whether this president is really serious about making changes in the war in Iraq and reforms in health care. America is a nation of employees. Stagnant wages, poor to no health care, and dwindling assets have left many frustrated and worried that the American dream is no more. To win the hearts and minds of the people, this president will need more than empty promises about health care. Unfortunately, as we know, it is very difficult to make sweeping changes when the treasury is in such disarray. There may be some fiscal pain ahead.

Jupiter and Saturn

Even with all the best intentions of the government, the truth is that citizens' actions alone have a limited ability to get the country back on sound financial footing. When it comes to the economy, it is the two titans of business, Jupiter and Saturn, that influence our financial destinies. Where they are placed and how they interact with other planets will spell the difference between recovery and recession.

Overview of Jupiter in Aquarius

Jupiter is the king of expansion, and when he is strong (by sign and position), the stock market goes up. Jupiter stays in one sign per year. During that time, the sector most closely associated with

the sign Jupiter is in has a mini bull run. In 2009, Jupiter will be in the sign that has one foot in the future, Aquarius. While in Aquarius, Jupiter will likely sew the seeds of hope for a brighter tomorrow. Aquarius is perhaps the most innovative of the signs. Therefore, we can expect that there will be more than a few great ideas out there. With some effort, we can hope that there will be more incentives to unravel the Gordian knot of our massive dependence on oil, and the byproduct of that dependency—global warming.

Air-sign Aquarius is one of the so-called "intellectual" signs of the zodiac. This means there may be some hope for our technical industries, including the computer industry; however, we will not see a return to the good old 90s, but instead a sense of reality returns to the market place. Throughout Jupiter's time in Aquarius, Jupiter's antiscion will land in the medical sign of Scorpio. We may see the lifting of the stem cell ban, as religion finally takes a back seat to science.

When in Aquarius, Jupiter has always been associated with inventions and inventors, particularly in the electronic field. Thomas Alva Edison was an Aquarius. Aquarius is especially related to electronics. Hopefully, we might see some potential breakthroughs in harnessing electricity for use in travel. Look for more positive innovations in the realm of electric cars from auto manufacturers. With a little bit of luck, more incentives will be made available so that we can become less dependent on gasoline, using electricity instead, or a combination of the two.

There is no field riper for change than the energy industry. Whether Jupiter's stay in Aquarius will help us tackle the oil shortage and global warming is anybody's guess, but it will not be for lack of effort. Look for green industries to see more growth, as well as alternative energy. There is some evidence that the cost of solar power may come down. Unfortunately, while in Aquarius, Jupiter is heading toward a conjunction with the largest of the outer planets, Neptune.

In modern times, we have given Neptune charge of oil. If such a large amount of money is being sent to some far away country just to get you to work, there is something seriously wrong. Some might interpret this as oil prices going even higher. This may indeed be the case—at first. However, energy has been on a run for some time. Once the contact between Jupiter and Neptune is made, we may begin to see energy reach peak prices. Hopefully, after this contact, we will begin to see more, rather than less ,supply come on to the market. This may bring hope for reduced prices toward the end of the cycle.

Aquarius has more to do with aeronautics than any other sign. While the United States economy has declined in recent years, it has been boom times in places like Saudi Arabia and China. Using less fuel than its closest competitor, Boeing may be in the right place at the right time.

Big Brother has his eye in the sky on you! In its negative side, Aquarius tends to expand controlling power of the central government. When we see Jupiter in Aquarius coupled with Neptune, and add a little dash of Pluto in Capricorn, it may mean big changes to our freedom. We got used to watching our enemies with the eye in the sky, but now those satellites will be monitoring us! In May of 2007, the Bush administration tentatively created an office to spy on us from the skies. Of course, officially, this office was created to coordinate with Homeland Security to protect us in times of crisis and terrorism. Yet, if Congress enacts this legislation, it will make it legal for Big Brother to watch your every move when you're out of doors, thus making the United States one of the most monitored nations in the world. Generally speaking, once created, such entities are rarely withdrawn. Still, investors will always make a profit. Thus, look for Boeing (BA), Google (GOOG) and Satellite Applications International (SAI) to benefit greatly from this homeland-spy program.

Unfortunately, Jupiter is only working at partial potency when in Aquarius, because he comes under the domination of the bearish Saturn. Even the greatest idea can go nowhere without funding. The sub-prime/derivative disaster has left lenders suspicious. In such a climate, whatever growth we can expect in markets will not come quickly, or easily. In fact, growth may not come at all if sensible fiscal policies are not put back in place in Washington.

Overview of Saturn in Virgo

Saturn is there to take away Jupiter's optimism, and Saturn stays for two-and-a-half years in each sign. During that time, as Jupiter's economic opposite, Saturn brings a sense of fear and loathing to whatever sign it is placed. We all remember the dotcoms bust in 2000, when Saturn was in technology-loving Gemini. Well, Saturn will be in Virgo, the sign of health, until the very end of October 2009.

Virgo is also the sign of small farm animals and household pets. With Saturn in Virgo, we will need to be especially vigilant about the companies we use to feed and care for our pets. Puppy mills and tainted dog food may be just the tip of the iceberg for pets, and feeding farm animals gets more expensive by the day due to the high cost of energy.

Saturn has to do with reality and Virgo has to do with accountability. New regulations have been enacted to make banks more transparent in their reporting practices. In other words, banks will no longer be able to report their assets based upon computer-driven models and past performance. Instead, regulations (FASB 157) will force banks to use actual market prices, which means that banks will have to reveal the true value of their assets. Many banks have been shifting capital from one asset class to another to hide losses. Given the greater public scrutiny, we may see more banks and funds go under.

Some banks have been "cooking their books" with million-dollar write downs for so long that they have come to think of it as "business as usual." Not any longer! As Warren Buffet says, "we will see 'which banks have been swimming with their clothes off.'" Thus, banking stocks may leave something to be desired, with the exception of Goldman Sachs, which seems, once again, ahead of the game. While this stock is very pricey, there are even silver linings in a down market, in that 70 percent of the market moves with the trend. Thus, look for dips in the market as buying opportunities for this excellent corporation.

The healthcare system in the United States has been under constant criticism for decades. When people have to choose between chemotherapy or their home ownership, there can be little doubt that the system is broken. The new administration and congress must get truly serious about providing quality, affordable health care for all citizens. However, talk is cheap. Health care has been the main platform of every single Democratic presidential candidacy since 1952!

We all know that enormous deficits have built up over the past three decades. How a country will be able to provide health care without money is anybody's guess. Part of the problem with the current system is the enormous costs of keeping the books. A doctor needs an entire staff to comply with government and insurance regulations, which is expensive. With all of the negative talk about health care, we may want to take a serious look at lightening holdings in health-maintenance stocks, if we own such. Given that Saturn will be moving into opposition with Uranus, and also considering that many drug patents are about to expire, we may not want to be holding big pharmacy stocks at this time.

Jupiter in Aquarius and Saturn in Virgo

Both Aquarius and Virgo are what astrologers refer to as "human signs." With Jupiter in Aquarius and Saturn in Virgo, we can expect the human element to return to government. We will hear a lot about change and cleaning up the system. However, what is good for the people is not always good for the marketplace because markets dislike anything having to do with "reform." This is because the market interprets scrutiny as restriction. Therefore, until some of the reforms are properly digested there may be some hurdles to overcome before American markets expand.

It is hard for Jupiter to grow when in Aquarius, because he is completely under the rule of Saturn. Intriguingly enough, when Jupiter and Saturn are in these signs, the reform principle is held in check because of the bottom line. Jupiter in Aquarius sets about trying to implement massive reform. Meanwhile, Saturn in earthy Virgo demands to know who is going to pay for it. These conflicting energies do make for governmental gridlock, which big business and the market prefer.

Historically, the combination of Jupiter in Aquarius and Saturn in Virgo means that people want to improve circumstances, but they have different means of doing so. Jupiter wants to promote the Big Picture, and criticizes Saturn for not seeing the forest for the trees. Ultimately, this conflict means that most proposals are thwarted. What we get are the seeds of tomorrow's reform, which brings about incongruities, like Belva Lockwood arguing before the U.S. Supreme Court, even though in most states she would not have the right to vote!

Jupiter and Saturn not only influence markets, but they also have influence over who will be sitting in the White House. The Democrats are the older of the two parties, and thus are ruled by the planet of age, Saturn. Meanwhile, with the elephant as their symbol, it is fitting that Jupiter will represent the Republican Party. What astrologers do is measure the respective strengths of each of the planets to determine who will win. Given that Jupiter is in Aquarius, a sign dominated by Saturn, this implies that we may see a Democrat sitting in the White House in 2009.

A Word on China

As of this writing we have seen the power shift in global power. Even though the United States is still a very strong nation, eight years of mounting deficits and rising energy costs have damaged the U.S. economy. For much of recent history China has focused on her own economy with a gusto that probably has never been witnessed in modern time. More countries are turning to China to negotiate economic conditions, and also foreign treaty disputes. As time goes on, we'll see China, not the United States, calling the shots in global affairs and in the marketplace.

With a trillion dollars in surplus, China is the indisputable manufacturer to the world. China has become the "darling" in investment portfolios. For the past few years the Chinese people have worked very hard to bring about the China Miracle we see

today. As a result of this, the Chinese market has been on fire. In one day alone, Petrol China became more valuable than Exxon Mobile! When everybody wants to own a piece of the action, the price goes up. As scarcity develops, the demand increases and prices skyrocket. As a result of this increased demand, bubbles develop. However, as we have seen in the United States—when tech got hot in the 1980s and 90s, followed by a booming real-estate market—bubbles burst.

What we are going to watch now is that instead of being the "worker" to the world, China will become "rich." This is problematic for America. After a period marked by a friendliness between nations, those who trade with China will be in a difficult position—finding, for example, that lead painted on our children's toys was not just an honest mistake. In a sense, we are now entering a new thirty-year-cycle, which returns us to one based on mistrust, only now they will be our secret enemies, rather than the out in the open enemies that they were in the past. With a major percentage our household goods imported from China, buyers beware.

However, what we are going to see in the next few years, due to the signs of short precession raising in China's chart, is a distinct shift in demographics. We are watching the people of China go from a worker society, where class structures are frowned upon, to a society where a distinct upper echelon will call the shots to a lower class below. Many changes are already taking place, like the beginning of real-estate sales, which is bringing about a middle class. However, with the luxury-loving Taurus now rising in China's directed chart, we shall see China going from a producer for foreign goods, to a nation of consumers. This shift in demographics is going to have an enormous impact on the world in the years to come as Chinese has three billion people. This translates into Chinese people having more financial clout. Unfortunately, it may not be evenly distributed. In the next year or so, with their wealth and their miracle, the Chinese people are going to experience growing pains and the desire for more freedom. Stay tuned.

Solar Eclipse of August 2008

The August 1, 2008, eclipse was visible over a narrow band that runs from the far northern reaches of Canada straight across and through the arctic regions of Russia; then the path turned south and passed directly over the area in which goods passed from China to the citizens of China in the first few centuries of the current era. This eclipse path is significant because the area under darkness was the main route used by merchants to carry silk to the citizens of Rome in ancient times.

The effects of an eclipse always take place after the eclipse, not before. Since this eclipse brought two hours of darkness to parts of the Arctic region and central Asia, the effects of this eclipse will be felt for a good solid two years. By obscuring this portion of the world, history repeats itself.

There are plenty of reasons why this eclipse is important, even thought it was not visible in the United States. The eclipse will be very important because it occurred in the royal sign of Leo. And at this time, whether we feel that way or not, the United States is the number one economy in the world. The U.S. has the "fiat" currency (inconvertible paper money made legal by government order). This eclipse has to do with oil, and not just the oil that will be pumped from the ground darkened by this eclipse. It will affect the spending of Americans as newly discovered oil begins to flow not west into the cars and furnaces of Americans, but east, to the factories and furnaces of China and other parts of Asia.

The eclipse falls in the first house of our nation's chart, but it is in an asterism of Cancer; therefore, any hope for an improvement in the real-estate market, may be in for some disappointment. The eclipse also indicates that for the year ahead, money may be in much tighter supply than we have seen in many years, given Saturn's position on the second house cusp of the chart .

The Fed, which has come to the rescue of the market over and over again, can only add so much liquidity to the market before its currency becomes worthless. This indicates that consumers will be tightening their belts. We have essentially given much of our money to our open enemies. It will take many years to bring industries back to this country, but this eclipse could see the beginning of this turn around. This is a good time to spend money on those things and only those things of real value to us. If it is not necessary, we don't need it. Getting out of debt seems to be the keynote here. The country from top down has been far too lax about saving. With this eclipse, we may see a change in values. It also warns of an increase in global warming.

Market Month

October 2008

Markets roil as everybody scrambles out the door. Any bulls left out there may be a shock or two this earning season. We knew it was bad, but we just didn't quite expect it to be this bad. We can expect losses in the drug and health care sectors. Some bright spots around the 16th, but for the most part, this month is troubling for investors. Don't take anybody's word for anything. Check the facts, and do not sign any important documents until after the 18th, when Mercury is once again traveling direct.

November 2008

Markets hate uncertainty, and this is not the start of a happy spending season. When debts are high, and savings are low, bankruptcy casts a long shadow. Look for slowing sales and potential labor unrest. Whatever the next administration plans to do with the health care crisis does not bode well for insurance or the drug industries.

December 2008

Markets open the month on a positive note as the incoming administration brings in seasoned economic advisors for the transition. Prices could peak as a sense of hope fills the air this holiday season. Look for more holiday bargains to tempt the consumer into spending. Energy remains high as the winter months begin. With more people choosing to let their fingers do the walking instead of spending on gas for their vehicles, online businesses experience a windfall.

January 2009

Energy prices act as a hidden tax. Whatever gains we made today, thanks to generous consumers this holiday season, may be lost due to high gas and energy prices. Do not sign on the dotted line after the 9th, when Mercury can turn coaches into pumpkins.

Uncertainties about the new administration hang over the markets like a dark cloud. Rumors do not tell the story. Experts can be wrong. As Jupiter enters Aquarius, there may be some bargains out there.

February 2009

Business takes a step forward when Mercury turns direct, but housing continues to weigh heavily against the market. Wise leaders will need extra precautions this month. There could be some shocks in high places. Debts don't disappear over night. Sacrifice will be called for. Is this the end of the ample dividend? The new president may discuss spending more money rather than less on defense to help bolster an over extended military. Tech may surprise during this cycle.

March 2009

The honeymoon between the market and the new administration may be over—for now. We may be at the dawn of a new age of embargoes and tight money practices; we may want to reexamine our international investments, and any idea that the new president will be soft on military spending may be dashed this month. With inflation harder to disguise, the Fed may make some moves that are a bitter pill for the market to swallow.

April 2009

Earnings continue to be meager. Troubles may erupt on the high seas, as Venus stations on shipwreck star, Scheat. Markets sour the second week with earnings still held in check by bad loans and high energy. Inflation is getting harder to disguise, prompting the Fed to make some moves that bring a gloomy outlook to the markets. Look for market carnage to ease after Venus goes direct around the 19th.

May 2009

Make certain that all important business is taken care of by the 6th, as Mercury turns retrograde shortly thereafter, casting a dark cloud over agreements. Do not sign any important documents in this climate. Look for more pain in the beaten housing sector the first week.

June 2009

It is always darkest just before the dawn. Bad numbers continue to mount on markets around the third. Mercury turning direct helps businesses inch forward again, bringing much needed improvement to the market place. Those who can keep their heads while losses continue may see some bargains once the dust settles.

July 2009

Tight-fisted policies may start to pay off if the softies at the Fed will let them. Only prudent monetary policy returns a sense of stability to a bubble-ridden market, though. Silver linings are out there. The less the American consumer spends, the less energy the developing world needs. Will this translate into lower prices at the pumps? Stay tuned.

August 2009

Tension mounts the first three weeks as troubled markets continue. It is always darkest just before the dawn, however. And technology may be the silver lining when some answers to the world's energy problems are revealed. Look for some recovery after the 19th. Good productivity numbers and stronger currency could begin to bring gold prices back down to reality. Better to wait until the dust settles before bone picking undervalued companies at the close of the month.

September 2009

More bad news from the housing industry brings the market to its knees. How long the over stock of houses will run its way through the market is anybody's guess. You cannot fool Mother Nature. Just renaming industries to hide pain only prolongs it. Oddly enough, the less American consumers spend, the less energy the developing world needs. This may eventually bring down prices at the pumps.

About the Author

Dorothy J. Kovach is a practicing astrologer, writer, and timing expert based in northern California. She acts as a consultant to individuals and businesses wanting success in their business and private endeavors. Her specialty is horary astrology, the branch of astrology that answers specific questions. She has been writing the economic outlook for Llewellyn's Moon Sign Book *since 2001. Her clients hail from around the globe, and she can be reached via internet at Dorothy@worldastrology.net and her Web site: www.worldastrology.net/*

New and Full Moon Forecasts

By Sally Cragin

Sometimes I feel as though I'm existing from Full Moon to Full
Moon. Hurry up—get it done—do some more—collapse—
do it again. I think part of this feeling comes from metabolism,
but also from living in the late Industrial Age. Before there was
electricity, illumination came from candles (expensive), kerosene,
and before that, whale oil. We did not have the option of a lot of
brightness at night except during the period of the Full Moon.

So what we've done as a culture (in one-third of the world anyway), is to artificially create "Full Moon" conditions, and the rhythms of pre-industrial life have been completely subverted.

Are we getting more done? Certainly a computer can tally up sums, figures, and equations much more quickly than Bob Cratchit doing the books in Scrooge's office. And e-mail, personal handheld computer devices, cell phones, CBs (yes, they're still around!), answering machines, voice mail, listservs, and other electronic communication trends are only on the increase. How many of you have more than one phone number? More than one e-mail address? As we get more and more wired, it becomes more and more difficult to have sufficient rest between lunations.

But you can get in tune with the rhythms of the Moon, and allow our closest satellite to guide your daily journey. The first thing we have to do is to notice what the Moon is doing. Begin by being aware of whether the Moon is waxing or waning. Here's the formula: When the Moon is light on the right, it's waxing. When it's light on the left, it's waning. Of course, Romantic poet Christina Rossetti said this much more elegantly:

> O Lady Moon, your horns point toward the east: Shine, be increased; O Lady Moon, your horns point toward the west: wane, be at rest."

Sometimes people get confused by the terms "first" and "fourth quarter" Moons because what we *see* in the sky is *half* the Moon illuminated, when the calendar says it is a quarter Moon. "Quarter" refers to one-fourth of the lunar cycle. The lunation cycle is about 29.5 days, and the first quarter Moon appears about seven days after the New Moon. The waxing (increasing) phases, therefore, are: New Moon (nothing in the sky), waxing crescent, first quarter, gibbous Moon, Full Moon. The waning (decreasing) phases are: Full Moon, fourth quarter, balsamic, waning crescent, dark of the Moon, and New Moon (nothing in the sky).

Phase Is Crucial

If you are starting a project, do so while the Moon is waxing. If you are concluding a project, do so when the Moon is waning. Farmers plant when the Moon is waxing, weed or harvest when the Moon is waning. Fish tend to bite when the Moon is waxing and close to the Full Moon rather than when the Moon is waning. If you end something on or around the New Moon, this project is more likely to be over for good. If you end something around the first quarter or Full Moon, you may reconsider when the Moon is waning, or after the next New Moon (especially if the Moon is in one of the indecisive signs: Libra, Gemini, Aquarius, or Pisces). Projects that reach a peak or are at their fullest potential during the time of the Full Moon are in tune with the phase. Beginning a project on or just after the New Moon gives you about twenty-eight days to explore your options, develop your ideas, make contacts, and otherwise reach out to the public.

Living Consciously During the New Moon

I'm going to write about the time just before and just after the New Moon, since it's wiser not to do too much separating of phases. The New Moon is an ending and beginning time all at once. This is an excellent time for meditation. During this phase, the Sun, Moon, and Earth are getting into alignment, although the Moon is behind the Earth, which is why we only see a sliver and then no Moon at all. However, this interlude can be emotionally draining, and a time when feelings are magnified. Beware of inappropriate pessimism or overreacting to adversity.

The waning crescent to New Moon period is a time when everything "shakes down," and sometimes relationships, projects, endeavors, and activities just need to come at an end. When things end during this period, you have an opportunity to contemplate the appropriateness of an ending. Sometimes it's easier to come to terms with a conclusion you may not have expected.

Living Consciously During the Waxing Moon Phase

This phase lasts until three or four days before the Full Moon. Optimism comes easily during this phase. When I've had clients born on or around that first quarter Moon, they're generally cautiously optimistic (as opposed to folks born on or around the Full Moon, who sometimes need lots of stimulation!). During this phase it's easy to get into a rhythm so "consciousness" is sometimes compromised. The first-quarter phase is a turning point for projects or relationships. Look back to days near the time when the Moon was new to see what started in your life. Where is it now, at the first quarter Moon? Sometimes the very day of the first quarter isn't the best time to take action, no matter how tempting.

Living Consciously as the Moon Races Toward Full

The gibbous Moon phase occurs between the first quarter and Full Moon, when the Moon really looks like a lopsided peach. This is when life gets very intense, and it's usually the day or two before the Full Moon that you hear people saying, "everything's so crazy—it must be a Full Moon!" However, this can be an excellent time to put the pedal to the metal in a number of areas in your life. Some people thrive on this energy, which can be the opposite of "living consciously." They hurtle pell-mell through their days in cars littered with empty coffee cups.

Full Moons—Do We Have a Choice?

Depending on how we react, my response is—not really! As conscious as one can be during the waxing Moon phase, something happens (and happens at mach-5) and we're lucky to be hanging onto the steering wheel.

Use the time during a Full Moon to work late hours, expand an operation, or extend the reach of a project. Even having a party means you're in the right zone with this phase. We all know that how we live our lives is very different from the way our parents did. Heck, even the lives we led ten years ago were different. It's been just about a decade since e-mail and cell phones have become commonplace items. As useful as up-to-the-minute information can be, sometimes we don't allow enough time for things to unfold in their own good time. And during a Full Moon, moving more slowly has got to be a conscious decision!

Remember that the Full Moon is in the sign opposite the sign the Sun is in. And when the Full Moon is in a particular sign, it can bring out that sign's attributes in darn near anyone. So a Full Moon in Aries can make people seem more impetuous than they mean to be, or a Full Moon in Virgo can make people seem pickier than they think they are, and a Full Moon in Aquarius is a time of wandering attention span for normally sharp-witted and grounded people. Are you reading this article during a Full Moon? Probably not—taking in information is easier when there's less illumination in the sky.

If you have pets, particularly nocturnal animals like cats or rodents, notice their activity during the Full Moon phase. They don't have to live consciously because they're in tune with natural processes. I have arboreal tree crabs for pets, and they invariably choose to change shells when the Moon is either new or full. There's much more clattering in the aquarium during these two phases as well.

Okay, When Will Things Look Up?

Frankly, there's no anticipating this. Sometimes you need to get the Full Moon behind you to be more efficient, to interrupt procrastinating, or to ward off the paralysis that comes from too many projects or deadlines looming at once. Some of my clients who were born during a Full Moon find that they feel lazy or distracted during the period before and after the New Moon. They prefer the excitement that comes with a Full Moon.

Living Consciously Between the Full Moon and Last Quarter/Balsamic Phase

It may take a few days to feel like your life is slowing down, because the days before and after a Full Moon have their momentum. But deceleration is in the stars. This phase can signal getting results. Are you cashing in on a project that began around the New Moon, or changed radically during the Full Moon? And if something in your life—a project, for example—isn't going to work out, this is the natural phase for it to fall apart. The fourth quarter to New Moon phase is about finishing projects. Lingering over problems may not be as expedient as cutting the cord, so to speak. If one is of a brooding state of mind, this is the period where it feels like life is slowing down.

It also becomes infinitely easier to regret words said or left unsaid, deeds accomplished or left undone. This is the natural time for cleaning out the clutter. Unless you're sentimental or acquisitive by nature, you should be able to discard unwanted items. If you're trying to phase out a relationship, you can put on the brakes now, or make yourself less available by phone or e-mail. But this is also a good time to look for bargains and to get goods for less than what they're worth—if you're in the mood to acquire, that is!

Quarter Moons, Coming and Going

I always look at the quarter Moon phases as opportunities to look back at events, projects, personalities, and relationships that became more prominent during the last lunar phase. For the first quarter Moon, look back on the New Moon and see if something or someone who emerged then is playing a larger role. First quarter Moons can also be a time of increased enthusiasm for a project. A feeling of hopefulness can come easily—also a drive for increased efficiency. Just before, you may have a difficult sense of "where you're going this month." Just after—acceleration comes easily.

Fourth quarter Moons bring an additional dimension because you can look back at your daybook or diary and see what you were doing during New Moon, first quarter, and Full Moon. Last quarter Moons should be a signal to slo-o-o-ow down—if you can. That waning Moon phase between fourth quarter and New Moon can also be a time when "the truth is finally revealed." Yes, the Full Moon can be a time of unexpected candor and frankness, but I've found that an urge to confess is prominent during the last lunar phase.

Here's a story. For some time, I've been conducting astrological tarot readings at an area health store, and I usually schedule my appearances around the time of the Full Moon, or just after. For the most part, this is a fine strategy because people come flying into my office during this period. But I wasn't always able to schedule my visits during the time of the Full Moon, and so I put in a session during the New Moon.

Talk about crowded! The most memorable day of doing these readings happened between the fourth quarter and New Moon and brought out people with chronic illness. Some of these folks were looking for a new way to think about their condition. Others were in a situation of coming to grips with the reality of their health. In short, the general theme was "confession," and I had a feeling that the folks I read for were having insights they might not have had during the Full Moon.

This was an excellent lesson and a reminder that every phase of the Moon has its use. The wise astrologer or individual pays attention to the nuances of each of these moments.

Back to the Beginning

I want to talk about the "dark of the Moon," which is that day before the New Moon (sometimes it's two days before the New Moon, depending on the actual time of the New Moon). This is an accident-prone time (Princess Diana's car crash was during this phase), but it's also an extremely useful time for figuring out what you want. Your subconscious wants to be heard during this phase, and if you do not make time for yourself, the universe (the Greeks called this "the Fates") will find a way to slow you down. It could be the stubbed toe, moving too quickly in a slow zone, or speaking too brashly or insensitively.

If the dark of the Moon falls on a Thursday or Friday, and there is pressure on you to complete a project, do your best but don't be surprised if you put the finishing touches on over the weekend or on Monday. And whatever preoccupies people (even you!) during this phase will be of limited interest once the Moon has turned new again.

So, even if you can never get it straight what sign the Moon is in, do pay attention to what it's doing in terms of phase. And be grateful we don't live on Mars, where we'd have to take into account the angles, phase, behavior, and eccentricities of both Phobos and Demos, the pair of Moons that circle the red planet!

New Moons, Birthdays, and Strategy

Here's an easy way to remember what sign the Moon is in when it's new: it's always the same sign as the Sun. So when the Moon is in your Sun sign during your birthday month, it's always the New Moon. And since New Moons are all about fresh starts, give yourself the birthday present of a new project or different perspective—at least for that lunar phase.

Who's In Tune with the Moon?

Animals! Watch your house pets. Nocturnal critters, like cats, get more agitated during a Full Moon, especially as it approaches. This is amplified if you live in a house that has mice, which are also active at night.

Lest We Forget . . .

Entire books have been written about the astrological, psychological, spiritual significance of eclipses, both lunar (when the Moon is full, and the Earth is between Sun and Moon), and solar (when the Moon is between Earth and Sun). The short take on all of this is pretty simple: Eclipses are, well—bad! Oh, you probably want some details. Traditional folklore associates eclipses with a fall from power or grace. It's a pretty easy interpretation: the almighty Sun or Moon is no longer visible. Therefore, something extraordinary has "seized" the power.

There were some interesting eclipses during 1971 to 1974, when the Watergate crisis was unfolding. For you young'uns, certain members of the Republican party and Nixon administration thought they needed an edge after the Pentagon Papers were published. Among their "dirty tricks" were bugging the Democratic National Committee headquarters at the Watergate Hotel and incidences of burglary and wiretapping, which those who were involved attempted to cover up. The nation was riveted to their televisions during the summer of 1973 and onward, as various Nixon administration operatives were brought to trial. The entire affair ended with numerous jail sentences for presidential staff and associates, and the resignation of Richard Nixon.

I've observed that eclipses usually precede a transition or power shift. In the case of Watergate, the White House Counsel John Dean told Watergate investigators that he and the president had discussed the Watergate cover-up dozens of times in early June of 1974. That month, there were both solar and lunar eclipses and when they were in process, Dean testified at length before the Senate Watergate Committee, which basically was the beginning of the end of the Nixon regime.

Read the entries later in this article to see how an eclipse spices things up. In 2009, eclipes will occur on:

- January 26 (solar)
- February 9 (lunar)
- July 7 (lunar)
- July 21–22 (solar)

- August 5–6 (lunar)
- December 31 (lunar)

Your short-term strategy during these unsettled periods should be caution, caution, and caution. Let others surge forward, even if it seems as though you should be receiving the credit.

Void-of-Course Moon During New and Full Phases

When the Moon is void-of-course it ceases making angles to other planets. This is considered a null time—not the best time to make decisions, not the best time to implement plans, but a great time to be creative or artistic. If plans change during this time, it's for the best. If you make plans during this time, chances are you'll have to readjust because it's very difficult to be "precise" during void-of-course Moon phases. The best way to interpret void-of-course times during the New Moon might be to see whether you're under real or imagined pressure because sometimes we're prone to unrealistic fantasies or thinking that things are more dire than they are. A Full Moon void-of-course is when people sometimes over commit. Don't ask for big favors during this time, but it's a great time to apologize because everyone's so spacey that it's difficult to remember exactly what the problem was!

New and Full Moon Cycles for 2009

Full Moon in Cancer, January 10

With Mars syncing up with the Sun this month, emotions could run high for water signs Cancer, Scorpio, and Pisces. Even so, this is an excellent period for introspection, meditation, and domestic goddess activity. Getting or giving a massage, baking bread, or kneading clay will be deeply pleasurable. Pisces folks may find that they're attracting attention from new places. Aries and Libra could reverse direction. Smile, and then reverse again!

New Moon in Aquarius, January 26

There's an eclipse attached to this New Moon, so air signs should be cautious about something that seems "too good to be true." But the general theme with this New Moon is making space for innovation. Quirky folks could turn up for dinner, or an e-mail from them may show up in your Inbox. Listen carefully to what they say because they might not be immediately clear. Aries and Libra, if you're not getting "your share," have patience because next month you may get more than you expect.

Full Moon in Leo (with Eclipse), February 9

Great day for advertising, playing with children, or getting in touch with the child within. Is there something you've been meaning to do with your hair? Beat the winter doldrums by throwing a party, or hanging with those folks who make you laugh. With Aquarius as this month's dominant planetary influence, plus another eclipse, the Leo Moon will divert attention from the ethereal to the real. More than usual, the shy will be overshadowed by the exuberant narcissists among us.

New Moon in Pisces, February 24

The end of the zodiacal year brings out that "you talkin' to ME?" defensiveness usually happily latent in both Sagittarius and Gemini. But this is an excellent day for art appreciation, especially photography. Don't be surprised if "backstage" gossip reaches your ears (especially from air- and water-sign folks who are naturally receptive to confidences). Hidden messages are also likely in the form of people saying one thing and meaning another. This is no fun for sweet and literal-minded earth-sign folks to interpret, so Taurus, Capricorn, and especially Virgo, hang in there.

Full Moon in Virgo, March 10

With the Moon and Saturn in lockstep, setting limits comes easily for Taurus, Virgo, and Capricorn. This means the rest of us might find these (usually predictable) signs "on a tear," as a friend from the

West used to say. Be productive and proactive in your endeavors by putting health matters first. Experimenting with vitamins, supplements, or a new kind of exercise could be a useful distraction.

New Moon in Aries, March 26

With the Spring Equinox barely in the rearview mirror, this New Moon will help projects take flight. Others are open to new ideas or new approaches, although attention spans could be compromised. Don't do the complicated explanation. Just stick to the "bullet points." It would be best to wait until March 28 if you want your actions to take root. Fire signs Aries and Leo are especially motivated for a change of direction; although, Sagittarius may be prompted into impulsive action that could turn a stumble into a fall.

Full Moon in Libra, April 8

This Full Moon would like to bring harmony to one and all, but resistance could come from Cancer and Capricorn folks, who may resent specific direction. If you're involved with either sign, give them space. Otherwise, useful phrases during this phase include, "On the other hand," and "It's good to hear a variety of perspectives." Activities involving persuasion (of one other person in particular) could be extremely successful.

New Moon in Taurus, April 24

Some lunar phases are very helpful for working with tools, so if you've been waiting for the weekend to spring clean, jump in now. Getting rid of items that are chipped, battered, or threadbare comes easily, and even possessive earth signs can let go of clutter. Banking activities are favored, and fire and earth signs have very good advice for others.

Full Moon in Scorpio, May 9

Spring fever hits with a vengeance, particularly water- and fire-sign folks, who could sizzle (separately, or together!). Getting to the heart of a matter is also easy to do and since this Full Moon occurs on a weekend, it's an excellent time to entertain folks who have strong opinions or passions. Gardeners should also be in the mood to rip out everything and start something new. Have you been craving a grotto or concealed fountain?

New Moon in Gemini, May 24

Even though Mercury is retrograde, this is an excellent period to get more information in a variety of arenas. Air signs are favored for this activity, but fire signs (who are feeling very passionate this month, thanks to a Venus-Mars conjunction) could also be dynamic and attractive to everyone. Pisces and Sagittarius folks, who could be indecisive and easily irked, are the exception.

Full Moon in Sagittarius, June 7

Adventures beckon to one and all, and even conservative Taurus folks feel like kicking up their heels. This Full Moon is super for planning (or embarking on) a lengthy journey, or exploring an exotic culture—perhaps hosting a barbecue with a variety of international spicy sauces. Pisces and Virgo may feel that others are setting needless limits with them. However, fish and virgins, try not to take idle remarks personally.

New Moon in Cancer, June 22

With the Sun's ingress into Cancer, this New Moon could find everyone mildly vulnerable, but open to meeting multi-faceted new folks, thanks to Uranus making a helpful angle to this Moon. Taurus could be the peacemakers right now, and it's an excellent week for making your home more cozy, or improving a living space that's outside.

Full Moon in Capricorn, July 7

Structural issues need a closer look and earth signs are in a practical mood. With a pair of eclipses this month, and another in August, the status quo will be shaken up. Aries and Libra could face surprising resistance from normally accommodating quarters this month. Cancer folks shouldn't let mild skepticism turn into paranoia.

New Moon in Cancer, July 21

Usually tough-minded folks could feel as vulnerable as a small child, but even with an eclipse in the works, there are super ingredients for launching a new product, idea, or campaign of persuasion. Air signs are particularly favored during this New Moon and could make difficult problems seem easy and curable.

Full Moon in Aquarius, August 5

Ready for another eclipse? This one could cause discomfort to Scorpios and Taurus folks, who usually seem so certain. Conservative ideas have little place for anyone right now and the wildest notions work best. Escaping into fantasy can sometimes seem like a needless indulgence, but restless spirits will be calmed by watching movies, or participating in any "crowd" situation. With the Moon and Jupiter in harmony, over-eating is also a danger. Think twice before taking seconds.

New Moon in Leo, August 20

Fire-sign New Moons usually put the sizzle into initiatives, new relationships, and other projects at that "tender" stage; and this month finds virtually every sign willing to take chances and explore novel ways of working. Sagittarius and Pisces could feel like others aren't listening (particularly mid-month), but on the whole, the planets are saying, "why not be social? Why not meet someone new?" This is also a terrific time to get a new toy (for yourself or a pet!)

Full Moon in Pisces, September 4

Trust is a two-way street, and harmony between Mars and the Moon means some of us may be called upon to be (emotionally?) braver than we've been before. Limits could be an unpleasant surprise for Sagittarius and Gemini. Fortunately, those two signs are flexible and will "pick battles carefully." Since Pisces rules photography, hidden places, and subconscious motives, you may want to look beyond the frame of the picture. If you're told something that seems too good (or even too bad) for your assessment of a situation, skepticism will help.

New Moon in Virgo, September 18

Feeling like you want to take a closer look? You're in tune with the Moon this week as Virgo influences other planets as well. Earth signs need more time to think than others (air and fire signs?) may give them. Assessing a health plan is a smart move. You should also gauge your own energy level when it comes to helping out a friend. Mercury continues to be retrograde, and has just slid back into Virgo, so others may interpret a noncommittal comment as willingness to fix or clean up a situation. Perfectionism could also be a theme when embarking on a new activity. If others try to make a joke of this, prickliness is also likely.

Full Moon in Aries, October 4

Here comes the Harvest Moon, and signs that will shine on include Virgo, Scorpio, and, of course, Aries. This could be the last weekend for a barbecue with new friends. Learning how to play a game, especially one that requires mental agility as well as physical fitness could be a pleasurable occupation. Capricorn and Libra could be mildly (even humorously) accident-prone. Signs that will need more than their usual amount of attention will be Sagittarius and Leo. (Archers have an attraction for eccentric folks this month).

New Moon in Libra, October 18

Seeing both sides is a useful exercise, but one that comes too easy for Libra and Gemini folks right now. As for the remaining ten signs, work on issues that strengthen partnership or trust; and if you've got a lot of air in your chart, try not to exaggerate or overstate the ease of a particular job. But if you're selling hope or optimism, you'll have eager listeners. Air-sign Moons bring out the curious side in cautious individuals, so this is a fine time to get information.

Full Moon in Taurus, November 2

This Full Moon is superb for improving home décor or finding "that perfect something" to complement a theme. Taurus, of course, is in full-steam-ahead mode, and the rest of us had best hang back because subtlety is lost on this sign. Changing banks or savings accounts is a temptation for all, but Leo and Aquarius need to be wary of "get-rich-quick" schemes. Value for money is what we all want right now, and the wise folks will take their time with investments.

New Moon in Scorpio, November 16

Psychic feelings or quirky insights are likely, especially for Cancer, Scorpio, and Pisces. Aquarius and Taurus could be impulsive in a way that costs money, but for the most part this is an excellent time to cut a budget or start from scratch. If you have plants or greenery that's past its prime, put it right on the compost. This New Moon is helpful for getting back to nature or exploring a (hidden?) erotic side. Have fun!

Full Moon in Gemini, December 2

The Long Night Moon is a tremendously chatty time for all, particularly Geminis, who are being given the benefit of the doubt here, there and everywhere. Overall, themes you'll focus on to your own benefit include partnership and improving how you communicate. Remember that writing short is harder do, but it's far more memorable. Overexplaining can cost valuable time or visibility.

New Moon in Sagittarius, December 16

The holiday spirit is in full gear with many planets in fire signs, and this New Moon says: "Where haven't you been? Why don't you go there?" Sagittarians are in a lively mood and could be infatuated with someone who turns up unexpectedly. This is a great day for planning an office party. If you don't give in to the lighter side, you could experience humorous digressions in an otherwise serious business environment.

Full Moon in Cancer (with eclipse), December 31

Full Moons around family-oriented holidays can bring out a passion and emotion that some folks find difficult to bear. As unlikely as this may seem, salvation or distraction could be achieved in a highly satisfying way by baking! This first Full Moon after the Winter Solstice wants everyone to howl, even normally conciliatory Cancers, so say yes to that New Year's party and then bring those cookies for others to eat.

About the Author

Sally Cragin writes "Moon Signs," an astrology column for the Boston Phoenix *newspaper in New England. She also writes about theater- and arts-related topics for the* Boston Globe.

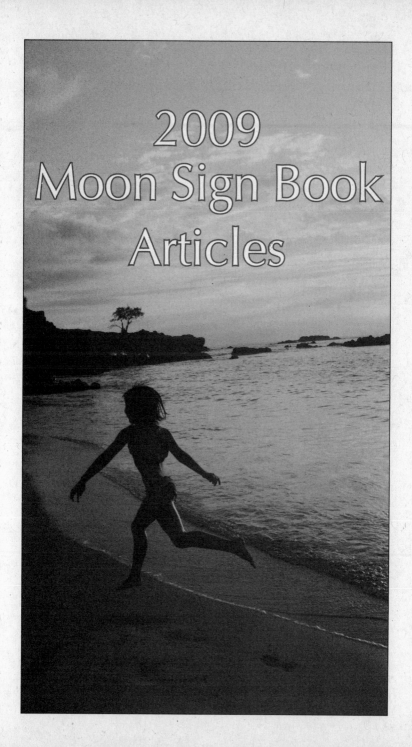

2009
Moon Sign Book
Articles

Decorating a Garden in the Age of Aquarius

By Janice Sharkey

It is a frosty December morning. Each blade of grass glistens, still with frozen dew. The garden begins its winter sleep but not all things are dormant. The ornaments we use are our way of creating a personal signature on the landscape, and every garden is a personal creation between you and Mother Earth.

Gardens are always a work in progress, a partnership between you and nature. That sundial or urn you laid down last year will change with time, becoming every bit as interesting and special as the first time you set eyes upon it. After all, ornaments, like the land itself, erode and change. That is part of their beauty.

The ancient word for "garden" or "enclosure" was *pairidaeza* from the Persian, which became *paradeisos* in Greek and links with the notion of paradise, a Garden of Eden, and a tranquil escape. Whether you use your garden for a purely pleasure-seeking place or a plot to grow vegetables, every garden space should have room for adornment.

Decorating our gardens is like putting icing on a cake. How we choose to add knick-knacks to our own outdoor spaces says something about us, and it seems that anything goes.

During the long history of horticulture, every conceivable material that can be made into something to garnish the garden—stone, wood, terracotta, to even glass—has been used. Anything is possible, and nothing is new. Like the fashion catwalk, we "clothe" the garden in ideas borrowed from the past, which are updated by adding a twist from the culture of today.

Take for instance the influence of Renaissance Italy upon Western gardening, in particular the inspiration of the classical style. It has been said that the Italian garden does not exist for its flowers, but that the flowers exist for the garden. What seems to matter more is the way architecture, mythological statutes, and terracotta pots direct the eye through a labyrinth of mini gardens to unfold a story, a journey within.

With each new era, we learn something about the necessity to change and the need to adapt to the new. The *hortus conclusus*, or "enclosed space," gave us a safe place to socialize and beautify. From the Renaissance came the formal expression of the landscape to the evolution of the necessity for the pottager or cottage garden. The cottage garden developed around the idea of a garden becoming not only practical and able to feed us, but also a place to reuse old objects. Pieces of wood were turned into benches and wire messes became molds to train up plants. Nothing in the country cottage garden really went to waste. During the Arts and Crafts Movement, skilled artisans married the garden influence with wood, metal, and glass to make beautiful objects—doors carved with fruits and floral art in a stained glass window, for example. Around 1900, Edith Wharton found "the old garden craft" that modern Americans were seeking in Italian Renaissance gardens. She claimed that the old Italian garden was meant to be lived in, with the grounds as carefully and conveniently planned as the house. She recommended that her readers think away "the flowers, the sunlight, the rich tinting of time" to find a deeper harmony in the fundamental design that of course included those extra trinkets or adornment.

Eclectic Décor and Garden Rooms

The smallest garden can become the most successfully decorated garden room, a favorite place for all the family to eat and play, if it is well planned. The most obvious difference between outside and inside rooms is, of course, planting. The other big difference is that inside floors are usually flat whereas the ground often has varying levels that will need steps or bridges to cross. Here, the choice of materials will structurally clothe the garden, so keep in mind the need to link house with garden through the color and material you incorporate into your garden. Often, materials shout at each other like grey stone walls with red terracotta pots. The color scheme and style of the house must link with the garden.

One way to bridge that gap between inside and outdoors is to plant up an old kettle and place it outside a window. The repurposed kettle will create a slow and natural transition from interior to exterior. It will also provide an unusual focal point when you are in the garden and look back toward the house.

Dividing the garden into mini-rooms is a good idea if you want areas for different activities. You can do this by varying the levels, or with low walls or trellis screens. Even loose hedging tied in an arch over a pathway and studded with flowers divides a garden into areas of interest, especially when it leads the eye to a focal point beyond which should always be an ornament or feature to surprise the onlooker.

The quickest way to introduce year-round color into the garden is to paint something—a bench, bird bath, or garden shed door, for example. Why not try your hand at al fresco art if there is a spare wall that looks like it needs brightening, or paint flowers on an outside door that looks onto a backyard. Bring out the artist in you!

Mosaics make perfect all-weather exterior art and can be made into pictures, sculptures, or even used to decorate tables. Anything can be made to adorn your outdoor living space. A scarecrow can be an outdoor sculpture. Pots piled upon one another can create the structure of a mini waterfall feature. Odds and ends of unused leftover what-nots can become reborn *objet d'art* (small, decorative art pieces) given the treatment and a little imagination. Stamp your style and be noticed. Just stick to a theme that links all manner of things together and it will look fantastic. Pay attention to the composition, and make the color scheme rich and complementary to the plantings.

There is no reason why gardener's tools should not be just as beautiful to look at as everything else. Good, well-looked-after garden tools have a beauty and integrity of their own. Try hanging some tools on a fence or the side of the garden shed. And why not try to make a plant pot out of an old pair of wellie boots that could be painted with flowers? Leave old weathered pots on a shelf with one planted up and the rest more for antique interest.

Garden Art in the Aquarian Age

At one time art deco, gleaming chrome, the architecture of Frank Lloyd Wright, or abstract cubism was all the rage. Maybe that is when modernism—in garden terms—with its emphasis on straight lines, concrete, steel, and gleaming pools really began.

Today, modernism in the garden appears as simplicity and harmony within its surroundings. Some of the most striking gardens of the twentieth-century have been created by writers and artists. Poet Ian Hamilton Finlay developed Little Sparta in Scotland in a nine-acre garden on the edge of moors, with sculpture-poems and inscriptions that are linked to themes such as the life of the sea and the sailor. Carved stones announce the words of Louis de Saint-Just: "The present order is the disorder of the future."

Modern roof-top gardens started with the idea that a garden can be anywhere and that modern materials such as glass, aluminium, or steel can sit well on chic city balconies. Nowhere more so than in the modern landscape is it a place to escape into and to create a fantasy world where planted ornaments play their role in the drama. What seems to work well in any modern sense is the marrying of the timeless elements of fire, earth, air, and water.

Sensual Ornaments

The sensuality of a garden space can be very obvious in a chic garden when a fresh trickle from a water feature draws your ear and eye to the feel of some velvety foliage. Artificial light plays its part in creating the right atmosphere in a modern living space, too. Ideally, any added lighting should be solar powered and positioned so it reflects in water. Modern gadgets should be functional, but they can also surprise us, like the sprinkler system that is activated as we pass by. A modern designed garden reflects the Aquarian signature of *avante guard* mixed with the need for innovative solutions.

Outstanding sensory delights can be achieved by combining soft plantings with garden objects. Something as simple as chimes can bring the garden alive with sound. Unusual birdfeeders are not only attractive, they also allow life to fly into your living space. Fragrance can come from planting at windowsills, doorways, and patios; and it can be added whenever you want with lovely mini pots of your own aromatherapy. Touch, too, can be stimulated by the contrast of ribbed pots to ferny foliage. Try to include a range of fleshy and feathery plants into a display, using a themed-style container, such as terracotta or metallic. Colorful mosaic tiles add tactile interest and color to a shady area in your back yard. And taste should not be forgotten either. When room is made for the barbecue grill and an eating area, al fresco dining can be enjoyed by all.

Exotic Themes

Recreating a themed garden can be fun when you let your imagination wander. The secret is to devote a small space to a specific style and let it speak for itself. It could be an artist's retreat with a shed at the bottom of the garden, painted pots, and a table and chairs sitting outside. Or maybe it could be a coastal theme with pebbles, a water feature, and the odd lobster pot as a hanging basket. Whatever you decide, remember that the best ideas are not always that expensive to fulfill. Stick to a theme such as tropical, formal, or natural, and keep the *objet trouve* (found objects that are modified) linked to that style. This can be done through choosing a color scheme, type of material (such as metal), or maybe it's the shape or age that gives it a certain image. With a little thought and a lot of fun, you can see it come to fruition.

Ornamental Junk

Beauty, they say, is in the eye of the beholder. What is junk but an opportunity to turn some discarded item into a quirky expression of beauty. What is expressed depends upon you. Junk pots can be made to reflect a new beautiful theme within your living space. You name it, the junk yard will have it. Junk comes in all shapes and sizes, from ceramic teapots to old metal buckets. There's no end to what can be used so long as you—the creator—has that innovative, visionary spark to see it planted up and taking on a new "life" as an *objet d'art*.

Creating a place for *objet trouvé* in your garden may seem daunting. Someone else's discarded junk could so easily look lost in amongst your planting. Yet once you're switched on to the magic of "planted junk," it can enhance the garden by adding that personal touch that is both an economic and creative reward. Start hunting through all those unused bits and pieces in your own home. Then explore the nearest demolition yard. From Victorian tiles to old vases, wicker baskets to old cookie tins—you never go away empty-handed.

Another trick is to be observant and choose ideas that have definite shapes or lines dominating the object and echo this with a shape or color of a plant. An old bright yellow plastic bucket with a few drainage holes in the bottom can be very vivid, but when planted with yellow cannas or calendulas, the yellow becomes really pleasing to the eye rather than brash—especially if placed within the background of a hedge or a white wall to show it off.

Whether you are spicing up an existing garden with a few bizarre planters or creating a more complete junk-style outdoor space, keep in mind that your "junk" should reflect the current style of your own home and garden.

. . . .

Gardens need ornaments. No matter how wonderful your planting is, if it lacks ornamentation, it lacks that personal signature that says you occupy that living space. Garden ornaments are a mixture of arty expression, whether it be the stately gazebo or merely a humble ceramic pot. What makes gardening so addictive and therapeutic is the relationship with nature and human expression. We commune with nature to ground ourselves and to make sense of our world. Those little artifacts, from the chipped gnome to the armless Venus de Milo, help us to accept that while time doesn't stand still, it can hold precious memories and become something more.

About the Author
Janice Sharkey is a keen Moon gardener. Having been a garden designer for a number of years, she enjoys making things—from clay ornaments to stained glass panels—for the garden. She now writes children's fiction and radio plays.

Labyrinths: The Beauty or the Beast?

By Sally Cragin

There are stunning examples of functional art throughout antiquity. The Valley of the Kings, with pyramids and sphinx. The Great Wall of China, the Labyrinth in Crete, which housed the mighty Minotaur in the center. We are fascinated with these architectural forms and the myriad cultures that create them.

Why do we do this? One thought is that a labyrinth is a useful tool for personal transformation, whether psychological or spiritual. One of my friends built a labyrinth behind her church during a period of personal challenge, and found the activity of creating the labyrinth as soothing as walking it.

Finding the right path is always a challenge and those of us who use astrological transits and information to enhance the journey are using both sides of our brains creatively. For me, writing in 2007 about the astrological transits forthcoming in 2009—well, that feels like navigating a labyrinth!

Some individuals, even some signs, are better-suited to a logical, methodical way of thinking, which is helpful when exploring labyrinthine forms. Virgo is probably the most obvious sign—methodical yet creative (due to being a mutable sign), and capable of routine, yet willing to think imaginatively if the stakes are high enough. Virgo likes neat lines and squared-off edges. Every present my son has received from his Virgo great aunt is beautifully wrapped, right down to the pieces of tape enclosing crisply folded edges that are exactly the same size. There's no information from mythology explaining whether Daedalus (the builder of the labyrinth) or Theseus (who entered the labyrinth unreeling a spool of thread so he could make his way safely to the exit) had autumnal birthdays. But one suspects both of these characters had a touch of the engineer in their nature.

A Primer on Labyrinths

Daedalus is a recurrent figure in Greek mythology. Best known for the Labyrinth at Knossos, on Crete, he also created artificial wings for himself and son Icarus. An Athenian citizen (his name means "cunning worker"), his darker side emerged when his apprentice, his nephew Perdix, showed great talent in building. Daedalus murdered him by heaving him off the Acropolis. After a trial at Areopagus, he was banished from Athens.

But a man with talents will always make a living, and he traveled across the Mediterranean to Crete, where King Minos and Queen Pasiphae gave him commissions. He built a wooden cow for the queen, in which she concealed herself while having amorous trysts with a white bull sent by Poseidon, lord of the sea.

Thus the Minotaur—half man, half bull—was born. Daedalus was ordered to build the labyrinth to contain the murderous monster and for years, King Minos demanded that youths from Athens be sent to the center to feed the creature. Finally, Theseus arrived to slay the Minotaur. He received help from Ariadne, the human daughter of Minos and Pasiphae, who gave him a flaxen thread to tie to the door of the labyrinth, so he could make his way out after slaying the Minotaur.

Minos was enraged, Theseus fled with Ariadne, leaving Daedalus to take the blame. The master builder and his son were confined in the labyrinth. Eventually, the hero Theseus came to Crete to slay the Minotaur. Ariadne, daughter of Minos and Pasiphae, fell in love with Theseus and asked Daedalus to help him. Daedalus gave her a flaxen thread for Theseus to tie to the door of the labyrinth as he entered, and by which he could find his way out after killing the monster. Theseus succeeded, and escaped Crete with Ariadne. Minos, enraged at the loss of his daughter, shut Daedalus and his son Icarus into the labyrinth. We all know what happened next. Daedalus constructed a set of wings made from feathers and wax, and though the pair flew off from the labyrinth, Icarus ventured too close to the Sun, and the heat melted the wax, sending him to Earth again. Daedalus, bereft, buried him and went to Sicily, where Daedalus built a stunning temple with a golden roof. The legend continues that Daedalus met King Cocalus (or Kokalos) and lived among the Sicilians.

But King Minos did not forget Daedalus and he sailed the Mediterranean sea in search of his former employee. Perhaps a puzzle would entice the master builder? Minos let it be known that the first person who could string a thread through a conch shell would receive a rich reward. Daedalus came up with an ingenious solution and drilled a tiny hole at the apex of the shell. He placed a drop of honey there, then tied a thread around an ant, which then circled through the chambers to the opening.

When Kokalos showed up to ask for the reward, Minos demanded Daedalus, who wisely refused to appear and instead assisted one of Kokalos's daughters to build a special pipe into a bath. When the tyrant stepped into the bath water, boiling oil descended and Daedalus was free for all time.

. . . .

In later history, we see the construction of labyrinths or mazes in great gardens or wooded spots. In the New World, the corn maze during harvest time has become a tradition. But you can find mazes and labyrinths in nature just by walking in the woods and turning over a fallen log. For example, wood boring beetles create magical passages and runic links in the wood.

Every culture seems to find its own labyrinth. The original design utilizes seven circles. During the medieval era, a labyrinth based on a pattern of eleven circles or "circuits" emerged. This pattern became extremely prevalent in the floor tiles of the grand churches and cathedrals of Great Britain and Europe. Chartres is a splendid example of the eleven-circuit pattern, and the original design featured a rosette at the center.

Penitents and pilgrims would walk this "pavement maze," or crawl on their knees, and their journey was meant to represent a path of spiritual quest and repentance. The Chartres labyrinth is divided into four quadrants, which represent a cross with arms of equal length. Psychologist Carl Jung, a great guide for astrologers, termed a labyrinth the "archetype of transformation." This circling path, or spiral, is meant to temporize a variety of spiritual or emotional states. But don't confuse labyrinth with maze. A true labyrinth is one path, while a maze has intentional dead-ends and diverse paths. You don't need to be logical to follow a labyrinth—you just "go with the flow."

Quirky Minotaur Story

I love checking the astrological "fingerprints" for events as much as doing natal horoscopes for clients. I am always interested when events are delayed. While researching this story, I found a variety of companies that use the term "Daedalus," "Minotaur" or "Labyrinth" for a product line. In the mid-1970s, "Project Daedalus" was a large-scale research study designed to create an unmanned spacecraft that could reach an adjacent star within fifty years (the length of a human scientist's working career). For a while, nuclear fusion research showed that the project had promise, but technology is still not capable of constructing this complicated rocket. But there is one successful space vehicle in this theme. One especially admires the Orbital Sciences employee who decided to use their classical background by dubbing a rocket "Minotaur." This little solid-fuel rocket was launched in 2006, but instead of consuming sacrificial Athenian youths, it neatly deposited satellites in the upper atmosphere. And just as the Minotaur was the only creature "launched" into the labyrinth, thus was the rocket Minotaur 2 heaved heavenward from Wallops Island, VA, the first launch in twenty-two years, and the inaugural launch from the new Mid-Atlantic Regional Spaceport.

About the Author
Sally Cragin's complete bio appears on page 262.

Signs from the Birds

By Robin Ivy

Stories of birds live in our conscious minds and in our memories. If you think back, chances are you have a notable bird tale or two. I have several that stand out as very significant to me. One is of a crow that was injured and hopping around my yard. As one of my dogs raced toward it, the crow didn't fly away, but instead hobbled to the fence that borders our yard. I called back the dog and wondered what to do next, but it was other crows that had the answer. They came to the yard and stayed with him, apparently protecting him from potential predators. A short while later, they had somehow urged or helped him up into a nearby tree where he sat and cawed loudly for hours. The other crows came back and forth many times that afternoon, visiting and

perhaps bringing him food. After a period of time, the injured bird made it up further into the tree, a limb or two higher each time. By evening, the crow flew! An amazing story of how community and friendship can be essential to survival played out before my eyes, right in my own back yard, literally!

Another very sad morning, I sat in my yard and held my dying dog in my arms. He had rolling seizures over the course of a few days, and I knew he would not survive another. In our last hours together, shortly after dawn, hundreds of birds came! Small brown sparrows flocked to my garden as I sat nearby dreading the inevitable loss of my pet. My dog had spent hours every day in that garden, playing, sleeping, and keeping watch. The birds seemed to come to say their goodbyes. Their appearance forced me to tune in to something greater than the terrible sadness I was feeling and put a spiritual spin on a very difficult day.

Bird Omens

Presumably, experiences like mine date back to the beginning of time, ever since birds have been a source of human interest, which is as far back as literature dates. Throughout mythological, religious, and folk stories, birds have acted as symbols and heralds, reflected human behavior and circumstances, and demonstrated great powers. In American folklore, birds are knowing creatures according to the saying: "A little birdie told me." Their actions are well timed, as in: "The early bird catches the worm." They are even reputed to make the right friends according to the adage: "Birds of a feather flock together." Birds, it appears, have lessons for us if we are willing to tune in.

Is there a bird that appears on your windowsill, feeds from the flowers in your garden or makes its home in the trees in your yard? Is there a bird that seems to call to you or makes itself known at significant times or in your dreams? Tiny or large, outspoken or subtle, seasonal or year round, the bird's appearance can help you tune in to the cycles and the energy most beneficial to you during any given period of time. Notice the traits and the timing as birds present themselves and you may discover a wonderful totem and find another source of spiritual guidance. Ahead, you'll find descriptions of some birds native to North America, that may be year round or seasonal residents of your backyard. The astrology sign(s) associated with each bird is determined by the birds' predominant characteristics.

Bird Totems

Blue Jay (Virgo, Gemini)

Blue jays are known for their color and their call. The jays' distinctive crest color ranges from mid- to lavender-blue, relating to the throat chakra, the energy center of vocalization. This connects the blue jay to planet Mercury, ruler of communication. And blue jays certainly know how to use their voices! Most often associated with a gull-like scream—their warning call—blue jays also make more subtle sounds to communicate when in close proximity. A member of the crow family, blue jays are aggressive and will attack larger birds of prey, or even humans who threaten their nests.

To understand the blue jays' lessons, consider how you can learn to communicate more directly. Is there someone you need to have an honest conversation with? Blue jay cries out in alarm to alert other jays or drive predators away. Does some destructive behavior or a predatory person need to be "called out"? It may be time to band together and ward off a threat by making it public knowledge. The blue jay will take on a bigger, equally bold competitor. Is it time to step up and make yourself known—loud and clear? Communication and vocalization is the teaching blue jay conveys.

Cardinal (Libra, Aries)

Cardinals are non-migratory birds that seldom live far from the place they were born. The male and female court each other, work in pairs, and communicate through song, one finishing or repeating the other's call. The male is territorial and aggressively defends the home area. He is also the red one with the black mask, while the female is olive brown with a paler mask and a dull shade of red on her wings and tail feathers. Cardinals win the popularity contest, as they are claimed symbolic bird by seven different states.

Male and female cardinals have a strong connection so cardinal is a favorable totem for couples. Not all female songbirds sing, but the cardinal female shares her partner's song! The two demonstrate affection and the male will share a feeder with his mate, and even put food in the female's beak. If cardinal is present and your relationship needs some attention, consider how to be more affectionate, balance responsibilities, and share with one another. The cardinal is also a symbol of popularity, so you two may live a very public, social life.

Crow (Cancer, Scorpio)

Commonly viewed as a bad omen and a pest, the crow is actually a very intelligent bird. A British study published by *National Geographic* suggests that crows may be as smart as apes. They are able to fashion tools to help them catch prey, they learn to trust and recognize individuals who provide them with food, and they seem to use memory to plan and predict other birds or animals intentions. The crow is also a creature of community in that crows often feed and sleep in groups, possibly for mutual protection during the times they are most vulnerable.

The aura of magic, mystery, and transformation associated with crow may be one way to interpret his presence in your life. However, remember that the crow is clever, watchful, and knowing as well. Ask yourself how you can be more innovative, connect with others who can support you, or predict your competitor's next move. The crow is often credited with intuition, but in fact, this bird seems to observe, experiment, and learn, as much as sense. When the crow comes, absorb all the information you can, be aware of your surroundings, and strategize, since that is how the crow outwits the enemy, finds his allies, adapts and survives.

Hummingbird (Gemini, Leo)

Most often considered a totem of joy and activity, the hummingbirds' life revolves around flowers. They visit gardens and feeders, their long bill adapted to extracting nectar, their primary source of nourishment. These birds are territorial when it comes to the feeding area, however they are known to play and interact with one another when competition for food is not involved! Hummingbird eats dozens of times a day and metabolizes very quickly. One of hummingbirds' messages is to pay attention to our blood sugars, and consume what we need to keep our energy level and metabolism high. This bird also conserves energy with rest, and can hibernate overnight, so hummingbird may be a sign you need more sleep or rest periods throughout the day.

Hummingbird does exactly what its name says: it hums! The sound comes from the vibration of its wings, which actually move in a figure eight pattern, like the symbol for infinity. Because they are so small and fly at high speeds, hummingbirds could be mistaken for insects when they appear in your midst. If you are lucky enough to observe one, notice its iridescent color along with its speed and ability to hover and fly in many directions. In fact, hummingbird is the only bird that can fly both backwards and sideways, indicating the significance of the past, present, and future. To sum up the message of this distinctive garden bird, stay busy, be versatile, and revel in both your work and play.

Owl (Libra, Cancer, Scorpio)

The nocturnal owl has excellent vision and hearing. Owl's acute senses and quiet flight help her hunt with great success. She also has sharp, well-developed talons adapted to carry heavier prey and tear through animal flesh. You'll know owl is nearby by its hoot, which is distinctive to each variety of the creature. However, you may not know where owl lives since many do not nest in the traditional way. They tend to take up residence in natural tree cavities including in hollows, rotted areas, in man-made structures, such as boxes or platforms, and in nests abandoned by other large birds or squirrels, which the owls will then fashion to suit themselves.

When owl appears, it is time to look beyond the surface of a situation. Owls swivel their heads to move their eyes and can turn far enough to see all the way behind them. Owl may turn up when you need to have "eyes in the back of your head." Their ears are unusual in that they are not the same size and are placed in different positions on each side of the head. Owl's ears allow her to sort out sounds and in some cases use a form of echo-location to zero in on her prey. If you're attuned to owl energy, you benefit from hearing beyond what is said and listening for subtle messages. Primarily night birds, owls operate in the cover of darkness. For us this represents the ability to find the hidden, discover secrets, and use extra sensory perception.

Robin (Aries, Leo)

A traditional sign of spring, the robin is generally a bird that migrates for feeding purposes. Robins are territorial, and the males will compete, usually by singing loudly, and sometimes with physical force. Robins also use song to attract mates and to announce the impending arrival of new baby birds, just before their pale blue eggs hatch. This common backyard bird also loves wilder, woodland areas and seems to prefer open ground, where insects are abundant for feeding.

Robins, as heralds of warmer days, symbolize spring and fresh growth. When robin appears, you may want to plant the seeds of something new, be an initiator, and seek opportunities. Robins' stance is cheerful and full of confidence, so it may be time to boost your self esteem, be assertive and request what you desire when robin comes. The red robin is the male of the species, while females are a duller, less noticeable color, so robin can be associated with Mars energy. Pioneering, making a breakthrough, and being that "early bird that catches the worm" are robin's domains. If robins seem to have a message for you, take a positive hopeful attitude and go for it!

Bird Correspondences

Astrologically, birds are associated with the air signs: Aquarius, Gemini and Libra. As messengers, birds naturally relate to Mercury, the ruling planet of Gemini and Virgo. However, some birds, because of their individual qualities, embody the spirits of planets Jupiter, Venus, and Pluto, and the Sun as well. For example, the inky-colored crow and raven represent the dark, transformative energy of Pluto. The eagle is often associated with the Sun in lore and legend, however eagle's size associates him with Jupiter, too. Songbirds have Venus/Libra traits, as do birds that mate for life. And though we most often consider them creatures of air, many birds are also land walkers and water dwellers. The loon is a powerful swimmer, and the turkey can fly but prefers the ground and is strongly connected to Mother Earth in Native mythology.

So, whether you are an earth-, air-, water- or fire-sign personality, one or more birds may attract you with traits you admire, behaviors you reflect, and unique talents you could develop.

About the Author

Robin Ivy is a radio DJ and an astrologer in Portland, Maine. Her morning radio program is a mix of astrology and alternative rock streaming worldwide online at www.wcyy.com.

The Buzz About Bees

By Janice Sharkey

Where would we be without the bee? We rely on them to pollinate our flowers. Bees are as old as the garden itself as they have been around for millions of years. They have been associated with humans for a long time and cave paintings depict the harvesting of honey as far back as 8,000 years ago. The Eastern honeybee was domesticated a long time ago in China. The Egyptians were also beekeepers and their methods spread throughout the Mediterranean and the Middle East. Egyptians used the Western honeybee, which is also the most widely used species today. The native bee (*Apis melliphera*) is one of many species of bee that belongs to the insect order *Hymenoptera*.

Honeybees are a Gardener's Friend

The honeybee in particular is truly the gardener's friend. While many species of insects consume nectar, honeybees refine and concentrate nectar to make honey. In ancient times humans observed honey bears and other mammals raid beehives for honey and then copied them. Once people found out how valuable honey was, they had to master the art of how to harvest it without being stung.

Honeybees are Crucial Pollinators

As the field bees forage for nectar, pollen sticks to the fuzzy hairs which are over their bodies. Some of this pollen rubs off on the next flower they visit, fertilizing the flower and resulting in better fruit production. Some plants will not produce fruit at all without the help of honeybees. In the U.S. alone, it is estimated that honeybees accomplish a quarter of the pollination needed for all fruit produced for human consumption.

Field bees stop periodically to groom themselves and collect the pollen on their pollen baskets. They remove this load from their legs when they return to the hive and the house bees store it in a special part of the comb. The pollen provides protein and other essential nutrients for the bees.

Why Bees Make Honey

Honey is produced from the nectar of flowers so bees will have plenty of food when it is unavailable from plants. Unlike other insects, honeybees remain active throughout the winter, consuming and metabolizing honey in order to keep from freezing to death. Flower nectar is one of two feed sources used by honeybees. The other is pollen. Both are gathered by the field bees as they fly about on their daily foraging flights.

Inside the Honeycomb

The honeycomb is a golden treasure trove of insect engineering. It consists of flat vertical panels of six-sided cells made of beeswax. Beeswax is produced from glands on the underside of the abdomens of worker bees when they are between twelve and fifteen days old. House bees take the beeswax and form it with their mouths into the honeycomb. The cells within the comb will be used to raise young and to store honey and pollen. The comb is two-sided, with cells on both sides and are perfectly uniform in shape as well as built a precise distance apart depending on whether they are meant to contain food or young bees. The nursery area of the hive is called the brood comb, and that is were the queen lays her eggs.

What Is a Beehive?

A hive is an elaborate nest almost like an ordered fortress, and every bee within the hive knows its place and function. In the wild, beehives can be found inside hollow trees. Man-made bee-hives are usually made from wood, such as cedar, which contains natural oils that help preserve the wood and protect against insect attack. Hives are also made from pine or deal, but beware of these as they can warp, split, and they are heavy to move. If you do want to start your own beehive, you will need protective cloth-ing and a "smoker" to make the bees sleepy before you open up a hive.

Bees are social insects that work together in a highly struc-tured social order. Each bee belongs to one of three specialized groups called castes. The different castes are: queens, drones, and worker bees. A hive can contain up to 20,000 bees during the summer season.

Queen Bees

There is only one queen bee in a hive and her main purpose in life is to make more bees. She can lay over 1,500 eggs per day and will live from two to eight years. She is larger than the other bees—up to 20 mm—and has a longer abdomen than the work-ers or drones. She has chewing mouthparts. Her stinger is curved with no barbs on it and she can use it many times.

Drones

These are male bees and, surprisingly, they have no sting. They live about eight weeks, and only a few hundred, at most, are ever present in the hive. Their sole function is to mate with a queen. A drone's eyes are noticeably bigger than those of the other castes. Their large eyes help them to spot the queens when they are on their nuptial flight. Any drones left at the end of the season are con-sidered non-essential and will be driven out of the hive to die.

Workers

Worker bees do all the different tasks needed to maintain and operate the hive. They make up the vast majority of the hive's occupants and they are all sterile females. When young, they are called house bees and they work in the hive doing comb construction, brood rearing, tending the queen and drones, cleaning, temperature regulation, and defending the hive. Older workers are called field bees. They forage outside the hive to gather nectar, pollen, water, and certain sticky plant resins used in hive construction. Workers born early in the season will live about six weeks, while those born in the autumn will live until the following spring. Workers are about 12 mm long and highly specialized for what they do. They have a structure called a pollen basket (*corbiculum*) on each hind leg, an extra stomach for storing and transporting nectar or honey, and four pairs of special glands that secrete beeswax on the underside of their abdomen. They have a straight, barbed stinger that can only be used once. It rips out of their abdomen after use, which kills the bee.

Kinds of Bees

Believe it or not there are over 25,000 kinds of bees in the world! Here are a few common kinds.

Bumblebee

There are about fifty different types of bumblebee (*Bombus sp.*) in North America. Much larger than other bees, some species are over an inch long. They are densely covered with yellow and black (and sometimes red) bands of hairs. Their long mouthparts allow them to gather nectar from flowers that have their nectaries buried deep within the petals of some flowers. They are social nesters, although they are not as highly ordered as that of honeybees. In contrast to honeybees, their nests are made anew each spring by solitary queens who hibernate through the winter. The large bumblebees seen in the spring are queens looking for food and a place to start a new colony. They will often take over an abandoned field mouse nest for their own.

Carpenter Bees

Carpenter bees look like bumblebees but they may be recognized by their dark, shiny (hairless) abdomen. The common North American species east of the Rocky Mountains is *Xylocopa virginica*. They are solitary nesters and make their nest by chewing tunnels into wood. Often, people will notice them burrowing into the rafters of barns or outbuildings. The males are sometimes seen patrolling near a nest in an obvious bobbing flight. The bee is looking for a mate, not a fight, and since it is a male it cannot sting you.

Leaf-cutting Bees

Leaf-cutting bees (*Megachile sp.*) have the interesting trait of chewing little circles out of leaves or flower petals and using these to construct small, thimble-shaped nests in a dry, protected location. They are typically dark in color, with whitish hairs running across the abdomen, and they range in size from 5 to 25 mm. There are 130 species in North America. Both leafcutters and mason bees are superior pollinators compared to honeybees. One leafcutter bee will do the same amount of pollination as twenty honeybees.

Mason Bees

Mason bees (*Osmia sp.*) typically use the abandoned tunnels of wood-boring beetles for their nest. These small bees are not social. They mate straight after hatching in the spring. The female then searches for an appropriate hole or crevice to build her nest. Mason bees are closely related to the leaf-cutting bees. To gather pollen, they both use a brush of hairs on the underside of the abdomen called a "scopa" instead of pollen baskets on their legs.

Honey-healing Food

Honey is a marvellous natural energizing food, which also helps digestion. It is known to settle nervous stomachs and can also be used to heal dry and irritated skin. Royal jelly is not only a wonderful luxurious honey that is full of nutrients, but it also is said to act as an aphrodisiac. Because honey holds natural sugar, it is slow to release in the body and is better for us than refined cane sugar. It is well known that a honey and lemon drink can help to heal sore throats and keep colds away. Honey is a natural Sun food and belongs under the sign of Leo. Its golden color even looks solar energized and, let's face it, most flowers that bloom do so with the help of the Sun to produce the nectar and pollen that goes into allowing bees to produce it.

Be a Beekeeper

Why not produce your very own honey? It makes the perfect present for friends. Just think of all the other products you can produce from beeswax to polish and candles to honey soap. The choice is yours. The options are endless. One things is for sure, though: honey harvests represent not just health, but eco-wealth.

About the Author

Janice Sharkey's complete bio appears on page 271.

Peaceful Eating for a More Peaceful Planet

By Judy McCoy Carman, M.A.

One day a shaman, who lives nearby, told me a story about energy fields and food that brought me to tears. He said that he was preparing to eat some meat from a cow. The shaman knew this cow had been raised with greater care and attention than most cows receive. Nevertheless, he decided to "feel" the vibration or energy of the meat before he ate it. When he did so, he experienced the cow's pain and sadness from the time she was taken from her mother, and the pain and fear when she was killed. The shaman did proceed to eat that meat, but it was the last time he would ever do so. He became very ill and realized he could no longer take such suffering into his body.

We are embarking on a new era of higher consciousness in these times in which we are living. Astrology, Native, and other religious prophecies, and many futurists say that we are being given an unprecedented opportunity to awaken to our true nature as divine beings, to actually evolve as a species to become a peaceful, nurturing, creative presence on the planet. In my book, *Peace to All Beings,* I propose that we can become Homo Ahimsa, the Kind Human, dedicated to living in *ahimsa*, the Sanskrit word for harmlessness, nonviolence, and unconditional love.

What does vegetarianism have to do with this "new humanity coming into form," as Pierre Teilhard de Chardin referred to it? Perhaps, Michael's story can shed some light on the answer. Michael Ho, a young man living in San Francisco, had recommitted himself to veganism after reading *Peace to All Beings.* Soon after that, he told me, "I witnessed a bird hit the windshield of a car and die on the freeway. It was the first time I really felt for this small creature and could identify with the pain it must have suffered. Before, I was numb to the pain and suffering of animals, because I think it was too painful for me to accept. I just blocked it out. But this was the first time I was courageous enough to open my heart up to this beautiful creature's suffering and horrible death. Your book has made me stronger and more courageous."

There is a concentration of energy in Capricorn and Aquarius as we enter this new year of 2009. While Capricorn is connected to meat eating and convention, Aquarius creates an energy of opening up to new ideas, leaving old thought patterns behind, and looking for truth and better ways of living into the future. In addition, the Moon evokes the maternal, feminine energy of compassion and nurturing. The Union of Concerned Scientists has urgently let us know that the future for all life on Earth depends on human beings finding a way to stop destroying and begin living in harmony with all life. As this new year dawns, with its Aquarian energy pouring forth, let us seize this opportunity to bring more love and peace to this suffering Earth and all the beings who dwell here with us.

Few subjects address so directly the heart of our challenge as that of pure vegetarianism and veganism. As most of you know, pure vegetarianism refers to a diet of plants, seeds, grains, and no animal products of any kind. Veganism is more than a diet, in that it is an ahimsa ethic by which to live. While it is nearly impossible in this world to do absolutely no harm to any being, vegans aim to do the least harm possible by not eating or wearing animals and not supporting companies that exploit them in laboratories, entertainment, factory farms, and the leather, fur, silk, and many other industries. This attitude of kindness extends, of course, to human beings as well and, therefore, does not support sweatshops and the many other forms of human exploitation. Likewise, ahimsa is extended to the Earth and all life upon it. Veganism is an ethic that is all encompassing in its respect for all creation and its awareness of the interconnectedness and oneness of all.

While there is clearly a physical aspect to the vegan life, the spiritual aspect is, perhaps, the most important and exciting part of this way of living, both for the individual and for the future of the planet. And it is an extremely important part of the great awakening that is taking place in the hearts of so many human beings. Dr. Gabriel Cousens explains in his book, *Spiritual Nutrition,* that we are being given the opportunity to integrate our body, mind, and spirit and, in doing so, become "superconductors" of divine energy. In his book, *Six Foundations for Spiritual Life,* Cousens lists veganism as the first foundation. He states, "we eat to enhance our Communion with the Divine." Cousens makes it clear that a pure vegetarian diet is essential if one is learning to quiet the mind, to become a clearer channel for divine inspiration, and to open the heart to universal love.

Many of you will remember the story of Queenie, the cow who escaped the Queens neighborhood slaughterhouse in New York City. Tina Volpe, in her book *Fast Food Craze,* describes Queenie's dramatic escape and the nationwide outcry to save her life that was covered on TV and in newspapers all over the country. Thanks to that massive public outcry of compassion, she now lives at Farm Sanctuary in New York where she is safe and can live out the rest of her life happily with the other animals living there.

To me, this story reveals something beautiful about human beings: we do sense our kinship with animals. Of course, we all know that children are naturally aware of this relationship. Nearly every children's book on the market is about animals.

From birth, we love animals and want to relate to them as our friends, but somewhere along the way, our culture works to harden our hearts to them and erects, as Will Tuttle so aptly describes in his book *The World Peace Diet: Eating for Spiritual Health and Social Harmony,* "a taboo against knowing who you

eat." This emotional shutdown causes great spiritual unrest. Closing our hearts to other beings is spiritually harmful to ourselves.

I believe that in these intense times, it isn't just personal inner peace we are all seeking anymore. *Moon Sign Book* readers and many other folks are seeing the bigger picture. The Earth herself and all life upon her are in trouble because of our destructive actions. We need to raise our vibrational, spiritual nature, not just for ourselves, but also for the world at large.

Erin Pavlina, author of *Vegan Family Favorites,* writes that early in life she wanted to help bring the planet to a state of love, peace, and harmony. Her spirit guides told her she would have to raise her vibration, and one powerful way to do that was to stop eating animals. They explained that eating animals lowers our vibration because we are taking into our bodies the torture and death of the animals. After a time of denial, Erin finally decided to try giving up meat but not dairy and eggs. She noticed that her psychic abilities did increase, but it wasn't until she tried a strict vegan diet that her "psychic abilities increased massively." She also noted that 95 percent of her chronic health problems disappeared, her sense of compassion increased, and so did her connection to Source. Today, she writes and works as a psychic medium at www. ErinPavlina.com, and is on track to fulfill her spiritual purpose.

Tuttle explains that we have allowed this destruction to life on this planet because of "our inner desensitization to vibrational energy frequencies—the numbness that keeps us from screaming or weeping when we bite into a hot dog or cheeseburger." Tuttle goes on to say that our social progress toward world peace is thwarted, because we pollute "our shared consciousness-field by the dark agonies endured by billions of animals killed for food . . ."

Zarinea of California noticed a shift in her consciousness when she became vegan. "I have become more compassionate towards all forms of life, and not just animals. I have become more sensitive regarding issues of the environment and human rights violations." Her experience certainly resonates with the Jewish saying, "The deed shapes the heart." She beautifully states, "My hope is that all human beings will not only walk in the light, but also come to an understanding that all life has meaning, and should be respected in all forms."

There are a growing number of families who are raising their children as vegans. One mom recently related a story about her daughter who, at the age of three, demonstrated extraordinary compassion. Sammi was playing with several children while the mothers visited, when suddenly she began to scream as if she herself were terribly injured. As the mothers rushed to the scene, they found Sammi crying and cupping her hands over a tiny ant. The boy next to her had already stepped on some ants, and Sammi was trying to protect this one from him. Sammi's mom, who was vegan before her children were born and whose two children have never tasted any animal food, states that her children are "protective of every living creature."

The theosophist, Charles Leadbeater, reported that he could see energy fields around people. When people were eating meat, he was able to see a darkness clouding their energy fields. Another New Thought pioneer, Charles Fillmore, who co-founded Unity Church with his wife Myrtle, stated, "The mind is incapable of vibrating at the higher frequencies and manifesting the higher aspects of mind, when a person eats dead flesh." The Fillmores established Unity Village near Kansas City, and only vegetarian food was served there. In addition, no leather covered Bibles were allowed in the church. The Fillmores were in the good company of many mystics, saints, and others who knew that one can only proceed so far in one's spiritual development while simultaneously supporting the domination and killing of animals.

Amy, a yoga teacher, gave up the flesh of land animals after seeing raw meat brought in to her table at a Japanese restaurant. Several years later, she gave up fish after awakening to the pain of a lobster being boiled alive. She states so beautifully that "at times it has been very painful, being so sensitive as there is so much suffering in this world. But along with the pain, there comes reverence for life, all life. What greater way to demonstrate that reverence than by refusing to use animals for food, clothing or any other purpose. Since purifying my diet from any animal pain or suffering, I seem to have a deep well of compassion for all living creatures, be it a fly or worm or polar bear. I watch with wonder and awe at spiders spinning their webs, at the snails moving in their shells, at the bees sucking the nectar from flowers, at the beauty of flowers, and all the way up the food chain. I see and feel the interconnectivity of it all."

The most joyful and rewarding aspect of vegan living is knowing that with this one simple act, we are making a monumental difference for all sacred life. We are all bombarded by news of wars, murders, parents killing their children, children killing classmates, genocide, the starvation of vast numbers of people, the impending death of the oceans and rivers from pollution and overfishing, the loss of habitat and homes for wildlife and indigenous people as giant corporations take over their lands, global warming, the cruel confinement of billions of innocent animals in factory farms, and the list goes on and on. Very few of us are in a position to stop the killing of the innocent Falun Dafa people in China or stop the giant drift-net ships from raping the seas. The dark energy that surrounds our planet at this time from all the dark deeds done can be overwhelming even when we are not consciously thinking about these tragedies.

But veganism is a simple action that we can take that is so powerful and so full of light energy that it can literally have an effect on every one of the tragedies listed above. We can lighten the dark energy field around the Earth, improve our own health, save the lives of starving people and the lives of around 100 animals per year, bring peace to our own hearts, and simultaneously draw all life closer to creating a paradise on this Earth. And this action doesn't even take any extra time out of our days.

Those who are paying attention and waking up to the crisis in the world know we are running out of time. Each one of us must participate in bringing the culture out of the old paradigm of domination and exploitation. It is we who will demonstrate how to live within the new paradigm of cooperation, love, and mutual respect. In so doing, we will, perhaps in our lifetimes, be able to see the old paradigm simply become obsolete and disappear. It has been said "we are the ones we have been waiting for."

We, the animals, indeed all creation, are here to praise and celebrate life together, not to make war against each other. Great thinkers through the ages have made it clear that, as Isaac Bashevis Singer stated so eloquently, "As long as people will shed the blood of innocent creatures, there can be no peace, no liberty, no harmony between people." The vegan life is a selfless commitment to literally bring heavenly peace to Earth. This year, with its Aquarian influence pouring forth wisdom and truth, may we seek the Light as never before, go forth with confidence, and say to all beings: "Greetings, earthlings. We come in peace. We are the new Homo Ahimsa."

About the Author

Judy Carman is an animal rights, environmental, and peace activist. She is founder of the Circle of Compassion Initiative, cofounder of Animal Outreach of Kansas www.animaloutreach-ks.org/, and cofounder of the Prayer Circle for Animals at www.circleofcompassion.org. She is author of Peace to All Beings: Veggie Soup for the Chicken's Soul *(Lantern Books).*

References

Cousens, G. *Spiritual Nutrition: Foundations for Spiritual Life and the Awakening of Kundalini* (North Atlantic Books, 2005).

Tuttle, W. *The World Peace Diet: Eating for Spiritual Health and Social Harmony* (Lantern Books, New York, 2005).

Pavlina, E. Blog at www.erinpavlina.com/blog/

SPEAK (Spiritual People Embracing Animals with Kindness) at www.members.dodo.com.au/~kritters/

Volpe, Tina. *The Fast Food Craze: Wreaking Havoc on Our Bodies and Our Animals* (Canyon Publishing: Parks, AZ, 2005).

Growing Heirloom Tomatoes

By Dallas Jennifer Cobb

I love tomatoes, that versatile vegetable that's really a fruit. I love them raw, cooked and dried. I also love to grow tomatoes. This love affair with tomatoes is relatively new. Many years ago I started to hate tomatoes, those tasteless, woody things at the grocery store. I avoided them. I wandered away when I saw them, steered clear of them in restaurants and social situations, and even banned them from my home. But a warm summer affair changed all of that.

At a local event, called a Heirloom Hurrah!, I was introduced to heirloom tomatoes. Dazzled by the variety of colors and shapes I found myself reaching out to stroke the smooth flesh. Gently holding the fruit, I brought it to my nose and was delighted by the bouquet. It actually smelled like a tomato. The scent lingered, stimulating my olfactory senses, making my mouth water. When a grower offered a taste I responded hungrily. When I put the juicy fruit flesh into my mouth the love affair began.

By the end of that afternoon I had tasted about twenty different heirloom tomatoes, each one possessing a unique personality. Subtly different from each other, the varieties possessed individual appearance, scent and taste. I ate heirloom tomatoes raw, in salsa, cooked into sauce, as part of a sweet jam like spread, and in a spicy chutney. Yum.

That night I lay in bed savoring the day, wondering how I could get some of those tomatoes for myself. I was curious to know all about the object of my affection, and I wanted to possess it. I wanted to have, and eat, tomatoes that tasted fully alive.

Heirlooms. Where did they come from? What made them taste so good? How did they get all those colors? How could I secure a source? My infatuation led me to research heirloom tomatoes, and this is what I learned.

What is an Heirloom Tomato?

Heirloom is the name given to a plant with a traceable history that stretches generations. Like family heirlooms that have been handed down from one generation to the next, heirloom seeds have been preserved and handed down within families and among friends, for generations. Individual strains have evolved and adapted over generations to the particular climate and growing conditions they have historically inhabited, developing natural resistance to insects and disease common to the area. Heirloom varieties exist all over the world, with each individual variety suited to the ecosystem it developed within.

Because of their adaptation, each heirloom variety is genetically unique, a strain ideally suited for the ecology and climate that shaped it. Natural adaptation and selection has produced robust breeds ideally suited to organic growing techniques.

Why Do Heirlooms Matter?

While the historic origin of heirloom seed saving was ordinary agricultural reproduction practices, these days it is considered an almost subversive practice. Multinational corporations have been trying to take control of agricultural stock and breeds, purposefully buying up, and suppressing, the available genetic diversity of food crops. In the past fifteen years many varieties of seeds have disappeared from seed catalogues. With the disappearance of a variety there is the loss of its naturally developed resistance.

Multinational corporations purchase seed stock in an attempt to gain control of the seed market. By developing hybrids and genetically modified seeds which are patented, and suppressing other varieties of seed, they can control the market selling only their patented varieties to farmers, gardeners and consumers. Under the conditions of the patent, such seed is licensed for one time use only to the consumer. This is almost a moot point because genetically modified seed is bred to be sterile and is generally unable to reproduce viable seeds. These practices facilitate market control and develop a dependence on the purchase of patented, genetically modified seed.

Because the DNA in these genetically modified plants has been artificially altered they lack a natural resistance to disease and pests. With increased crop vulnerability, the grower of hybrid and genetically modified seed needs to purchase herbicides and pesticides to treat crop problems.

Coincidentally, these herbicide and pesticide products are produced by the same multinational corporations.

The Heirloom Movement

A lot of common heirloom varieties were brought to North America by our ancestors when they immigrated, and others can be traced to their indigenous first nations roots. Today, many heirloom seed savers are not just farmers or gardeners who want to grow food, but visionaries who are unwilling to allow corporations to control seed stock, and our heirloom inheritance.

Seed saving has taken on an almost subversive identity. Heirloom seed savers are often vocal advocates, educating the public about the perils of monoculture, genetic modification, and the corporate ownership of food sources. Frighteningly, the genetic diversity of the world's food crops is being quickly eroded, with strains of hardy vegetables and fruits disappearing after thousands of years of adaptation, development, and survival.

Genetic diversity and adaptation enables plants to evolve to resist emerging modern diseases and pests. Without genetic diversity and naturally acquired resistance, food crops are vulnerable to infestation and epidemics. Like bugs in the human system, there are strains of disease developing that are immune to plant "antibiotics." In the agricultural sector such super bugs could wipe out entire crops, varieties, and breeds. We're all familiar with the Irish potato famine. While this blight spread across Europe, only in Ireland were the consequences so drastic. This was due to a country-wide reliance on a limited genetic pool. The potato crops had little or no genetic resistance to the emerging disease, and crops were subsequently wiped out. Starvation prompted widespread Irish immigration and migration to other more abundant areas.

Not Just A Few Seed Savers

By preserving heirloom varieties mány seed savers believe that they are investing in insurance against another disaster like the Irish potato famine. This advocacy and preventative practice is being taken on not just by a few seed savers or gardeners, but by renowned scientists and citizens concerned about genetic modification and the possible impact a limited seed stock could produce.

Jack Harlan, a world renowned plant collector and preservationist wrote:

> These resources stand between us and catastrophic starvation on a scale we cannot imagine. In a very real sense, the future of the human race rides on these materials. The line between abundance and disaster is becoming thinner and thinner, and the public is unaware and unconcerned. Must we wait for disaster to be real before we are heard? Will people listen only after it is too late.

The Council for Responsible Genetics is comprised of scientists, lawyers, public health advocates, and citizens concerned about the social, ethical, and environmental impact of new genetic technologies. They drafted the following Safe Seed Pledge:

> Agriculture and seeds provide the basis upon which our lives depend. We must protect this foundation as a safe and genetically stable source for future generations. For the benefit of all farmers, gardeners and consumers who want an alternative, we pledge that we do not knowingly buy or sell genetically engineered seeds or plants. The mechanical transfer of genetic material outside of natural reproductive methods and between genera, families or kingdoms, poses great biological risks as well as economic, political, and cultural threats. We feel that genetically engineered varieties have been insufficiently tested prior to public release. More research and testing is necessary to further assess the potential risks of genetically engineered seeds. Further, we wish to support agricultural progress that leads to healthier soils,

genetically diverse agricultural ecosystems and ultimately people and communities."

Grow Your Own

Maybe you are worried about the declining seed stock, and the possibility of widespread crop destruction and subsequent starvation. Or, maybe, like me, you are hungering for a tomato that really tastes like a tomato. Either way, heirloom tomatoes may be what you are looking for.

The easiest way to start growing heirlooms is to purchase seedlings from a renowned grower. Ask at the nurseries in your area if they know who sells heirloom seedlings, then go and visit that greenhouse. Seedlings allow for a quick start. You take the seedling home, find a suitable location in your garden after the frost, and concentrate on the care and feeding of your tomatoes.

If heirloom seedlings are not available in your area, or you are a skilled gardener who enjoys starting plants from seed, a few contacts for heirloom seeds in Canada and the United States are listed at the end of this article.

Seed Saving

Once you have grown your own heirloom plants, seed saving is easy. You don't need special equipment, and it requires little effort and space. Learning to save your own seeds can save money, increase self sufficiency, and give you access to your favorites from year to year.

The Seed Savers Exchange (www.seedsavers.org) published a handy guide to seed saving. *Seed to Seed,* written by Suzanne Ashworth, is a valuable information source for the home gardener. It is widely available through most bookstores. The following information is summarized from *Seed to Seed*.

Saving Tomato Seed

Through the growing season, and the eating season, decide which varieties you like the best. Watch for a perfect fruit from one of these plants, one that is well shaped and colored, typical of the variety. Wait until it's fully ripe and pick it then. Slice the tomato open and remove the gooey part in the center that contains the seeds. Spread the goo out on a dry paper towel, and use your fingers to separate the seeds from the pulp. Let the seeds dry for two days and store them in a small glass jar with their name clearly labeled, and the date. Store these in a cool dry place, ready for next year's planting.

Heirloom seeds produce the same type of fruit that the parent plant produced, so you will grow the same kind of tomato next summer that you took the seed from this summer. Don't bother saving seeds from hybrid plants because they will only produce a plant similar to one or other of the parents, but not similar to the hybrid plant.

Starting Seeds

Count back six to eight weeks from the date when the last frost is expected in your area. Seedlings can't be transferred to the garden until after the last frost.

Whether you use individual pots, or large flats, sow your seeds into a sterile planting medium, covering them with a quarter inch of moist potting soil. The seed can't dry out, or it will die, so water lightly after planting, and cover the pots or flats with plastic covers to create a mini greenhouse, keeping the moisture in.

The temperature for germination of tomatoes seed is between 70 and 90 degrees Fahrenheit. Tomatoes also appreciate bottom heat, so many growers put their pots or flats on top of the fridge or freezer. During the germination stage sunlight is not necessary, as it's the temperature that signals the seed. Once germination has occurred and sprouts begin to appear move your pots or flats into bright light. This will stimulate the above ground growth of the plant.

It's time to transplant seedlings from the flats when the first set of true leaves appear. Working carefully so you don't injure the seedlings, transfer them to a 3- to 4-inch pot. If you planted seeds directly into 2-inch pots they can stay there a week or two longer before they move to a bigger pot. During the transplanting, add nutrient rich compost to the new pot so the seedlings get natural fertilizing.

Young seedlings still need full light, but appreciate a lower temperature of 60 to 70 degrees Fahrenheit. The coolness keeps them from growing too tall and spindly. Be sure to water regularly allowing the soil surface to dry to the touch in between waterings.

A week before they go outside, plants need to begin hardening off, acclimatizing to outdoor conditions. Start by putting them outdoor during the day in a sheltered southern exposure location. At night bring them inside to a cool location, or cover them if they are staying outside. Once plants begin to look darker and sturdier, they can be considered hardened off.

About Tomato Plants

Heirloom tomatoes are vines, or 'indeterminate'. This means they produce fruit all season long and will grow into a tangle of stems if left alone. Pruning these vines will help to produce earlier, larger fruit. The main vine of a tomato plant is called the "mother stem," which develops "leaf stems" growing off of it at right angles. Leaf stems grow leaves where photosynthesis takes place. Flower clusters grow in the middle of a leaf stem section, coming directly off of the vine. The flowers eventually become the fruit. Suckers are the little branches that grow out of the crotch of the right angle leaf stem. The name "sucker" should alert you to the fact that you should pinch them off so that they don't suck too much energy out of the plant and away from the flower and fruit. When you find these, just pinch them off and compost them.

A healthy, productive tomato plant is one with a strong mother stem, and two long main leaf stems. The leaves are necessary for photosynthesis and shade which protects the developing fruit.

Lunar Growing Tips

If you are interested in growing heirloom tomatoes, why not learn a little about lunar gardening. The cycles of the Moon aid plants by focusing their energy appropriately on the specific task at hand.

While the New Moon is generally considered a good time for planting seeds, tomatoes prefer to be planted a few days before the Full Moon because they are annual crops that produce above ground with their seeds contained inside the fruit.

In the few days before the Full Moon, lunar gravity pulls water up, stimulating seeds to swell and germinate. The Full Moon allows for a focus then on above ground growth, stimulating the development of the primary stem and leaves.

As the Full Moon wanes in the third quarter, lunar energy is drawn down, and the focus shifts to root development. With the high gravitational pull, the soil retains moisture better, supporting root development. This is a good time for transplanting because root growth is stimulated and that helps the young plant overcome the shock of transplanting. The third quarter is also a time for pruning leaves because the vital energy is focused on the root, and the plant won't be made vulnerable by the removal of sucker vines.

The fourth quarter Moon phase is a resting period when there is decreased gravitational pull, and decreased moonlight. This is the time to prune to retard growth, harvest ripe fruit or seed, or transplant a plant.

Late in the summer, when you are harvesting ripe tomatoes, to save the seeds, take a moment to admire the abundant inheritance you have been given through heirloom seeds.

Cut the tomato, set aside the seeds, and think of a friend that you can pass some seeds on to, for next season. Share your inheritance, and preserve the heirlooms that belong to us all.

Where to Buy Heirloom Seeds

Baker Creek Heirloom Seeds
2278 Baker Creek Rd., Mansfield, Missouri 65704
417-924-8917 or www.rareseeds.com/

Deep Diversity (Peace Seeds)
P.O. Box 15700, Santa Fe, New Mexico 87506

800-957-3337 or fax: 505-438-7052
www.seedsofchange.com

Terra Edibles
Box 164 Foxboro, Ontario K0K 2B0
613-961-0654 or fax: 613-961-1462
www.terraedibles.ca

Cottage Gardener Heirloom Seed
4199 Gilmore Rd., RR#1, Newtonville, Ontario L0A 1J0
905-786-2388 fax: 905-786-2204
www.cottagegardener.com

Seeds of Diversity
Canada Box 36 Stn Q, Toronto, Ontario M4T 2L7
905-372-8983, toll free 1-866-509-7333
www.seeds.ca

About the Author
Dallas Jennifer Cobb lives in Wellington, in Ontario, Canada. She loves to garden and prepare fabulous food for her family. You can contact her at gaias.garden@sympatico.ca/

How Light Affects Social and Breeding Behaviors of Birds

By Carole Schwalm

Previously, here in New Mexico, in my little corner of the world, lovely birds sang the most beautiful songs that lulled me to sleep like a mama's lullaby. In the morning, families of quails lined up and marched into the front yard for their daily fresh water and birdseed. Not long after that another family of little birds came for their food and thanked us with a song that sounded like, "ebert, ebert, ebert." That was then. This is now. The birds are no longer here and they are noticeably missed. Besides my little feathered visitors, according to The Audubon Society report, the population of mountain chickadee is down in New Mexico by 83 percent. The meadowlark down by 57 percent. The pinion jay down by 54 percent.

The question is: Why is the Earth losing her birds? One reason is that bright lights upset hormonal levels and confuse breeding and migration patterns. You'll understand if you look at the cities at night, with their street lights, house and building illumination, outside lighting of walkways, and thousands of car headlights. Birds naturally fly to the brightest part of the sky, but nature meant that to be the Moon and the stars, not city lights. Light is nature's message to the bird's circadian system that tells them when to migrate.

But urban light imitates, then confuses birds. Instead of migrating, birds stay and end up trapped by cold weather. Available food sources disappear. They've built nests, thinking that winter is spring, and deaths are doubled because both adult and chicks freeze and starve. Those that do begin to migrate follow the city lights and fly north, when they should go south. Lights alter hormonal levels, and hormones are toxic in the wrong levels. This too, results in premature breeding.

Migrators, or birds in urban habitats, encounter danger in other ways, too. Michael Mesure, of the Fatal Light Awareness Program, estimates 100 million birds are killed annually crashing into man-made structures. Their vision and magnetic perception systems skewed, disoriented birds fly into lighted buildings. Fifteen hundred birds a night crashed into Chicago's John Hancock building, until they turned off the ornamental lighting. This is only one structure in the cityscapes across the country. In 1954, 50,000 birds were killed in one night, when they followed a beam of light at Georgia's Warner Robins Air Force Base.

The increasing greenhouse gases contributing to climate change have driven 30 percent of species to extinction. April 2, 2007, the U.S. Supreme Court ruled that the Environmental Protection Agency must consider greenhouse gases as pollutants and deal with them through the regulations the Bush administration fiercely opposed. There were five votes in favor and four against. Don't you wonder what those four against were thinking when you consider the risk of harm that is "actual" and "imminent," as judge John Paul Stevens wrote?

Cell phones require towers that emit microwaves, which skew a bird's magnetic compass. This is only one example of "waves" that can short-circuit a bird's steering sense. Witnesses have seen birds fly straight into the ground, or they will crash into each other, trying to reorient themselves.

One-third of 1,900 North American bird species use wetlands—138 species actually can't survive without them. Wetlands are breeding areas. They offer shelter, and are vital to long migrations. The rising sea levels have swamped natural wetlands. On the other hand, drought conditions mean a 50 percent decline in breeding waterfowl. Over 100,000 acres of wetlands are destroyed every year. Eighty percent of hazardous waste sites drain into wetlands, and wetland areas are becoming filled for building projects.

Migrators and flying birds risk even more. A segment of Mega Disasters aired on the History Channel on October 20, 2007. Scientists addressed pandemics like bird flu in the context of cosmic micro-organisms that float through the air, like specks of dust we see in the house when sunlight shines brightly through the windows. Some believe the organisms originate from things like asteroid or comet debris. Of course, flying birds absorb the alien organisms, depleting their populations, possibly doing the same for our own, because there is no cure, yet.

Jet contrails may be another hazard to birds. NASA Langley Research says that jet contrails are just "water vapors and ice crystals." Maybe. On the other hand, the Air Force released a report in 1999 stating: "Planes were dumping fuel before landing," perhaps a cause of the contrails. Like car exhausts, something has to be ejected. Jet fuel consists of a toxic, ethylene dibromide. People living in high-contrail areas have experienced respiratory infections that can't be cured with antibiotics. People in high-contrail areas have also reported an extraordinary amount of plants and trees dying, which endangers bird habitats and nesting areas.

"So," some people might say, "a few birds die!" There's much more to it, though, than just birds crashing into the illuminated buildings. Those birds fall to the sidewalks and in the alleyways. Scavengers, like mice and rats, scrounge on the dead birds, and rodent populations thrive as bird populations decrease.

Birds eat "gazillions" of insects every day! That little chickadee you see in the yard (a bird whose population declined 83 percent last year in New Mexico), eats 200 to 500 insects every twenty-four hours. This is in addition to 4,000 eggs and larvae that, if left, would grow to be adult insects that would produce new insects. Multiply those numbers times the 100 million birds we lose annually. Migrating birds eat a tremendous amount of insects both before and during their journey. Some species of birds eat tree-leaf-eating caterpillars. The tiny hummingbird can eat one-fourth its body weight in aphids, daily.

Animals are natural adaptors—if they have the luxury of time to do so. But it may take generations for the remaining species to move their habitats. And as birds move into new territories, other animals, plants, and insects must shift, as well.

What Can You Do?

We have to save our remaining open spaces and wetlands. We have to address global warming and energy policies. On an individual level, we can decrease decorative illumination at home. See what you can do to help the Campaign for Dark Skies in your own community. Contact some of the Web sites listed under "Resources" at the end of this article. Learn about programs and what you can do. Write to your local and national politicians, on the off-chance they just might listen now and then and enact something that helps the environment. We can hope that the Capricorn/Virgo earth energy will make people more conscious of the Earth's delicate condition, rather than promote the amassing of financial power.

If you have a yard, feed and water your birds. In New Mexico, in October 2007, I bought 20 pounds of birdseed for $3.50. This is a small price to pay for the reward of watching and feeding the birds.

Fresh, clean water is a necessity for birds. We use saucers designed to go under plant pots because they are inexpensive and can be replaced often to avoid pollution of any kind. The long containers that go under window-box planters are perfect bird baths. Birds need to take baths in the winter as well as in the summer. As the owner of Wild Birds Unlimited says in a local radio commercial: "A fluffy, clean bird is a warm bird."

Once you begin feeding the birds, they depend on you. You must be a responsible steward. You can't simply forget, or just stop feeding. They come every day, trusting that you'll be there for them. In return, besides their beauty and their music, each one will eat 200 to 400 insects (and more) a day. Wouldn't you rather have more birds than insects? Wouldn't you prefer owls to mice and rats? Birds scatter seeds for you. They make more birds. They symbolize good chi as they fly around your home. They deserve our tender, loving care.

Decreasing Populations

A study released by the National Audubon Society (Santa Fe New Mexican, June 17, 2007) reported that twenty common American bird populations are only half what they were forty years ago.

- Everglades wading birds—some down 80 to 90 percent
- Mountain Chickadee—down 83 percent
- Sanderling—down 80 percent

- Loggerhead Shrike—down 74 percent
- Whimbrel—down 60 percent
- Bobwhite Quail—down 57 percent
- Meadowlark—down 57 percent
- Pinon Jay—down 54 percent
- Boreal Chickadee—down 50 percent
- Field Sparrow—down 50 percent
- Dowitches—down 40 percent

Resources

- National Audubon Society
- "Campaign for Dark Skies" at www.britastro.org/dark-skies /wildlife.html
- www.birdola.com/bird facts.html
- www.birdlife.com
- Contrails at www.usatoday.com
- Contrails at www.geocities.com
- Fanny Carrier, Supreme Court at www.terradaily.com

About the Author

Carole Schwalm lives in Sante Fe, New Mexico. Her interest in gardening comes from following after her grandfather, a life-long farmer. The accent on every element but earth in her astrological chart made it mandatory for her to get her hands in the sod or risk floating away in the clouds of dust or drowning in a tidal wave of emotion or spontaneously combusting.

Earthly Powers

By *Janice Sharkey*

To the better furthering of
the gardener's travails,
he ought afore to consider,
That the Garden earth be
apt and good,
well turned in with dung,
at a due time of the year,
in the increase of the Moon,
she occupying an apt place
in the Zodiack,
In agreeable aspect
of Saturn, & well-placed
in the sight of heaven . . .
for otherwise his care
and pains bestowed about
the seeds and plants,
nothing availed the Garden.

THOMAS HILL,
THE GARDENER'S LABYRINTH (1577)

What on earth is your soil like? If we feed it, it will in turn feed us. Without healthy earth teeming with life, our world as we know it would crumble. Your soil will say a lot about what is possible. If it is overworked, and underfed, it will become impoverished. The only natural way is to organically maintain, and increase the fertility of the topsoil by encouraging organisms into the soil and thereby converting inactive minerals and water back into it. It is this cycle of life which regenerates and builds up humus-rich, water holding loamy soils which is the real sign of fertility. Chemical fertilizers and overworked soils destroy this natural store of living organisms for a short-term quick fix—a bit like someone living on vitamin pills instead of a good wholesome diet.

Capricorn, being an earthy sign, is naturally rooted in the soil. After all, Saturn was not God of agriculture for nothing; he had a purpose to sow words of wisdom to us mere earthlings: "As you sow, so shall you reap." Capricorn is a reasonably good sign to plant under, favouring root crops. Ruled by Saturn, its element is earth and is the ideal time to apply organic fertilizers. Culpeper's definition of Saturn is "of a cold, and binding nature." Many herbs fall under Saturn rulership because they offer medicinal healing such as limiting bleeding, like knapweed, or cooling inflammation from nightshade or moss and in some cases helping to heal bones from holly. Capricorn relates to the knees and bones in medical astrology, while in plants it rules the bark and structural material, so plants like Solomon's Seal, the elm tree, holly and fumitory, to mention a few, can help heal the joints. Saturnian nature is coldish, preferring to remain a little distant, and that is exactly how Culpeper described where to look for Capricorn plants: "Herbs grow along waysides, hedges and ditches." Comfrey ideally grows near ditches and is a strong pest resistant herb that is pleasing to the eye and replenishes the soil when done. Hemlock and henbane are wayside lovers, too, both ancient medicinal herbs, where were used to look after the humours. That's not to say that the old goat is bereft of humor, although there is still much superstition about Saturn being the bringer of bad luck. However, halting progress is Saturn's way of bringing wisdom and teaching until we learn to listen.

Soil, and the condition of it, is the concern of Capricorn. Worms and all manner of insect strata belong down in that often forgotten dark space—earth. With healthy soil we reap the rewards. When poor, it limits growth. Therefore, take heed of Capricorn's wisdom; feed the worms by having that wormery; feed that soil with a compost heap; use natural soil improvers and let the myriad of microcosms within the earth do the work.

Comfrey: An Earthy Tonic

One comfrey plant in your garden will repay you tenfold. Why? It is not only an attractant to bees; its leaves are harvested, it will make a wonderful fertilizer, and it will help to decompose the compose heap. Making a liquid manure from comfrey involves harvesting about half the leaves of one plant and shredding them before putting them into an old tub (preferably with a lid, as comfrey does smell a little). Add some rainwater to cover the leaves and allow them to steep for three to four weeks. Then drain off the liquid and use at a rate of 1:20 with fresh water. Store any unused liquid in a plastic container. All that remains is to water the garden with it and watch the flowers grow.

Soil

You can get your soil in good condition by adding organic matter and digging only when it really needs it. An organic gardener feeds the soil so that it can feed the plants. There are a range of organic fertilizers to choose from including dried blood, bone meal, blood, fish and bone meals, hoof and horn, and seaweed. One way of measuring how good your soil is to dig a few spade's full and count how many worms are present. Ideally for a meter's length you should have about twenty worms, but this will vary depending upon the weather and season. There will be fewer worms in a dry spell.

One crucial fact you need to discover is your soil's pH. Buy a soil tester kit from a good garden center and discover the soil type in your garden. Try different areas in your garden to see the variations of pH in the soil. There are three basic types: acidic, neutral, and alkaline. In most cases, it is best to not fight nature, but to go along with her. If the soil type is strongly acidic or alkaline, for example, it is best to choose plants that flourish in that type of soil.

The No-Dig Method of Gardening

There are more benefits from not digging. Apart from avoiding the usual sore back, there are other rewards. No digging preserves the soil structure and over time this allows the soil to improve naturally. Left to itself, the soil encourages organisms to develop and find a balance in the earth below our feet. By leaving the soil alone, less organic matter and moisture are lost. As if that wasn't enough reason to stop digging, consider that fewer weed seeds are brought to the surface, which means fewer weeds will grow. The soil may need turning over at first if it has been neglected, but once improved it can benefit from switching to the no-dig way. This approach is really beneficial when gardening with raised beds, such as in a kitchen garden plot.

Green Manures

Green manures are easily-grown plants that are dug into the soil before they mature, which adds organic matter to your garden. You will also need to add a general-purpose organic fertilizer such as pelleted-poultry manure. Green manures, such as red clover or mustard seed, have many other benefits. They also help break up the soil and bring nutrients up from the depth. Using an overwintering type will reduce leaching from the soil. They're not only good ground cover, they prevent weeds, give bees lots of nectar, and attract many more insects to feed.

Convert to Composting

Recycle all garden and raw household waste into a compost bin (preferably have two). There are probably a multitude of ways to successfully compost, but one essential tip is to ensure you have a balanced mix of organic matter. Ideally, you want waste that is high in nitrogen like grass, nettles, leaves, and weeds with tough woody waste (like shredded prunings). Adding kitchen waste that is raw and uncooked is ideal. By mixing both together you get more air microbes and insects breaking down the waste into compost. Once the first bin is full, tip the top waste into the second bin, which should be decomposed and ready for use. Start filling the empty bin again until full. Place the cover back on and leave until the heap is nearly rotted; then, repeat the process.

Compost bins come in various shapes and sizes, from drum tumbler bins to twin wooden composters. There is also the leaf-mold composter, which is made from wire meshing and decomposes at a slow rate, taking up to three years before leaf mulch is ready for use as compost. To quicken the process, put in some leaf decomposer, such as liquid comfrey.

Tips For Successful Composting

A rainproof lid is essential. Use a mixture of twigs and snappy material at the bottom for drainage. Use a strong container with few gaps in the side and a rainproof top. Chop or shred larger materials. Try to layer with grass cuttings, then kitchen waste, then shredded debris. Empty out and refill the container to turn the contents. Add water if too dry, or add drier ingredients if too wet. Use a compost activator (i.e., comfrey leaves or organic powder composed of herbal preparations, or seaweed or honey, which is mixed with water and helps to quicken the decomposing process to achieve fertile friable compost).

Semi-quick Route

Separate waste materials and layer at least 30 centimeters and try to get a mix of soft and tough materials. Spread the materials to the edges and firm down, or wet the material if it's too dry. If you are only adding kitchen waste, cover it with torn up newspaper. Thereafter, just leave to decompose.

Quick Route to Compost

Collect enough garden and kitchen waste to fill your bin on one go. Add manure, neighbors' weeds, and chapped rough wood, using a shredder if available. Mix all materials before adding to the bin—especially grass mowings, which exclude air—with drier items. Add water if needed, or dry waste if too wet. With this new supply of air, it allows fast-acting microbes to continue working.

Worm Composting

A wormery is an easy and efficient way of turning your kitchen waste into high quality compost all year round. Worms will eat their own weight in waste every day. The result is richer material than the original due to their unique digestive process. All organic kitchen waste, including cereals and bread, can be composted together with other garden waste. However, only small amounts of material at a time work best in a wormery as the tiger worms can only cope with a steady but small stream of waste to break down. If the material seems too acidic, a handful of dried seaweed can be added or extra shredded newspaper to reduce moisture and acidity. The wormery also needs a frost-free location. The final compost can be used as a top dressing or in potting compost. It is important that half of the material in the container is kept so that there are enough worms to breed and keep your wormery in production.

Making Your Own Wormery

A homemade wormery isn't too expensive. Find a small plastic dustbin and drill some ventilation holes into the lid and down at the bottom. Have a tray catch the liquid, which you can dilute with rainwater and use as a fertilizer. Stand the worm bin on top of a couple of bricks. Cover the bottom with a 4 centimeter layer of well-rotted compost, or use coir compost as bedding. Then, just put in the worms. Brandling or manure worms are most productive, or you can get some worms from a fishing tackle shop. A cheaper still alternative involves searching the top of a healthy compost heap and finding your own worms. Keep your wormery at 60 degrees Fahrenheit and protect it against the extremes of heat or cold. If there is a risk of frost, put hessian sacking or some fleece over the bin at night.

Your Soil Is Your Garden's Soul

As a gardener there is something magical about being in touch with the earth. Our soil is in many ways the garden's "soul." It holds the very cycle of life, and if looked after, it regenerates fertility back into the earth. When we dig in "magic muck," such as compost or manure, we are breathing life into all those myriad of microcosms that enrich the earth. Whatever soil type your garden is, be aware of its needs and give it an eco-boost with natural compost and it will repay you in a bountiful reward of flora and fauna.

About the Author
Janice Sharkey is an organic moon gardener who above all enjoys observing nature. She is a writer who gets therapy from gardening.

Garden Alchemy: Reclaiming Barren Spaces

By Pam Ciampi

Are you the type of gardener who loves a challenge? Who sees a forsaken plot with poor soil, a few half-dead plants and a forest of weeds and begins to rub her hands together with glee?

If the answer is yes, welcome to the Garden Alchemists! The mission of this unique group of unknown gardeners is to magically transform bare and unproductive areas of dirt into flourishing gardens. Read on to find out what kind of magic can make this happen.

The beauty of starting with nothing is that it's a win-win situation. Since you are starting at ground zero, any effort is guaranteed to be a big improvement and is sure to produce howls of approval. All of my gardens have started out as barren spaces. Although now most people would call them beautiful, they all began as either a newly cleared pine forest or a gravel and trash filled backyard. The soil was acid, dry, and either covered with a blanket of dead pine needles or choked with weeds. With plenty of patience and a little magic, all of them grew slowly but surely into beautiful and magical spaces. All you need to qualify as a Garden Alchemist is a challenging plot of any size that is mostly comprised of uninspired weeds and dirt. You can even be a member of the group if your garden is flourishing and in full bloom. The reason why is because every garden has that one difficult spot where no matter what you do, it seems that the garden devas have decreed that there nothing will ever grow.

"Show me your garden and I'll tell you who you are" refers to the idea that if looked at in a certain way, the smallest parts of our lives can be indicators of universal truths. Taking a long, hard look at your garden can be a very revealing experience. Is your garden formal or spontaneous, cared for or neglected? Do you like prickly or soft leafed plants? Are you a flower or a vegetable gardener, or do you favor long-lived perennials over flashy here today gone tomorrow annuals? The answers can be a real surprise!

Besides beautifying your environment and making your backyard a magical space for rest and relaxation, reclaiming barren spaces through garden alchemy is one of the easiest and least expensive ways to heal the barren parts of your inner self and help get your life back on the road to harmony and balance.

The practice of chemical alchemy goes back to medieval times, when there was a great interest in attempting to turn the lower energies of metals, such as lead, into higher energies, like gold. Alchemy is also found in astrology, where the idea of turning something that is dead into something full of life is reflected in the star-sign of Scorpio.

The Phoenix in the Garden

Garden alchemy has its roots in ancient times with the story of the mythical Babylonian bird called the Phoenix. The Phoenix story is about a beautiful and magical bird that was completely burnt up in a devastating fire. The Phoenix had fabulous hidden powers that, after its death, enabled it to rise up from the ashes of the same fire that caused its destruction. The Phoenix was reborn and would never die again. Like the amazing resurrection story of the Phoenix, the alchemical gardener creates something new out of something that is, for all practical purposes, dead. Creating life out of death is the essence of gardening magic.

To see how Mother Nature performs this amazing feat, let's take a look at the Jack pine tree, a native of the forests of the Great Lakes states. The following information was found on the National Park Service Web site under "Fire Management." The Jack pine tree is unique because the pinecones that carry its seeds are primarily released through fire. The majority of Jack pine seeds remain in closed waxy cones that stay alive on the branches for up to twenty years. But when the rare fire occurs, the intense heat that is created causes the wax to melt and the scales of the pinecone to open and release the seeds. Because the fire has already destroyed much of the existing vegetation and litter under the tree, the seed falls onto the ideal seedbed, which in turn ensures the continuation of the Jack pine.

Timing is Everything

Garden transformation begins with clearing the space to receive the seeds, the same way the fire did in the Jack pine story. The first step is getting rid of any litter, weeds, or rubbish. I once heard an old gardener remark: "My definition of a weed is anything I don't want in my garden. I don't like roses so I call them weeds."

Clean-up techniques, for roses or other "weeds" can include slash and burn, pruning, clear cutting, and many trips to the dump or recycling center. (One memorable garden clearing began by getting rid of all the old tires the previous tenant had left lying around the garden.)

Garden clean ups go better and more quickly when you are in tune with natural rhythms. Timing your garden activities to the zodiac signs of the Sun and the phases of the Moon is the next step in alchemical gardening. When the Sun and the Moon appear in certain fire and air signs, (Aries, Gemini, Leo, Sagittarius, and Aquarius), it is a signal that the time has come for cutting down, weeding, pruning, digging, and clean ups. This celestial wisdom has a practical basis, because fire and air are elements that correspond to hot, dry conditions. It follows that the times when things are brittle and dried up are the easiest times to cut them down and to get rid of or destroy them.

The seasons of choice for burning, clearing, and preparing the soil are spring and fall. As soon as the ground is ready, it's time to get your hands dirty. The alchemical gardener borrows the wisdom of the Native American tradition and only digs a hole where something will be planted. After the holes are dug, compost or fertilizer (a dead fish was the choice of Native Americans, but today fish emulsion is easiest to come by) and water are added to the hole Then, the plant is set in. This method has worked for centuries; and while it will magically cut down on time spent over a shovel, it will also save precious back muscles.

The key to finding the magical days for garden clean-ups and working the soil is choosing the right the season of the year and the phases of the Moon, and then combining them with the correct sign of the zodiac. Because these days change from year to year, it will be necessary to consult an astrological calendar or almanac when planning your garden each year.

Garden Activity Dates in 2009

The key days for garden clean-up and preparing the soil for planting in spring are when the Sun is in Aries and the Moon is waning and in fire or air signs (Aries, Gemini, Leo, Libra, Sagittarius, or Aquarius). Those dates are:

> March 12–13, 16–18, 21–23
> April 9,13–14,18–19

The key days for garden clean-up and preparing the soil for winter are when the Sun is in Virgo or Libra, and the Moon is waning and in fire or air signs. Those dates are:

> September 6–7, 11–12, 15–16
> October 4–5, 8–9, 13–14, 17

Mulching by the Moon

After you have finished cleaning up and carting off the trash, the next step in garden alchemy is to protect the newly exposed soil by applying a heavy dressing of mulch. The mulch will provide a covering that protects against the elements and allows the soil the time it needs to heal. Mulching is the process of laying down a protective covering of organic material over bare dirt. Mulching prevents erosion, keeps in moisture, and enriches the soil for planting. Either kitchen compost and/or commercial mulch can be used, and free mulch is often available for pickup from local farms and even zoos.

Because the purpose of mulching is to enrich the soil, apply mulch when the Sun is in Pisces, Scorpio, Taurus, or Libra (a semi-fertile sign); and when the Moon is waxing and in Cancer, Scorpio, Pisces, Taurus, or Capricorn. The best dates to apply mulch in the spring and fall are:

March 1–2, 5–7, 28–30
April 2–3, 26, 29–30
September 21–22, 26–27
October 1–3, 19–20, 23–25, 28–30

Watching and Waiting

Now it's time to let your barren space take a rest. Think of it as "in the oven" and it's time for you to leave it alone to "cook." The time will vary from two weeks in the spring to six months if the mulch was applied in fall. This is the wintertime of garden alchemy; a dark and silent resting period that allows the soil to absorb the nutrients is a vital and necessary part of any successful garden transformation.

Practical Magic

But while the garden is resting, you are not. Now is the time to decide what kinds of plants are going to live in this magical space. The first rule of garden transformation is to go with, not against, the flow. And no matter where you live, the best advice you will ever hear is to go with native species.

If you plant species that are compatible with the zone where you live, they will fill up the space twice as fast and your work time will magically be reduced by at least half. To find out the names of these plants and where to buy them, talk to your neighbors to see what looks good and grows well in their gardens. Your local nursery is another great source of this information. The hard part is giving up your garden dreams and accepting the limits of practical magic. I happen to love bee balm, a crazy Dr. Seuss kind of flower that attracts hummingbirds and butterflies. In my rainy East Coast garden, bee balm flourished in four different colors.

But now that I live in the dry Southwest, growing bee balm, while not totally impossible, would be an unrealistic and time consuming challenge. The solution? Morning glory and passionflower vines both grow like weeds in the dry Southwest, and the garden is still filled with hummers and butterflies.

One of the most important but overlooked points in transforming a barren space is to remember to pay attention to the height your plants will grow. By planting the tall plants in the back and the shorter ones in front, you can save yourself hours and days of transplanting time. The moral of the story: it's not magical, but it really helps if you read the directions!

One last suggestion is a bow to the gods of the four winds. Please treat yourself and your garden to wind chimes. I once had the privilege of visiting a very special magical garden high above the ocean in the mountains of Big Sur. This unusual spot, where orange and lemon trees grew at 1,500 feet, had at least a dozen chimes ranging from a deep mellow alto, that had pipes over four-feet long, to a tiny chime in the upper soprano notes. The women who owned, lived, and gardened on this spot for over fifty years told me that once, when someone asked her if she was ever afraid to live in such a remote location, she answered: "Why would I be? I have my chimes to protect me!" Take the sage advice of this alchemical gardener and purchase a magical security system for your home and garden.

A Time to Plant

It is ancient knowledge that there is also a direct correlation between the Moon phases, the signs of the zodiac, and times for planting in the garden. While planting is best done under the waxing Moon, digging and fertilizing and planting root crops and perennials are best done under the waning Moon.

The season of choice for planting is late spring, but according to your weather and gardening zone, planting and seeding times

are best carried out during times when water and earth signs—Taurus, Cancer, Scorpio, Capricorn, or Pisces—are emphasized by the sign of the Sun and/or the Moon. That is because water and earth elements have special connections to the wet and dark conditions that nurture the life force and promote growth at the beginning of life.

For gardeners in the hotter regions, the best days for planting annuals (plants that live for one season) are when the Sun is in Capricorn and the Moon is waxing in water or earth signs. The best winter dates are: January 8–10, 18–19.

The best days for planting spring and summer annuals are when the Sun is in Taurus and Cancer, and the Moon is waxing in water or earth signs. The best days are:

March 1–2, 5–7
April 26, 29–30

May 3–4
June 23–24

The best days for planting fall annuals are when the Sun is in Virgo (even though it is considered semi-fertile), Libra (because it is considered semi-fertile), and Scorpio, and the Moon is waxing in water and earth signs. In the fall, the best days are:

September 21–22, 26–27
October 1–2, 19–20, 23–25, 28–30

Perennials form the heart of an alchemical garden. Perennials are plants that produce for many years because the bulk of their energy remains below ground in their root systems. Perennials include bulbs, root crops, roses, and shrubs. Even though perennials have shorter bloom times than their more showy annual sisters, they are like good friends and keep coming back year after year with little or no additional work. They provide the foundation that you can build your other seasonal plantings around.

The best planting days for spring perennials, bulbs, and root crops are when the Sun is in Pisces or Taurus and the Moon is waning and in water or earth signs. In the spring, the best days are:

March 14–15, 19–20
May 13–14, 18–19

The best planting days for fall perennials are when the Sun is in Virgo or Libra, and when the Moon is waxing in water and earth signs. In the fall, the best days are:

September 5, 8–10, 13–14
October 6–7, 10–11

It is my wish that these comments have provided you with some of the keys to garden alchemy that will help you beautify your environment and transform the barren spaces in your backyard into magical gardens.

May you be blessed with the patience not to rush the process, the flexibility to plant only what fits your environment, and the knowledge to time your activities to the natural rhythms of the seasons of the Sun and the phases of the Moon.

About the Author

Pam Ciampi is an astrologer who lives, works, and gardens in southern California. She welcomes your comments and suggestions at: www.pciampi-astrology.com/

Maximize Your Creativity

By Donna Cunningham, MSW

Do you yearn to be more creative—to release your inner artist? Human beings are made in the image of their Creator and so are creative by nature. If you don't see yourself as talented, you may be limiting your view to the traditional fine arts, for there is room for creative inspiration in every area of life. Gourmet cooks who make up their own recipes are artists, as are those who decorate their boudoir according to their favorite fantasies, gardeners who design a beautiful flower garden, or amateur carpenters who come up with ingenious storage spaces.

The trick is to discover your special gifts and make the most of them. Analyzing your astrological chart can provide hints not only to your niche but to times when those gifts can bear fruit. We'll also survey other metaphysical tools—some you may already know, others not so familiar—to develop that creativity to its fullest extent.

Finding Gifts in Your Astrology Chart

The birth chart is a rich source of insight into your talents. A part of the chart that describes some of them is the fifth house—the house of self-expression and leisure activities. So, for instance, if you have Venus or Libra planets there, you probably have a talent for the visual arts and a desire to create beauty and romantic expression. The fifth house also shows what conditions will foster your gifts, and in the case of Libra, you'd be most inspired when you worked in partnership. The Sun or Leo planets there might show a flair for drama. When Virgo is featured, that well-known fine eye for detail and precision often lend craftsmanship. Cancerians' love of mementos and memories might lead them to pursue scrapbooking.

When the third house, Gemini, or Mercury are in high-focus in your chart, you doubtlessly have the gift of gab and may even have writing potential. When the Moon is strong, especially in the earth signs Taurus or Virgo, you may be a gourmet cook or master gardener. Neptune is the planet most associated with imagination, inspiration, and mystery, so the person with Neptune or its sign Pisces strongly featured might well be a poet, musician, or dancer.

Each sign and house has its own special interests and abilities, and we don't have space to cover all the possibilities here. If you're a student of astrology, you can analyze the chart for yourself, but if not, a session with an astrologer focused on this question can give you direction and a boost of confidence in your abilities. A computerized horoscope with a detailed analysis might also clue you in to some of the possibilities. (My booklet, *So You Want to Write*, gives more detail about astrological factors that correlate with various types of writing, writer's block, and best astrological timing for writing projects.)

Committing to Your Craft

The most important part of becoming a writer, actor, or musician is taking yourself seriously by forging an identity of yourself as an artist. What is powerful is making a consistent commitment to pursue your art and honing a belief that you can do it. For instance, if you want to commit to being a writer, subscribe to *Writer's Digest* or *The Writer,* and join a writing group or class where you have the reinforcement of a group of others who have the same goals and where you can learn from one another.

Be prepared, however, for the eventuality that when you begin to take yourself seriously as an artisan and commit to that path, your true life issues can come up—the very same blocks that have gotten in the way of other important goals you've wanted to achieve. Addressing issues like self-confidence and self-sabotage with healing tools like those we'll be discussing can result in a breakthrough, not just in the work but in other long-standing barriers to fulfillment. Thus, it's transformative to become aware of patterns of thought and behavior that stand in your way, rather than concluding that painting or singing is too hard, or that you don't have the gift. You'll doubtlessly find that your creative outlet is a form of healing as well, in that the most moving works of art are those that powerfully express emotions.

Intention Work

Intention is just about the most powerful instrument an artist or writer can use, and all the tools that follow have it as their underpinning. Dr. Wayne W. Dyer, who wrote the important best-seller *The Power of Intention*, says that intention is a field of energy that flows invisibly beyond the reach of our normal, everyday, habitual patterns. We all have the means to attract this energy to us and to experience life in exciting new ways. Some prominent researchers believe that our intelligence, creativity, and imagination interact with the energy field of intention rather than just being thoughts or elements in our brain. Everything in the universe has intention built into it. (*Vibration Magazine,* a free online quarterly, dedicated an entire issue to using the power of intention to enhance other metaphysical tools. See it at www.floweressencemagazine.com/nov05/)

Once you declare your intention about your creative work, thereby firming it into an energetic arrow, the universe starts sending the things you need your way. If you get really firm and committed about a creative project, that intention starts pulling relevant material in energetically, like a spiritual lightening rod. You automatically magnetize exactly the people, information, ideas, and experiences that pertain. To apply the power of intention to a particular project, think about what it is you plan to create, and write a concise statement of 100 words or so about it. Then create a loose outline if you write, a preliminary sketch if you draw or paint, a floor plan if it's a decorative project, or small model in clay if you sculpt.

I do this before starting a book or major article, and the data comes pouring in, bringing endless amounts of input. New clients call whose issues are exactly the ones the piece will address; I overhear conversations or receive random e-mail discussions on an e-list. I go to a doctors' office and the magazines are torn to shreds and two years old, but one of them has an article that precisely clarifies what I needed to know. Or, in meandering around the library, a book on the return book cart catches my eye. A colleague calls whom I've never spoken to before who is working on a similar issue, and we exchange views. I wake up with ideas that don't come from me but are inspired by guides or my Higher Self. A statement of intention is a potent form of magical magnetism.

Establishing a Sacred Space for Your Work

Organizing a sacred space for your creative work is another part of letting the universe know you are serious. It goes to honing that intention. Just like you go to a specific place in consciousness when you meditate or journal, going to a specific place in your home to paint or draw or write music creates a climate of readiness. A dedicated space creates a mood and an expectation that while you're there, you'll focus on the work and only the work.

Do you wonder where you'll find a space in your crowded home? It's important to do so, even if it's just a converted closet, a desk under the stairs, or a corner of your bedroom that you screen off. Clear off a desk, put up shelves, get a new filing cabinet, or create a folder on the hard drive. Fill it with images, objects, and books that inspire you.

If you do energy or light work, keep clearing that space. Reiki level two is a big organizer, as is rose-pink light. Green is the color of both creativity and abundance. If you place crystals around the room to enhance your focus, soak and energize them periodically. Some people find that arranging their workroom according to the principles of feng shui keeps their creative energies flowing better and creates a sense of peace and harmony. If you want more abundance to come from your work, you might put a crystal or something green in the north corner of the room.

Maintaining order in the workspace increases order in the thought processes and reinforces your intention. Clutter and chaos make it hard to think clearly. A valuable best-seller called *Getting Things Done: The Art of Stress-Free Productivity* talks about "open loops" and how they jam up the mind and make it harder to accomplish anything. An open loop creates a nagging list in your head that leads to a feeling of overwhelm. Unfinished bits of business cluttering up the desk, for instance, detract. A filing system (even on the hard drive) helps, as does a list of current work, somewhat like a to-do list, but one that contains for each project what your next action will be. The list keeps what I call the Virgo mind from nagging you by cycling through those loose ends over and over.

Dreams and Inspiration

Famous artists, writers, and inventors have often remarked that their most inspired ideas came to them while they were asleep. Albert Einstein, one of the great geniuses of all times, was open about the fact that his dreams were the source of many of his ideas and provided the solution to some of the knottiest unanswered questions in developing his theories. If paying attention to your dreams has proven a source of insight and guidance in the past, you need only focus your intention on using them as a means of tapping into creative projects. Before you go to sleep, direct your Higher Mind to go to work on any puzzles or knots in the progress of your work. Keep a notebook or sketch pad on the night table, and whenever you wake up—in the middle of the night or the morning—immediately jot down those thoughts before they fade with the demands of the day. If you've never seriously worked with dreams before, get a book or search online for techniques.

Releasing Work

Sondra Ray taught an excellent healing technique for releasing blockages in your life—one that goes several steps beyond the simple act of creating affirmations, because it gets to the bottom of negative programming. When you analyze how the obstacle arose, you may uncover a prohibition, traumatic event, or decision that has impacted your creative expression. For instance, perhaps you were ridiculed by peers for your dreams of greatness or had jealous siblings who picked on you when you did well, so you decided way back then to keep a low profile. Or, you got a negative review that made you decide to close the door on your talent.

When you have a sense of what that decision was, create a statement that cancels, dissolves, and releases it. Write it seventy times a day for seven days—not necessarily seven consecutive days. As you do so, you will uncover memories and specific examples of how that prohibition came about, which you may then want to work through with a variety of healing tools.

For example, many who want to write have been afraid to do so because of family secrets that they were forbidden to talk about, on pain of being severely punished. They learned the hard way to keep their mouths shut and not to say the truth, yet when they write, the truth just comes out. For a seriously traumatic family history, of course, some kind of healing work is likely to be needed, but here we're talking about countermanding the negative programming.

The helpful statement could be: "I give myself permission to tell the truth about my life and family history" or, "I release all programming I've had that interfered with my writing." It's not just our families that condition us not to rock the boat and not to make trouble by telling the truth, it's our whole culture, so include cultural programming in your review of blockages. The technique isn't limited to writing blocks, but you can tailor your statement to your own creative gifts. Here, again, a good writing group or a community of actors or artists can be an invaluable aid. What a difference it can make to have the support of like-minded souls who validate your perceptions and support your goals.

Flower Essences

Also known as flower remedies, these healing liquids are based on the energy fields of plants. They are not to be confused with aromatherapy, which involves essential oils based on aromatic extracts from plants. Essences bring about changes in our ways of handling such common issues as self-esteem or guilt.

A number of essences have well-deserved reputations as enhancers of creativity. In particular, Iris is recommended by the various makers who provide it, such as FES (Flower Essence Services). I have taken Iris essence often and also give it to artists, writers, and musicians who are blocked. Creativity depends on an almost child-like spirit of playfulness, and Zinnia is a flower essence for enjoying more playfulness. Indian Paintbrush gives a fresh outlook when creative work has gone stale. Peppermint and Hornbush relieve mental fatigue, as does the homeopathic cell salt Kali Phos. Madia and Blackberry lend focus, concentration, and follow-through. Shasta Daisy helps in synthesizing information from various sources, and Buttercup and Sunflower strengthen self-confidence. (All those listed here are available from FES.)

If this healing method intrigues you, an excellent free resource is *Vibration Magazine*, an online educational quarterly that I have co-edited since 1989. We have over 350 articles in our archives— including a collection of articles about astrology and essences. The current issue can be accessed at www.essences.com/vibration/

Chakras

The chakras are energy whorls located in the energy body (aura), and they regulate the energy we take in and give out. Each of the creative arts has a chakra primarily associated with it, although some of the chakras, like the solar plexus and the heart chakras, need to be strong and vital in order for an individual to be comfortable in putting their inspirations out for the world to appreciate.

The first, or root chakra, is located at the tip of the tailbone; and it is associated with domestic arts, like cooking, pottery, or textiles. The second, or sacral chakra, is located at the navel and is linked with dance. The third, or solar plexus chakra, is in the waist area and it governs the performance aspect of arts like acting. The fourth, or heart chakra, empowers the healing arts. The fifth, or throat chakra, is for speaking, singing, and other forms of vocal expression. The sixth, or brow chakra, is located at the third eye and has two halves. The left half is associated with the visual arts and the right with writing. The seventh, or crown chakra, is located on top of the head and is allied with the psychic arts and inspiration that comes from higher sources.

A creative block—such as the so-called "writer's block"—is usually also a chakra block, and when you apply yourself to your art, long-standing issues that have gotten in the way of self-development may start to come up. Many psychic individuals are able to see an individual's chakras as well as any blockages and to attune to them to find out the reasons for them. In the hands of a healer, chakra work is a powerful way of clearing out barriers to successfully expressing your creativity. (The November 2006, issue of *Vibration Magazine* had articles about each of the chakras and essences to clear and strengthen them. See the article at www.floweressencemagazine.com/nov06/)

To give an example of how working through a chakra blockage can open up creative expression, Mercury is the planet of communication. With tough Mercury aspects, like to Pluto or Saturn, the throat chakra may need clearing. When I first started speaking around the country, I came down with laryngitis every time I traveled to speak. I went to a healer named Phil Deal who pulled past lives out of the chakras. Every time he worked on the throat, it would be revealed that I was beheaded, hung, garroted, or strangled, all for speaking out about my beliefs. (Apparently, I have been a troublemaker in many lives!) The work was successful and I was able to lecture comfortably all around the world. (If you believe that you've pursued your creative talent in other lives, as many gifted people have, you might want to have a past life session to learn whether traumatic events or karma from that time are getting in the way.)

Metaphysical Tools

This article could only briefly introduce you to metaphysical approaches that can open the path to the personal fulfillment that finding and expressing your creative gifts can bring. If you're a student of metaphysics, you doubtlessly are already familiar with some of them, you may just not have applied them to your innate gifts. If some are new but intriguing, look into them now by visiting a New Age bookstore or searching online. Llewellyn's guidebooks in many of these areas can help you explore them in more depth. Developing your talents is a rich source of joy and pleasure—embrace the process!

About the Author

Donna Cunningham, MSW, is an internationally-known astrologer and the author of nineteen books and thousands of articles and columns about astrology and flower essences in which she combines her forty years of metaphysical studies with her master's degree in social work. Her new online seminars are designed to support people who wish to write about astrological, metaphysical, and self-help topics. See her books, writing tips booklet, and more about her seminars at www.moonmavenpublications.com/

The Business of Being You

By April Elliott Kent

In 1991, I left a cushy office job to become a professional astrologer. It's a path that's had its ups and downs, including many slow years when my idea of success was earning enough money to pay my rent. Today, thanks to a combination of time, hard work, and luck, I'm fortunate to work with a wide range of clients on a variety of astrology-related projects. I've even developed an unexpected sideline business as a Web site designer. But this modest success has introduced a dilemma that would have seemed like a godsend back when I started my practice: I'm a bit too busy these days, so much so that it's difficult to get everything done in a timely fashion.

Such was my plight as the deadline loomed for this article. Despite working seemingly around the clock, I couldn't bulldoze my way through the stack of folders on my desk. Then, when I finally found a moment to begin writing, disaster struck when it became obvious that my intended topic was simply not working out. With just days to go before my deadline, my article fell apart.

I brought my predicament to my patient editor, simultaneously seizing the opportunity to commiserate about the utter impossibility of daily life. "I see all these people who seem to get so much done," I wrote to her, "and I have no clue how they do it." She emphatically agreed, adding, "I'd love to read an article about that!"

Actually, so would I. But as a writer with a deadline to meet, I decided to write one instead. Perhaps, I thought, writing this article might help me figure out where I've gone wrong. Am I just disorganized, or is my life moving in the wrong direction?

You, Inc.

The question, "where is my life headed?" may seem a trifle lofty for those of us who are just trying to get through each day and earn a living. But as Pluto, the planet of transformation, settles into career-oriented Capricorn for a nice long stay (2008–2024), it may be exactly the right one to ask. Outsourcing and globalization have already eliminated many career options, a trend that will likely intensify during the Pluto in Capricorn years.

The reality is that most of us are free agents in the job market. And while this new career paradigm lacks the appealing security of the old days, it has the advantage of encouraging a more proactive and entrepreneurial approach to life. In fact, viewed in a certain way, your entire life is actually a sort of corporate enterprise—call it

"You, Inc."—and you are its CEO. Forgetting for a moment what you do to earn a living, what business are you really in? The business of raising a family, selling goods or services, traveling the world, or educating people? While Pluto is in Capricorn, it's time to find out, and to formulate a plan for making your "corporation" a success.

Pluto in Capricorn: The Mogul

Along with Aries, Cancer, and Libra, Capricorn is known as an "executive" sign, with a formidable gift for assessing opportunity and initiating action. In order to feel satisfied, Capricorn needs a sense of purpose and direction. To a lucky few of us, this sense of personal destiny comes easily and with a dedication that holds no hint of doubt or hesitation. For most of us, though, settling on a direction, in business and in life, can be a difficult process.

Are you ready to meet the challenge of the Pluto in Capricorn years? Do you have a clear direction in mind and a plan for getting there? The astrological symbol of Capricorn offers several strategies to help you get on track.

First, Define Your Core Principles

What is important to you? It seems like an embarrassingly simple question, but the answer can be deceiving. Sometimes, what we say is important to us may bear little relation to how we actually spend our time. Your days may be busy, but do you feel you're really accomplishing anything? There is a huge difference between success that feels earned, authentic, and meaningful, and simply crossing a lot of tasks off a "to do" list. Unless you operate from a sound platform built on values that are deeply important to you, you may well achieve all your goals without actually feeling like a true success.

Defining your core principles requires a peek under the hood at the psychological motivations that drive you toward achievement. In large part, you learned them from your family while growing up in the astrological territory of Capricorn's opposite sign, Cancer. Often, we're unconsciously motivated by family expectations rather than by what is truly right for us. For more insight, think back to 2003 through 2005, when Saturn was moving through Cancer. What did you learn about the needs that motivate you, and how to get them met? Now is the time to put that information to work for you, and . . .

Formulate a Plan

Capricorn loves lists, agendas, and mission statements. Just as a corporation prepares an annual report for its shareholders, and a wise shopper drafts a list before going to the grocery store, "You, Inc." can benefit from a written plan of action. A list of New Year's resolutions (traditionally made when the Sun is in Capricorn) is just one example. Sometimes it can help to break your plan into more manageable chunks covering a month, a week, even a day.

Don't be ruled by your lists, though; a Dayrunner is not the Ten Commandments! In fact, your plans should be dynamic, reflecting new developments in your daily life. And there's no need to feel like a failure if you don't complete every task on your list. The mere act of creating a plan is a powerful tool to remind you what business you're in and to keep you pointed in the right direction.

Take Stock of Your Capital

Capricorn is the king of resource management. Like his symbol the goat, which can turn almost anything into food, Capricorn is the master of using resources wisely (or doing without altogether). But while a goat can live on tin cans, you presumably need somewhat different resources in order to reach your goals. Some ventures require cold hard cash to get them off the ground, but almost none require only a financial investment. In many cases, your most valuable capital will be your physical energy and stamina, a particular set of skills or knowledge, or the people who know and care about you.

So take inventory of your capital: physical, spiritual, financial, and intellectual. As you move toward your goal, knowing exactly what you require and what you already have will make it obvious what is still needed.

Delegate!

I've been driving my husband bats for days, wandering around chirping "Delegate!" at random moments. I can't help it. As a mild control freak, I find the simple concept of delegation fresh and bewitching. I'm increasingly convinced that delegation is among the most powerful tools for achieving success.

Remember that Capricorn is the sign of the executive. How many executives do you know who type their own letters or make their own travel arrangements? Although this work is important, it can be delegated much more easily than some other tasks. (Not to mention that you might be a terrible typist and too impatient to negotiate with hotels and airlines. No one is good at everything!)

Decide which of your obligations can reasonably be entrusted to someone else, at least in part, and even if only temporarily. And then let them go. This may take practice and will certainly require trust, but without delegation, it can be difficult to scale the heights of Capricornian success.

Work Smarter

Like many entrepreneurs, you'll wear many hats in the beginning. At first, the person to whom you'll likely be delegating is you. Fortunately, as Pluto begins its long journey through Capricorn, hard-working Saturn is moving through Virgo (2007 through 2009)—the sign of efficiency and service—for the first time since the late 1970s. Just as the development of microprocessors during that decade set the stage for the personal computer revolution, which simplified the automation of routine tasks, one of the challenges of this Saturn in Virgo transit is to liberate yourself from tedious, repetitive duties. How can you work smarter so you are free to focus on treasured goals?

While Saturn is in Virgo, we must employ all that sign's shrewd skills of logic, discernment, and problem solving in the service of a larger purpose. Ruled by Mercury, the planet of communication and skill, Virgo is well suited to analysis, systems development, and problem solving. So while Saturn is in Virgo, it's time to get organized, to ferret out the underlying causes of the clutter and knots of daily life, and to become more efficient.

Whereas Capricorn is an executive sign, Virgo (along with Gemini, Sagittarius, and Pisces) excels at administration, carrying out plans of action with aplomb. While Saturn is in Virgo, you can lay the groundwork for your long-term goals by:

Downsizing

The less stuff you have, the less time you must spent maintaining it. Some friends of ours recently moved overseas, a huge relocation that required them to get rid of most of their possessions, including their house. It was a wrenching process but also, they confirm, a liberating one. Using Virgo's litmus test as your guide—Is it useful or practical?—cull through your belongings and get rid of as much as you can. You're not losing "stuff," you're gaining time!

Creating Systems that Work

Virgo delights in organization, and of course you need a few sturdy, simple systems for organizing your important papers and supplies. But don't go crazy. At one time or another, we've all heeded the siren call of the office supply superstore, wandering the aisles and lusting over complex filing systems that promise to put our lives in order. It's easy to become enthralled by the constant challenge of "getting organized," until it becomes just another delicious distraction instead of a means to a larger end.

Using Time Wisely

Virgo's ruling planet, Mercury, rules transportation. Where I live, no one walks and public transportation is slow and inconvenient. Consequently, I drive a lot, and for even the simplest errands. It takes some planning, but I'm trying to organize my trips so that I'm not constantly getting in and out of the car and fighting traffic just to pick up a loaf of bread. Combining trips saves time—not to mention gasoline (and patience).

Mercury also rules written communication, so consider streamlining the time you spend reading and answering e-mails, updating your blog, and surfing the Internet. When I recently spent a few days out of town with limited computer access, I couldn't believe how much calmer I felt. I'm experimenting now with limiting my interactive computer time to two hours each day. I still spend a lot of time working at my computer, but with my Internet browser and e-mail program closed. I'm surprised by how difficult this has been to do—but I'm also a lot less overwhelmed by incoming projects and questions.

Letting Go of Perfectionism

Imagine that in forty-eight hours you will welcome guests to your home for a one-week stay. The house is a mess, you haven't done your grocery shopping, a mountain of laundry needs to be tackled, and there are several small but crucial handyman tasks that need to be handled. How will you get it all done?

The correct answer is: Imperfectly. This is not an answer that pleases Virgo, who prefers a sparkling house, a refrigerator full of healthy food, drawers full of crisply folded laundry, and a house free of creaking doors and balky latches. But let's face it: You don't have days and days to shop and cook and fold your guest towels with origami-like precision. Make the place presentable, wash the guest towels and sheets, and stock up on a few tasty convenience foods to supplement home-cooked meals.

To paraphrase television chef Ina Garten (The Barefoot Cont-essa), your friends won't enjoy their stay any more just because you practically killed yourself preparing for their visit.

Perfectionism has its place; it can be the difference between raw creative talent and a beautiful work of art, for instance. But Saturn is a planet that insists we set limits, and Saturn in Virgo reminds us perfection is not always practical, or even necessary. Sometimes, "pretty good" is good enough.

Going With the Flow

While Saturn is in Virgo, the pull toward Virgo's opposite sign, easy-going Pisces, will be strong. Like all signs, Pisces has its strengths and weaknesses. Falling under a negative Pisces spell can make us disorganized, impractical, and undependable. But when we develop positive Pisces characteristics, such as flexibility and creativity, we can be formidable! The Pisces people I know well are exceptionally accomplished, educated, creative, and involved in a wide variety of interests. How do they do it all?

As far as I can tell, they do it by respecting time and schedules without being enslaved by them. They trust the day to open up enough space to accommodate all the tasks, fun, and people that are important to them. They're spontaneous. They use stray bits of time creatively. And they remember to make time for themselves—to get a massage, see a movie, or have lunch with a friend.

Best of all, Pisces has vision. Once, when I was feeling depressed that I hadn't achieved more success in my career, a wise friend stopped me in my tracks by asking, "What would success look like to you?" It's a good question. Without a clear vision of suc-cess, how can we recognize it when we get there?

. . . .

In the end, it seems there is no single solution to getting things done. Having a vision (Pisces), identifying your role in the world (Capricorn), understanding your emotions and motivations

(Cancer), and using practical skills to adapt your dreams to reality (Virgo) are all important tools to help us make the most of the years ahead—and of all the years of our lives.

As for me, I'm still struggling to get my deadlines under control and trying to keep my eye on the whole forest instead of just a few trees. But then, as I write this Saturn has only peeked into the earliest corners of Virgo. I'm confident that by the time he's through with me I'll have simplified my life, loosened my vice-like grip on overscheduling and perfectionism, and even sampled the joys of delegation.

And after all that, the reign of Pluto in Capricorn will still be in its infancy. By the time it's over, I'll be sixty-three years old—nearly the traditional age of retirement. But that doesn't mean my work will be finished. I've been a full-time astrologer since 1991, but April, Inc. has been in the business of figuring out the cosmos since 1961. It's a career path I warmly recommend—and one that I expect to follow for many years to come.

About the Author.
April Elliott Kent, a professional astrologer since 1990, is a member of NCGR and ISAR and graduated from San Diego State University with a degree in Communication. Her book Star Guide to Weddings *(Llewellyn) was published in February 2008. April's astrological writing has also appeared in* The Mountain Astrologer *(USA) magazine, the online journals MoonCircles and Beliefnet, and Llewellyn's Moon Sign Book (2005, 2006, 2007, 2008). April lives in San Diego with her husband, two cats, and—buried somewhere underneath a huge stack of paper—a very nice desk. Her Web site is: www. bigskyastrology.com/*

The Full Moon Keeps Me Awake at Night!

By Gretchen Lawlor

The Full Moon, a huge circle of creamy light, slowly climbs from the horizon. Stars and planets fade, trees and meadows take on a silvery sheen and we walk through them without the aid of a flashlight. Emergency rooms gear up for an extra load of work, and murder rates increase. Even the most sane of us stay up longer, wake earlier, feel restless and volatile. So, what happens to us as the Moon reaches its full illumination? How can we prepare? And what are the best ways to use this energy?

First, let's take a look at the physical relationship between the Sun, Earth, and Moon during the approximately twenty-nine-day lunar cycle. As the Moon moves around the Earth, one half is always lit by the Sun and one half is dark. We, on planet Earth, view the two halves from different angles during the month, seeing more or less of the light half, depending on the Moon's phase.

When the Moon is directly between the Earth and Sun, we see only the dark side. This is the New Moon. When the Moon is on the opposite side of the Earth from the Sun, we see the fully illuminated side, or the Full Moon. The Moon's orbit is slightly tilted (about 5 degrees) relative to the Earth's orbit, so it usually passes to the north or south of the Earth's shadow.

When the Moon enters the Earth's shadow, we get a lunar eclipse. These occur at least twice each year and, unlike solar eclipses, a lunar eclipse can be viewed (if the Moon is passing over our location and it's nighttime). The Moon is always full on the day of the eclipse. Be aware that an eclipse both intensifies and extends the effect of a Full Moon.

The Mythological Full Moon

It is the very error of the Moon:
She comes more nearer Earth than she was wont
And makes men mad.

~William Shakespeare, from *Othello*

Madness was associated with the Full Moon for centuries before Shakespeare. For instance, everyone "knows" that werewolves transform at that time, but did you know that, in Iceland, pregnant women were advised against sitting facing the Full Moon for fear that their children be deranged?

"Lunacy," "lunatic," and "loony" are all derived from the Latin word *Luna*, which means Moon. The belief in the connection between madness and the Moon was so strong that not only did early psychologists call extra staff into asylums during the Full Moon, but an English laborer who committed a number of murders at the Full Moon in the late 1880s was acquitted on the grounds that he was under its spell! This man, Charles Hyde, was one of the inspirations for Robert Louis Stevenson's story of split personality, *The Strange Case of Dr. Jekyll and Mr. Hyde*.

Though Moon madness is no longer an excuse for crime, studies conducted at the University of Miami have shown a strong correlation between murders and the phases of the Moon, increasing with the waxing Moon and decreasing as it waned. In Philadelphia, a report by the American Institute of Medical Climatology to the police department stated similar results over a broad range of crimes, including arson, dangerous driving, and kleptomania.

There are, however, a number of positive traditions to look at. Ancient Greeks considered that day to be the most propitious for a marriage ceremony; and, in the second century, the Greek physician Galen stated that those who were born when the Moon was sickle-shaped were weak and short of life, while those born during the Full Moon would be vigorous and sure to live to an old age.

The Astrological Full Moon

In your natal chart, the Moon shows you the qualities of your emotional self, the self that was strongly influenced by your mother and the world you grew up in. Children are explorers and miniature scientists and they like to figure out the world around them—observing, drawing conclusions, and forming hypotheses and theories about reality. These observations and conclusions, etc., become the unconscious basis for our reactions to the world.

Some theories about reality may be accurate, some may not be. A child who is told repeatedly that he is a "bad boy" or that she is "stupid" may accept those labels as fact. If a child hears often enough that "there isn't enough food," he or she may see the world as a place of lack and hunger. Or conversely, if a child's every whim and desire is immediately satisfied, he or she may expect life to continue in exactly the same way, and be quite indignant when it doesn't.

This deep, unconscious, emotional self rises to the light at the Full Moon. Like the Moon itself, the unconscious, emotional self may overwhelm its environment, demanding attention and refusing to take no for an answer.

You feel a pull on you that can cause tremendous tension. It's a difficult time, and to cope, you may attempt to drown out the anger, fear, or sadness by turning up the TV or playing a few extra computer games. But as awareness of the unconscious self increases, so does the potential for healing and integration. We can use our objectivity to keep from being overwhelmed by the flood of emotion and our power of conscious choice to transform the issues that gave rise to it.

You may find yourself being less rational than usual, and less able to stand back and be objective about yourself or your friends and family. Reactions may be quick and instinctive. You may find yourself flooded by emotions, surprised by their strength or the way they sneak up when you'd planned on being much more in control.

If you live in close contact with others, you might find yourself picking up on their emotions, too. This "bleeding" of anger or fear can play havoc with your own life if you're not able to separate those issues from your own. And be aware that someone else may be expressing something you've repressed yourself.

Just as the Moon is reflective, buried issues can also come into our lives dressed as other people. The overbearing mother you don't want to face could enter your life as someone at work. The lover you left ten years ago could show up as a casual encounter with someone who punches the same buttons.

Annoying? Of course. But the gift is one of closure. The message is: You need to deal with this and be free of it. Now.

Preparing For A Full Moon

Your opportunity to turn the Full Moon to your advantage starts two weeks earlier, during the dark of the Moon and the New

Moon phases. This is the time for taking a dispassionate look at your life and deciding on the intentions you want to set, the areas you want to "illuminate"—make visible—in the increasing moonlight.

Intentions are your sanity points, your instructions to yourself. They act on both the conscious and unconscious parts of your mind. Write them down, cut out pictures that represent them, make an altar that embodies them, buy a piece of jewelry that seems to express the life you're trying to create and wear it often.

During the week before the Moon reaches fullness, schedule some extra time for yourself on the day of the Full Moon, or close to it, both for dealing with emotional upheavals, for nurturing yourself, and forgiving whatever shortcomings you see in ways that are physical and concrete.

The day before the Full Moon is often one of anticipation, of building tension. You may become more aware of the gap between where you are and where you want to be. You may find yourself saying and doing things that don't fit. Ask yourself: "Why am I doing this?" And prepare for some letdown and fatigue afterwards. Once you pass through the "gate" of the Full Moon and you're starting to integrate, you may need quiet and downtime. Plan for it.

Handling Emotions During A Full Moon

This is a time of emotional power, with great possibilities for joy and happiness. But you're going to be aware of your blocks and your negative emotions, too. You may feel, sometimes, as though you're being knocked about by one wave of emotion after another. What can you do? Become a surfer. Don't fight the swells and breakers; find your balance on top of them.

Afraid something may happen? Turn it around and look at what you want to happen. If you're afraid of losing your job, you obviously want to keep it. Start brainstorming all the ways you can make yourself more valuable to your employer. Or perhaps you realize you'd really prefer another job. Start focusing on what you need to move toward. Either way, you gain a sense of power.

If you're grieving a loss, even a small one, give yourself time to grieve, then do something physical. Set a timer, go to the beach for a half hour, sit in a garden during your lunch break. Write letters to anyone who is a focus of the emotional upheaval you feel. Pour your heart out. Then get rid of the letter. You may find that walking is a good way to gain a sense of movement while still leaving your heart and mind free to process and integrate. Thoughts and emotions can well up, overflow, and then you can "walk away from them." If you can, stroll through the woods or by the seashore, and allow the healing energies of nature to wash away your pain.

Above all, be gentle with yourself (and your Inner Child). What's called for is cheers and celebrations for each bit of progress.

Conversations with Your Inner Child

Children theorize and generalize what they learn. They may also take on their parent's ideas and perceptions without question. "People are cold and distant," or "people are patient and kind." The Full Moon is an excellent time to look at these assumptions, some of which may be mistaken and need reworking.

But your Inner Child can be extremely attached to these perceptions and changing them can produce a great deal of fear. Allowing it to speak in its own language, through movement or gestures or music, can be very helpful. Listen carefully to the words that come up instinctively at the Full Moon.

Be ready to give some space for whining and complaining, too. Our Inner Child doesn't necessarily fit into daily life, doesn't behave politely and reasonably. There may be an annoyingly persistent whine of "I want _____," or "I'm hungry (tired, bored)," or "Why can't I_____?"

On the other hand, you may have to do a bit of coaxing to get your Inner Child to talk. After being ignored for years, it may not trust you enough to speak clearly. Here's an exercise to draw it out.

Sit down with a sheet of paper and make a list of your

- Ten favorite toys
- Ten things you liked to eat as a child
- Ten things you really liked to do as a child

Give yourself a minute for each list, no longer. Then, take your Inner Child out for a treat.

Celebrate, Appreciate, Give Thanks

The intentions you set at the New Moon will continue to unfold, to grow, and develop. But as the Moon reaches its greatest light, they are fully born into the physical world and you can clearly see how those intentions are affecting your life. This is a high point, a culmination of two weeks of preparation.

Give yourself a few minutes or a few hours, or even a whole day to appreciate. You've done your emotional work and you're beginning to integrate your new realizations. The next step is to give thanks for the light that is shining on your life.

Small rituals, even a moment of pause, solidify your gains and stabilize your newly-born intentions. You can look around you and see the new possibilities, the new life you've gained; you can feel the joy and gratitude well up in your heart and overflow.

One of the best ways to express this gratitude is with a gift, a concrete expression of your thanks to the universe. You might make a donation to a food bank, or write checks to your favorite non-profit organizations. You might do a random act of kindness for a stranger.

When you share this moment of abundance with others, it multiplies.

Playful Celebrations

Then, give a party for your Inner Child. You can praise and celebrate its unique gifts with bright colors, candles, anything that means play and fun to you. Even buying yourself a balloon can lift your heart.

Since the Full Moon amplifies and clarifies the need to nourish your child self, this is the time to brainstorm celebrations. What feeds your heart? How do you like to play? Special music, sleeping outside, dancing on the beach, a trip to a florist for roses? And don't be shy. Be wild, be imaginative, be yourself! Incorporate these elements into your ritual.

Breakdown to Breakthrough

When the Full Moon falls in the same sign as your own birth Moon, powerful and often unsettling experiences and urges surface in order to draw your attention to core emotional issues.

This amplified experience of energy flow and blockage on the day of the Full Moon is a powerful challenge (invitation) to cultivate a healthier emotional equilibrium. Is it that bright globe illuminating the dark that makes emotional imbalances so excruciatingly obvious? Meditation, vigilant awareness, and any reflective pause are particularly helpful for catching these Full Moon "aha" moments.

About the Author
Gretchen Lawlor has been writing, teaching, and guiding clients all over the globe with astrology for nearly forty years. For more about astroplay, lifemaps, consults, and classes, visit her Web site at www.gretchenlawlor.com

Career Transitions: Discover Your Passion

By Alice DeVille

People who love their work experience a greater degree of self-actualization and happiness than those who settle for "the status quo." These individuals are healthier, more productive, and motivated as they achieve one meaningful goal after another. What's the secret? Passion—the driving force behind the whirlwind who finds the dream job after channeling the enthusiasm to make a break from a familiar safety net. Where did the passion come from? It's a personal thing. There is no magic formula for identifying what it looks like. The path to career change calls for going through significant metamorphosis that starts on the inside, alters your mindset, and sets you free from the fear of the unknown. When you recognize it, you're ready to roll!

One of the nice things about having a career you love is the satisfaction and feeling of accomplishment that surrounds you each day. You probably know someone who made the leap and enjoys reminding you that "It doesn't feel like work," or "I can't believe how much I'm paid for doing what I love." Of course, they are usually compensated generously and experience greater independence in life.

This article takes a very different perspective from previous material I have written on the subject (as referenced in the last section of this piece). Here I want to help you set the stage and do your homework so you'll be aware of important steps that will help you make a *successful* career transition. I have considerable experience as a business coach, helping people find ways to maximize human capital so the company has a continuous flow of resources in the pipeline and the employee feels fulfilled. The bottom line for enthusiasts of career change is that they need to feel accountable for the outcome of their career and take steps to create the environment that allows them to pursue their quest for the perfect job.

Who Makes Career Changes?

Let's start with you and your acute awareness of current reality. Do some deep soul searching and make hard decisions regarding the work that is leaving you tired and bored. As the principal, you have to acknowledge that the career is not meeting critical needs and the desire to stretch has intensified. You know there is so much more you can offer and you would like to do so.

People who are casualties of downsizing or reorganization make good candidates for career change. Some organizations offer them opportunities for retraining or career counseling to help with the transition (highly recommended). Loyal retiree candidates who have given many good years to the company find they have an abundance of energy for pursuing a new career. Those who want careers requiring additional degrees, certifications, or other educational requirements enroll in classes and make plans to leave the mediocre career when they have completed the coursework.

Perhaps the motivation for any individual comes from enjoyable hobbies, part-time jobs, or long-held dreams. Employees fired from their jobs go through initial shock, yet many of them suggest the sudden termination was probably the best thing that happened to them in terms of reassessing their careers. Once they are psychologically ready to explore options, they find a wealth of information at their fingertips.

Those returning to the job market after a long sabbatical (often to raise children or after recovering from an illness) have the desire to switch career fields.

And the Internet is a wonderful tool that will facilitate your search for an alternate employment.

How to Know if You're Ready for Change

Your birth chart gives clear indications of the career paths that are open to you. No chart offers only one or two career options; in fact, the trend is away from grabbing a job for life, getting raises on schedule, and retiring at a predetermined age. I have seen clients' astrology charts that showed success in five or more careers (the new norm), and charts that indicate the client is performing successfully in two or more ongoing careers. That's why it should be no surprise to hear of individuals making drastic career changes at different points in life. I predict that with the increasing life span, the changing work world, and communication technology, many more individuals will have multiple careers—it is already happening!

Certain astrological houses relate more strongly to your career path than others. Yet it is possible for houses not normally associated with your life work to carry more weight because they hold large clusters of planets (called stellia) that more specifically describe work that appeals to you. Typical houses that address careers are the second house of income and resources because it indicates how you want to be compensated for your efforts and reflects the value you place on your personal, psychological, and spiritual worth; the fifth house of risk-taking because of its focus on leadership, entrepreneurs, and those who thrive on having their own businesses—stock market speculators, fund investors, and those in the entertainment or recreation fields; the sixth house of work routines and techniques, coworkers, and contractors, attitudes about work or conditions of the work environment; the tenth house of career goals, recognition, achievement, and the desire for rewards in your chosen field; and sometimes the eighth house of depth and probing, because transiting aspects to this house have you looking within to find answers to confirm your suspicions that it's time to leave the current work place. Since this house relates to debt, what you owe triggers the impetus to work a part-time job, or get your feet wet in another career. If you're at an age when you're close to retirement, the eighth house helps you calculate your net worth and determine how much income you'll need to live comfortably. For additional insight on retirement strategies see Llewellyn's 2009 *Sun Sign Book* for my article "Rendezvous with Retirement."

When the workplace becomes unsatisfactory, you'll know it is time to move on. It will be hard to ignore the clues. From an astrological standpoint, your natal chart seems to "sizzle" and reflects a significant share of challenges from transiting planets that have been brewing for a while, urging you to develop your next steps.

In Search of the Perfect Career

First, pay attention to your desires. You're the designer. If you had a choice of any career, what would you do? It's up to you to identify jobs to put excitement in your future. Do on-line research to find the top 100 careers where expanded hiring is likely to take place in the next ten to fifteen years. You'll find information like this on lists called Hot Jobs, Top 100 Careers, The 10 Hottest Metropolitan Markets, or Snapshots of Today's Hot Fields. See if you have skills to match the requirements. Find out what employment markets (key metropolitan areas) are hiring in these fields and offer security. Are these markets close to you geographically, or would a move be necessary? If you are game, then create real, positive changes to achieve the life you want.

Every two years the U.S. Department of Labor updates the Occupational Outlook Handbook (OOH), which provides descriptions for approximately 270 major jobs covering about 85 percent of the workforce. I've had recent experience with several agencies in the Department of Labor, as a consultant providing workforce analysis, examining person/job congruence, executive coaching, management solutions, and talent development. At the time of this writing, the U.S. Department of Labor cites the following fields as the hottest job markets:

1. Health care
2. Educational services
3. Computer systems design and related services
4. Internet service providers, Web search portals, and data processing services
5. Employment services
6. Management, scientific, and technical consulting services
7. Child care services
8. Software publishers
9. Arts, entertainment, and recreation
10. Social services (excluding child daycare)

By researching these fields you will be able to find thorough information, additional links, and statistics that describe average earnings, percent of job growth, and significant points about the discipline, the nature of the career field, job outlook, and the fastest growing hot jobs in each area. A further search will provide you with dominant cities that offer desirable employment, a snapshot of economic performance in the area, the percentage of the employed population, and median income. Search for position descriptions that outline the major duties and cite the level of education needed to qualify. Many sites list broad job categories, such as Computer Support Specialists, and then list the hottest fields where they work: Computer Systems Design and Related Services, Educational Services, Software Publishers, Employment Services, Internet Service Providers, Web Search Portals, and Data Processing Services. Take your search to the next step and you'll find the job postings.

If you're an entrepreneurial career seeker who likes to freelance and are converting your skills into independent consulting, look for companies that outsource, hire by contract, or want you to have a fully-equipped workplace at a remote site (normally your own home office). Also look for opportunities as a sub-contractor with a company that generates the long- and short-term work contracts and offers employment until the services are delivered. I have at least two dozen clients who have made a successful transition from one career into the realm of government contractor. Some of them have fixed-retirement income with benefits and are now earning a very lucrative second salary.

Educational Aspects

To grab the brass ring, be someone who is determined, flexible, and willing to learn new skills. In some way, whoever interviews you for your new career is going to be asking questions to figure out if you have these qualities. In some cases, you may not have the acceptable educational degree or the specialized certification to move right into the desired career. In the former case, you may be able to parlay your extensive work experience into a good fit for a position that gives you access to the new field and perhaps gives you a chance to work on your degree. If you go into a field like real estate, you will have to take a series of courses and then pass a state test. Once you have the required license you have to find a broker who will hire you. When you succeed and place your license with the broker, you normally attend agency-sponsored classes designed to accelerate your integration into the real-estate field before the broker gives you access to the world of buyers and sellers. Even though you're book smart from immersion in the recent classes, you need the experience. A real estate coach or mentor is the perfect solution.

While you're online, look for skills-match quizzes, and tests that measure personality and employment preferences to get a feel for where you fit. Most people are familiar with Holland tests, Kolbe A Index, and Myers-Briggs. Many candidates interview well and have impressive resumes but they don't have the most critical qualities for the new career. Employers want you to have the natural advantage when you're in action mode. Today, savvy companies, even at the executive level, test potential hires to make sure the incumbent has the qualities needed for the position, a strategy used to avoid expensive turnover or early termination after an unsuccessful probation period.

The Networking Advantage

If you are looking for work after a period of unemployment or because you're ready for a new challenge, tell everyone you know and find out where there are openings. Those who have a specific career in mind have better success contacting specialists or employers in the chosen field, arranging meetings, lunch dates, or facility tours to gain perspective of the daily routine. Your network of contacts may be largely concentrated where you currently live. If you move to a new area where you don't know anyone, you'll lose an important advantage in job hunting. If possible, choose a location where you know a few people or have a network that can provide leads and introductions. Check out the networking opportunities in the prospective city—does it offer access to professional and civic organizations where you would feel at home? A terrific source for obtaining local information is the city's Chamber of Commerce Web site, which is normally very detailed and can save you hours of phone calls or written correspondence.

Mentors and Other Helpful People

Establishing rapport with a trusted advisor early in your career gives you an encouraging ear when you are seeking options to grow or make a desired change. Be sure you don't make the mistake of using an HR staffer as your sounding board—they are not your friends—they work for management and may feel compelled to let the boss know you are thinking of leaving or are unhappy in your present job. Mentors fulfill many roles depending upon your circumstances. They can be coaches or advisors who help you lay out a strategic plan for advancing within the career field or outside of it; they may serve as liaisons between you and outside contacts in firms that hire for the career you're seeking; they can be part of your networking group; or they may be employed as executive or development coaches who work with you one-on-one to help you prepare for the impending change. In the latter case, you pay for their services, which will help you streamline your search. Other helpful people are those contacts you've told about your desire to make a change and who pass on job leads to you. They may also be employment agencies with whom you have registered.

The Transition Plan

Let's start with the riskier career changes. If you are used to having benefits paid by your employer, determine how many of them can be matched by the new employer. If you have a pension plan or 401K, be sure you can transfer the assets so you don't lose financially. Exercise stock option payouts if you have that perk. Talk to benefits personnel so you don't miss any important transfer deadlines. If you lost your job, find out how long you can carry the very necessary benefit of health insurance and how much time you have before you must find your own replacement insurance.

Going to start your own business? Have you figured out how much you'll need to earn to pay not only your bills and overhead, but also the cost of health care coverage, insurance, and contributions to a retirement plan? Unless you have a large cash reserve, it is easier to start a business if you do so while you are still employed in another field, or have a significant other who can pay the bills while you grow your business. The same is true if you go into largely commission based careers such as insurance, financial planning, real estate, mortgage banking, auto sales or other fields requiring risk-taking and uncertain paychecks. Some enterprises pay a small salary while you are learning the ropes but after a few months, you're on your own. You'll have to generate enough business to stay solvent and keep those commission checks coming. Targeted goal-setting and a clear vision help tremendously as you get established in a speculative career.

If you have a partner, it is a good idea to discuss beforehand the income adjustment and the anticipated lean months you'll experience while you're assimilating the new information. Never accept a job of this type without a heart-to-heart talk and a common understanding of what it is going to take to get started. I have seen beautiful relationships deteriorate when one of the partners did not disclose the facts behind the financially lean period. It takes passion and stamina to excel in a field where you are just as likely to be rejected as you are to make a huge sale—the jumbo mortgage, the McMansion, or the Mercedes-Benz.

An insightful real-estate broker puts reality on the table before offering sales associates a position with their firm. Brokers let candidates know it can be six months before the first commission check appears and usually ask how the new hire is going to pay the bills in the interim. In down markets especially, the broker advises candidates to have a second income or a solid source of income. Why? If you are worried about making mortgage payments and keeping food on the table, your sales effectiveness erodes and you'll be unable to sustain the momentum needed to be a top-notch professional.

If you are in a situation where you have been let go, couldn't stand the workplace any longer and had to make the break, or you are uncertain about how well you would do in the new career, register with a temp agency that caters to your field of specialization. You would be surprised how many temporary positions evolve into full-time employment and open up a world of benefits and job satisfaction.

Success!

You'll have it if you follow this advice! Let's speed ahead to see how you did. Your research has been fulfilling and you have identified the perfect career and an incredibly compatible employer. The wish list speaks magic. You sent your polished resume forward, were selected for an initial interview, and liked what you saw when you visited the firm. While you waited for your second interview, you got in touch with your passion and visualized yourself happily settled in your new workspace. Now your employer of choice calls you back to negotiate on any items not covered in the first interview, gives you a tour of the facilities, offers you the coveted position, and meets all of your salary expectations with a generous compensation package. You feel like someone just handed you the recipe for getting your life back. Congratulations! You created the road map for personal success.

Joseph Campbell said, "The privilege of a lifetime is being who you are." Acknowledge your strength and go for it!

For further information, see my previously written articles in *Llewellyn's 2003 Sun Sign Book*, "Catalysts for Career Change," which discusses a variety of careers affiliated with planets in each of the houses and "Charting a Lunar Career Choice" in *Llewellyn's 2000 Moon Sign Book*, which offers a career transition assessment and lunar insight regarding the career and emotional satisfaction derived from enjoying what you do.

About the Author

Alice DeVille is an internationally known astrologer, writer, and consultant with a B.A. in sociology. In her busy Northern Virginia practice, she specializes in relationships, government affairs, career and change management, feng shui, real estate, and business management. Alice has personally made a number of career transitions that include: banking, mortgage lending, federal government, change agent, real estate, employee recruitment, civil rights, freelance consulting and writing, training and development. She has worked under contract with the federal government and numerous businesses as an executive coach and management consultant. Alice, is a licensed Realtor. She has developed and presented over 160 workshops and seminars. Alice's writing appears on the StarIQ.com Web site and other nationally known venues, including Learning Escapes. Her work has been translated in numerous languages, and her material on relationships has been cited by Sarah Ban Breathnach in Something More, Oprah's Web site, and in material used by The Federal Executive Institute and The Franklin Planner. Contact her at DeVilleAA@aol.com.

Get Organized

By Lynn Sellon

Planning, organizing, and working toward new horizons is the planetary theme in 2009. Thinking ahead will make a tremendous impact this year, and this applies to everything from moving, renovating, or just keeping up with the everyday demands around your home. January starts off with planets Mercury, Mars, Jupiter, and Pluto in the sign of Capricorn, while Saturn, the "task master," is in the sign of Virgo. This means that, in the home, taking a businesslike and innovative approach rather than a sentimental approach toward getting things done will help you accomplish the goals you set.

The Moon plays an influential role in household routines and organizational patterns. As the Moon moves through the heavens the impact of its daily rhythms on your home is similar to the Moon's tidal effect on the ocean. "Surfing" with the energy of the Moon will keep you ahead of the waves for a smooth ride through any household organizational plans.

The following monthly guide simplifies using the Moon's energy to assist you in getting organized. Suggestions each month give optimal days to focus attention on specific areas in your home and dates during each monthly lunar cycle to maximize efforts in planning, starting projects, and completing them.

January Focus: Research, Plan, Set Goals

This year January and February provide key planning time to set organizational strategies for the year ahead. Set goals in January, refine them in February, and then follow the plan. Take things one step or room at a time month by month, and you will be amazed at how much you can accomplish by the end of 2009!

Start the new year by pulling out a calendar and begin planning. If this is not the way you usually organize, try it, and you will start reaching your goals. Optimize productivity by research-ing new ways to stream-line paying bills and other monthly rou-tines. This includes anything from planning meals to shopping habits. For instance, if you have been shopping every few days for supplies, this may be the year to join a discount wholesale club and shop for bulk cleaning supplies and staples once a month. If you already do this, review where you shop and make sure that the routines you have been following are still working. The time you spend this month orchestrating the way you run your home will save you many hours throughout the coming year.

There are plenty of opportunities this month to clear out and store holiday decorations before moving on to planning.

January Optimal Days	Organizational Activities
1, 2, 3, 8, 9, 14, 15	Closets and storage areas (attic, basement)
1, 2, 3, 20, 21, 22	Clothing, furniture
23, 24, 25	Consult an expert
23, 24, 25	Coupons, Tag sales
13, 14, 15	Family living areas
1, 2, 3, 9, 10, 11, 23, 24, 25	Landscaping and gardening
8, 9, 10, 11, 14, 15, 23, 24, 25	Organizational overhaul in any area, home office work

February Focus: Recycle, the Garage

It is not too late to research, revise and set goals for the year. Seek advice from friends and associates, and let them help you focus your energy. Survey your friends on recycling methods to see if there might be a new idea that you can begin to implement.

There is a good period of time this month to organize. Focus-ing energy on the garage is a great place to start. If the garage is the storage center for everything but the car, then use the high-powered energy this month to make room for the car. Recycle, donate, or throw out all "non-garage" items. To help distribute

unwanted items, plan to take time midmonth to make a list of charities that take donations or are willing to pick up. Keep this list handy along with an inventory of any contributions you make during the year.

February Optimal Days   Organizational Activities

10, 11, 12, 22, 23, 24, 25, 26	Closets and storage areas (attic, basement)
17, 18, 19	Clothing, furniture
17, 18, 19	Consult an expert
10, 11, 12	Coupons, tag sales
19, 20, 21	Minor repairs
10, 11, 12, 19, 20, 21	Organizational overhaul in any area, home office work

March Focus: Basement, Creating Peaceful Space, and Taxes

Make peace with chaos this month. March provides plenty of opportune moments to clean out areas you have not wanted to deal with. This is an excellent month to convert a basement area into a fresh new living area or, at the very least, clean it out. Even if you deal with one small area you will be amazed at how the planetary energy works with you this month. Simply sorting through a neglected pile of things you thought you wanted, and letting them go, can have a therapeutic affect.

Financially, March is an ideal time to review your finances as April tax time is just around the corner. On March 14–15 the Sun will form a positive aspect with the Moon in Scorpio directing extra energy to help in a search for hidden papers needed to organize tax information.

March Optimal Days	Organizational Activities
5, 6, 7, 14, 15, 16	Bathrooms
11, 12, 13, 21, 22, 23, 24, 25	Closets and storage areas (attic, basement)
11	Complete projects
11, 12, 13	Construction, kitchen, cooking
19, 20	Consult an expert
14, 15, 16	Family living areas
5, 6, 7, 14, 15, 16, 23, 24, 25	Landscaping and gardening
19, 20	Minor repairs
14, 15, 16, 19, 20	Organizational overhaul in any area, home office work
3, 4, 5, 11, 12, 13, 23, 24, 25	Painting, works of art, bedrooms
26	Start projects

April Focus: Kitchens, Start a New Routine

Spring cleaning starts with the kitchen this month. Empty out cabinets and start tossing out any unused or expired items. Painting and renovations of the kitchen should not begin until the planet Venus, which rules beauty, moves into a more favorable relationship with the Moon around April 17. The Full Moon on April 9 will help bring completion to at least a part of any kitchen project.

If you are not planning a major kitchen renovation, this is the month to review the way the kitchen is organized. This applies to everything from getting rid of counter top clutter to meal planning. Each night this month make a note of the meals you create along with the ingredients needed to make them. This list will be a meal planner and shopping time saver in the months ahead. At the end of the month set aside a time to review your meal preparation routines and make an effort to reorganize so that the time spent in the kitchen is highly effective.

April Optimal Days   Organizational Activities

April Optimal Days	Organizational Activities
1, 2, 3, 10, 11, 12, 28, 29, 30	Bathrooms
8, 9, 10, 17, 18, 19, 26, 27, 28	Closets and storage areas (attic, basement)
20, 21, 22	Clothing, furniture
9	Complete projects
1, 2, 3, 15, 16, 17, 24, 25, 26, 28, 29, 30	Construction, kitchen, cooking
15, 16, 17	Coupons, Tag sales
1, 2, 3, 10, 22, 12, 20, 21, 22, 24, 25, 26	Landscaping and gardening
1, 2, 3, 15, 16, 17, 26, 27, 28	Organizational overhaul in any area, home office work
24, 25, 26	Painting, works of art, bedrooms
25	Start projects

May Focus: Landscaping, Bringing a Plan to Life

Focus on the garden this month. On May 18–19, consider designing a meditation garden. Enjoy designing the landscape and then moving the earth to make it happen. In an apartment, consider a window herb garden. Pay particular attention to the visual and sensory impact of the colors and scents the garden will produce when it matures. At the end of the month, planting colorful annuals will give any garden a beautiful finishing touch.

Remember to include in any plans a practical way to feed the birds or local fauna; this may require a new feeder or new type of food. May 10–15 is a great time to consult local naturalists on recommended feeding methods as well as advice on planting.

May Optimal Days	Organizational Activities
10, 11 , 12	Clothing, furniture
5, 6, 7, 19, 20, 21	Closets and storage areas (attic, basement)
19, 20, 21, 28, 29, 30	Construction, kitchen, cooking
10, 11, 12, 13, 14, 15	Consult an expert
12, 13, 14, 15	Coupons, Tag sales
18, 19, 28, 29, 30	Family living areas
5, 6, 7, 12, 13, 14, 15, 18, 19	Landscaping and gardening
12, 13, 14, 15, 24, 25, 26	Organizational overhaul in any area, home office work
5, 6, 7	Painting, works of art, bedrooms
24	Starting projects

June Focus: Change of Season, Research and Planning

This is the perfect month to switch seasonal wardrobes and scour the papers for spring sales. Pick a couple of priority areas in the house for spring cleaning and devote several blocks of time to clearing them out. Move out any piles that have accumulated and are taking up space in the hallways or on the stairs. Without getting too caught up in details, sort through old items in a closet. If you plan to clear out all of the closets, attack them one at a time.

If there are children in the house, this is the season to purge old school work and keep only special memories. Take some time to research and plan any design changes you may want to make in a child's room or family room; any actual changes can be done in July and August.

June Optimal Days	Organizational Activities
22, 23, 24	Bathrooms
8, 9, 10, 11, 14, 15	Closets and storage areas (attics, basements)
7	Completing projects
6, 7, 8, 21, 22, 29, 30	Clothing, Furniture
16, 17, 18	Construction, Kitchen, Cooking
6, 7, 8, 21, 22, 29, 30	Consult an expert
8, 9, 10, 11	Coupons, tag sales
16, 17, 18	Family living areas
14, 15, 16, 22, 23, 24	Landscaping and gardening
8, 9, 10, 11, 21, 22, 23, 24	Organizational overhaul in any area, home office work
14, 15, 29, 30	Painting, works of art, bedrooms
22	Start projects

July Focus: Home, Cooking, and Family Living Areas

This month focus on tailoring the areas in your home where you spend the most time. This is a good month to paint the family room or main living area. If painting is not in the plan, simply shifting around furnishings that you already own can have a big impact. Adding a comfortable chair or reorganizing your photographs to be displayed may make you feel more at home.

The middle of July offers some time to cull through old recipes and experiment with new ones. Try your new culinary skills out on friends or, better yet, ask them for their favorite family recipes. At the end of the month you will be able to organize a grand list for meal planning.

July Optimal Days	Organizational Activities
20, 21, 22, 28, 29, 30	Bathrooms
11, 12, 13, 14, 15, 26, 27, 28	Closets and storage areas (attics, basements)
30, 31	Clothing, furniture
7	Completing projects
6, 7, 8, 13, 14, 15, 20, 21, 22	Construction, kitchen, cooking
30, 31	Consult an expert
20, 22	Family living areas
1, 12, 13, 15, 16, 17, 20, 21, 22	Landscaping and gardening
1	Minor repairs
6, 7, 8, 30, 31	Organizational overhaul in any area, home office work
15, 16, 17, 26, 27, 28	Painting, works of art, bedrooms
22	Start projects

August Focus: Creative Areas and Kids' Rooms

Take a walk through your home on August 1 using a visitor's eye. Make a list of places in your home that could use a new painting or novelty item. If you are traveling this month, shop for items that feature local craftsmanship.

Concentrate on space for creative hobbies and interests. Organize an area that is designed so that you can gain easy access to projects. Reorganize existing craft areas this month as well. August 18–20 are great days to find a way to display any of your own personal creations.

Finalizing and realizing the plans that were set for any changes to a child's room is another important focal point this month. August 16–18 are excellent days to do a complete overhaul on a child's room. Framed children's artwork or designating a shelf to display the sculpture work of a young artist makes quite a statement.

August Optimal Days Organizational Activities

16, 17, 18, 24, 25, 26	Bathrooms
4, 5, 6, 7, 8, 9	Closets/Storage areas (attics, basements)
1, 2	Clothing, Furniture
1, 2	Consult an expert
6	Complete projects
9, 10, 11, 16, 17, 18, 23, 24	Construction, kitchen, cooking
18, 19, 20	Family living areas
7, 8, 9, 12, 13, 14, 16, 17, 18, 30, 31	Landscaping and gardening
2, 3, 4	Minor repairs
1, 2, 3, 4, 16, 17, 18, 30, 31	Organizational overhaul in any area, home office work
4, 5, 6, 20, 23, 24	Painting, works of art, bedrooms
20	Start projects

September Focus: Adjust Routines, Clean Closets

Planetary energy encourages change this year. Think of each change as an opportunity to streamline the time and effort you spend on the mundane business of making the home run smoothly. The work you do this month to refine your procedures and routines will serve to make things easier to handle in the coming months. The first three weeks of the month provide time to review your existing routines and evaluate what is working and not working. September 26–28 are excellent days to implement any changes you uncovered during the first part of the month. Stop doing what is no longer working. Shred old papers that have been cluttering up your desk. This is also a great month to research electronic filing and online banking options.

Plan to spend at least one weekend digging through a closet or two. Start by sorting through clothes that you no longer need while preparing to make a seasonal switch. Designate a box for clothes that you haven't worn all season or perhaps for many seasons: this is the time to let them go. Donate unwanted items to a local charity; let someone who can use them have them.

September Optimal Days   Organizational Activities

September Optimal Days	Organizational Activities
13, 14, 21, 22, 23	Bathrooms
1, 2, 3, 4, 5, 16, 17, 18, 19, 20, 28, 29, 30	Closets and storage areas (attics, basements)
4	Completing projects
13, 14, 26, 27, 28	Construction, kitchen, cooking
26, 27, 28	Consult an expert
16, 17, 18	Coupons, tag sales
14, 15, 16	Family living areas
3, 4, 5, 8, 9, 10, 13, 14	Landscaping and gardening
16, 17, 18, 26, 27, 28	Organizational overhaul in any area, home office work
14, 15, 16, 19, 20	Painting, works of art, bedrooms
18	Starting projects

October Focus: Closets and Bedrooms

The beginning of the month should be spent finalizing any changes to home office procedures and reorganizing the closets. While working on the closets, keep a running list of items you need so that when you are out shopping you know what additions to the wardrobe are essential. This list should include accessories you need to complement your wardrobe as well as gift items that you can begin to pick up for the upcoming holidays. Keep the list with you at all times so that when you are out you will not be tempted to impulse shop.

By midmonth, once the closets and home business routines are in order, it is time to focus on making the bedroom a peaceful place to retreat to each night. Just clearing away the clutter that often accumulates will make a huge difference. A fresh coat of paint at the end of the month can make a significant impact.

October Optimal Days   **Organizational Activities**

18, 19, 20	Bathrooms
6, 7, 10, 11, 12, 28, 29, 30	Closets and storage areas (attics, basements)
20, 21, 22	Clothing, furniture
4	Complete projects
6, 7, 10, 11, 12, 14, 15, 16, 23, 24, 25	Construction, kitchen, cooking
10, 11, 12	Consult an expert
23, 24, 25	Coupons, tag sales
16, 17, 18, 19, 20, 21, 22, 23	Family living areas
28, 29, 30	Landscaping and gardening
26, 27, 28	Minor repairs
6, 7, 16, 17, 18, 28, 29, 30	Painting, works of art, bedrooms
10, 11, 12, 14, 15, 16, 18, 19, 20, 23, 24, 25, 26, 27, 28	Organizational overhaul in any area, home office work
18	Start projects

November Focus: Join Forces, Remodel Bathrooms

There is a shift in energy this month with Saturn, the "task master," moving into the celestial sign of Libra, bringing on a subtle change in atmosphere. There will be a lot of lunar energy to capture this month to help accomplish projects. This new energy encourages working with others.

Making changes to or reorganizing bathrooms is a great way to utilize the Moon's cycle this month. This can be as simple as getting rid of unnecessary clutter and giving any bathroom an intense cleaning. Enlist the help of the kids, a partner or a friend, and the bathroom will sparkle in no time.

Planning for work on a bathroom should be done in the beginning of the month. November 14 is an ideal day to begin work. If all goes well, even small changes will cause quite a transformation by December 2.

November Optimal Days   Organizational Activities

14, 15, 16	Bathrooms
10, 11, 12, 22, 23, 24, 27, 28	Closets and storage areas (attics, basements)
17, 18, 19	Clothing, furniture
2	Completing projects
19, 20, 21, 22	Construction, kitchen, cooking
10, 11, 12	Coupons, tag sales
14, 15, 16, 19, 20, 21, 22	Family living areas
6, 7, 12, 13, 14, 15, 16, 24, 25, 26	Landscaping and gardening
4, 5, 6	Minor repairs
6, 7, 10, 11, 12, 19, 20, 21, 22	Organizational overhaul in any area, home office work
4, 5, 6, 12, 13, 14, 24, 25, 26	Painting, works of art, bedrooms
16	Start projects

December Focus: Furniture, the Big Picture

Work with another member of the household to make a grand sweep through the house; place any loose or unwanted items in boxes and set furniture the way you would like it. December 4–5 are the best days to make a clean sweep. If you take advantage of these days, you will be amazed at how great the house looks.

Think on a larger scale this month. Make a list of all the gifts you are giving—this should include everyone—even the mailman. Make sure to carry it with you throughout the month. Hold on to this list and after the holidays, label it "December 2009," and file it away. You will be able to reference this list in 2010 as a snap shot of your 2009 gift giving.

December 16–18 is a great time to send holiday greetings. Set up a holiday card assembly line and the process will be completed very quickly. Mercury, the ruling planet over mail delivery, is getting ready to play havoc with the mail December 26. It is best to get the correspondence out before then. Or wait until mid-January to send out cards for the New Year.

December Optimal Days   Organizational Activities

December Optimal Days	Organizational Activities
4, 5	Bathrooms
10, 11	Closets/Storage areas (attics, basements)
14, 15, 16, 29, 30	Clothing, furniture
2, 31	Complete projects
4, 5, 24, 25, 26	Construction, kitchen, cooking
14, 15,16, 29, 30	Consult an expert
14, 15, 16	Family living areas
4, 5, 11, 12	Landscaping and gardening
16, 17, 18	Minor repairs
4, 5, 16, 17,18, 31	Organizational overhaul in any area, home office work
10, 11, 19, 20, 21	Painting, works of art, bedrooms
16	Start projects

About the Author

Lynn Sellon has studied astrology since childhood. She has degrees in sociology and education; she is a professional member of the American Federation of Astrologers (PMAFA), and a Level IV consulting astrologer through the National Council for Geocosmic Research (NCGR). Lynn is the coauthor of Simply Math: A Comprehensive Guide to Easy & Accurate Chart Calculation. *She maintains a professional astrological practice in Connecticut.*